The Quantification of Bodies in Health

The Quantification of Bodies in Health: Multidisciplinary Perspectives

EDITED BY

BTIHAJ AJANA
King's College London, UK

JOAQUIM BRAGA
University of Coimbra, Portugal

SIMONE GUIDI
National Research Council, Italy

United Kingdom – North America – Japan – India – Malaysia – China

Emerald Publishing Limited
Howard House, Wagon Lane, Bingley BD16 1WA, UK

First edition 2022
Editorial matter and Selection © 2022 Btihaj Ajana, Joaquim Braga, and Simone Guidi.

Individual chapters: © 2022 the authors Published under an exclusive license by
Emerald Publishing Limited.

Reprints and permissions service
Contact: permissions@emeraldinsight.com

British Library Cataloguing in Publication Data
A catalogue record for this book is available from the British Library

ISBN: 978-1-80071-884-5 (Print)
ISBN: 978-1-80071-883-8 (Online)
ISBN: 978-1-80071-885-2 (Epub)

Printed and bound by CPI Group (UK) Ltd, Croydon, CR0 4YY

ISOQAR certified
Management System,
awarded to Emerald
for adherence to
Environmental
standard
ISO 14001:2004.

Certificate Number 1985
ISO 14001

INVESTOR IN PEOPLE

Contents

List of Figures and Tables

About the Contributors

Btihaj Ajana is Professor of Ethics and Digital Culture at the department of Digital Humanities at King's College London. She is a former Marie Curie Fellow at the Aarhus Institute of Advanced Studies. Her academic research is interdisciplinary in nature and focuses on the ethical, political and ontological aspects of digital developments and their intersection with everyday cultures. She has written on the effects of technology on issues of identity, embodiment, governance and cultural representation. She is the author of *Governing through Biometrics: The Biopolitics of Identity* (2013) and editor of *Self-Tracking: Empirical and Philosophical Investigations* (2018) and *Metric Culture: Ontologies of Self-Tracking Practices* (2018). Ajana is also a filmmaker and uses film as a way of exploring social issues while bringing scholarly ideas to wider audiences. Her most recent films include *Quantified Life* (2017), *Surveillance Culture* (2017), and *Fem's Way* (2020).

Joaquim Braga is a Researcher and Professor at the Department of Philosophy of the University of Coimbra. He is also a Member of the Research Unit Institute for Philosophical Studies. His research activity covers the fields of Aesthetics, Picture Theory, Philosophy of Technology, Modern and Contemporary Philosophy, with a special interest in symbolic thought. His works include, among others, *Die symbolische Prägnanz des Bildes. Zu einer Kritik des Bildbegriffs nach der Philosophie Ernst Cassirers* (2012), *Rethinking Culture and Cultural Analysis – Neudenken von Kultur und Kulturanalyse* (2013), *Leituras da Sociedade Moderna. Media, Política, Sentido* (2013), *Símbolo e Cultura* (2014), *Bernard de Mandeville's Tropology of Paradoxes: Morals, Politics, Economics, and Therapy* (2015), *Antropologia da Individuação. Estudos sobre o Pensamento de Ernst Cassirer* (2017), *Conceiving Virtuality: From Art to Technology* (2019), *Teoria das Formas Imagéticas. Ensaios sobre Arte, Estética, Tecnologia* (2020).

Laura Corti is a PhD Candidate in Science and Engineering for Humans and the Environment at Campus Bio-Medico University in Rome. She is part of the Research Group Qua-Onto-Tech (Qualitative Ontology and Technology) at the University of Florence and of the Research Unit Philosophy of Science and Human Development at the Campus Bio-Medico University. Currently, her research is focussing on the philosophical issues of introducing qualities, such as sensation or emotions, into expert and robot systems. Her main research topics are post-phenomenology, philosophy of science and ethics of AI and Robotics.

Alessandro De Cesaris is a Post-doc Research Fellow at the University of Turin. He is also scientific collaborator at the Collège des Bernardins in Paris (Department of *Humanisme numérique*). He coedited a collective volume on Hegel's logic (2020) and wrote essays in Italian, French, English and German on his main research interests: Classic German Philosophy, Media Theory and Anthropology of Technology. His current research project is focussed on the notion of 'hypermodernity' and on the socio-technical imaginaries connected to the Information Revolution.

Lorenzo De Stefano is a Teaching Assistant in Theoretical Philosophy and in Ethics and Theory of Big Data at the Department of Humanistic Studies, University of Naples Federico II. His research interests focus on metaphysics, phenomenology, philosophical anthropology and philosophy of technology. He holds a PhD in Philosophical Sciences from the University of Naples Federico II and was a Visiting Researcher at Eberhard Karls Universität of Tübingen, Albert-Ludwigs Universität of Freiburg and Johannes Gutenberg-Universität of Mainz. His current research interests are concerned with the anthropological, ontological and ethical aspects of emerging technologies.

Zeena Feldman is a Senior Lecturer in Digital Culture in the Department of Digital Humanities, King's College London. Her research examines the ways digital communication technologies impact analogue concepts – for instance, belonging, mental health and food. She has published widely, including in the *European Journal of Cultural Studies, Information, Communication & Society, Celebrity Studies, TripleC, The Independent, OpenDemocracy* and *The Conversation*. She is Co-editor, with Deborah Lupton, of *Digital Food Cultures* (2020) and Editor of *Art & the Politics of Visibility* (2017). She runs the Quitting Social Media project, which explores digital overload and detox.

Simone Guidi is a Researcher at the CNR-ILIESI (Italy). In 2019–2020, he was an Assistant Professor in Philosophy at the University of Coimbra and is a Full Member of the same University's Instituto de Estudos Filosóficos. He received his PhD in Philosophy from the University Sapienza of Rome. His research deals with the History of Modern and Contemporary Philosophy, and particularly with the genesis of the Cartesian mind-body dualism. He is the Managing Editor of the international journal of philosophy *Lo Sguardo*. He received the Italian National Scientific Qualification (ASN) as Associate Professor and as Full Professor of History of Philosophy.

Amanda Karlsson is currently working as an External Lecturer at the Institute of Communication and Culture, Aarhus University in Denmark. She recently completed a PhD project on women's engagement with period-trackers. She has a background in media studies and her research interests revolve around the sociotechnical practices of everyday life and the effects of technologies on these. She focusses on topics such as the quantification of bodies through digital technologies, how various digital technologies ascribe meaning to life transgressions and how we come to understand these entanglements and intertwinements of digital communication, privacy, embodiment, gender and data.

Rachael Kent is the Founder of Dr Digital Health consultancy and corporate wellbeing (https://www.drdigitalhealth.co.uk/), and a Lecturer in Digital Economy & Society Education at the Department of Digital Humanities at King's College London. Having empirically researched the impact of digital technology on mental and physical health for over 15 years, her first book '*The Health Self: Digital Performativity and Health Management in Everyday Life*' is forthcoming with Bristol University Press. Her research regularly appears in press and podcasts including *BBC News, Forbes Magazine, The Independent, Runners World, BrainCare, Metro UK* and *Metric Life*.

Ana Carolina Minozzo is a PhD Researcher at the Department of Psychosocial Studies at Birkbeck, University of London and holds undergraduate and postgraduate degrees in Psychoanalytic Psychology and Psychosocial Studies at the same university. Her research crosses the fields of medical humanities, continental philosophy, eco-feminism and psychoanalytic theory in relation to diagnoses and experiences of anxiety in and outside of the clinic. She is also a Clinical Practitioner in the field and part of the Psychosis Therapy Project (PTP) in London, UK.

Phoebe V. Moore is Associate Professor of the Futures of Work at the University of Leicester, School of Business. She is a globally recognised expert in digitalisation and the workplace. Her most recent book *The Quantified Self in Precarity: Work, Technology and What Counts* (Routledge 2019) is a ground-breaking piece, analysing the use of wearable tracking technologies in workplaces and the implications for human resources and working conditions. She is a Policy Advisor and Commissioned Author who works with several institutions in the European Union including the European Safety and Health Agency; the European Parliament; the United Nations International Labour Organization; and the Chartered Institute for Personnel Development on the integration of big data, artificial intelligence systems, and old and new technologies into workplaces and spaces, and the risks and benefits these pose for working people.

Introduction

Btihaj Ajana, Joaquim Braga and Simone Guidi

Over the last decade, we have witnessed rapid development and widespread of digital tracking devices, apps, and platforms, together with the emergence of global health movements, such as the Quantified Self. Millions of people around the world are now routinely using such technologies to track, document and analyse their physical activities, vital functions, and daily habits, all with the aim to assess and improve their health, productivity, and wellbeing. And with the current Covid-19 pandemic, the uptake of such technologies has accelerated, as tracing apps, biometric techniques (such as temperature monitoring, thermal imaging and facial recognition) and health data gathering and analysis have become important *dispositifs* for managing the pandemic at the governmental and personal level.

At the heart of such fast-growing trends lies the *quantification of the body* deemed as a key element in both medical practice and personal self-care. Although the latest developments in metric and tracking technologies have dramatically expanded the scope and reach of body quantification, quantification itself, as a process, is not unique to the current era and its technological prowess but is inherent in the history of modernity itself. As Noji, Kappler, and Vormbusch (2021, p. 261) argue, 'the history of modernity is also the history of increasing instrumental knowledge about the human body and its "health status"'. And generally, people have long reflected on the state of their bodies and health for centuries using analogues devices and diaries (Sysling, 2019, p. 108).

From a historical perspective, quantification became all the more important thanks to Galilei and particularly to Newton, the first to conjugate mathematical reasoning and strict observations based on measures of natural facts and phenomena. But such development could not have been conceived and introduced without a preliminary work of application of measurability on a key place of ancient natural philosophy, that is, the human body. A special kind of body among the bodies that constitute the physical world, the human body is such that – in the wake of the Vitruvian view of a *physis* structured by proportions – classic philosophy made of it the 'natural parameter' for the measurement of nature. According to the Roman architect, Vitruvius, even human artefacts had to follow 'an exact system of correspondence to the likeness of a well-formed human being' (Vitruvius, 1999, p. 42).

The Quantification of Bodies in Health: Multidisciplinary Perspectives, 1–12

Copyright © 2022 by Btihaj Ajana, Joaquim Braga and Simone Guidi

Published under an exclusive license by Emerald Publishing Limited

doi:10.1108/978-1-80071-883-820211001

In no way both modern natural scientists and epistemologists could approach nature through abstract signs and measures without a preliminary reduction of the body to a quantitative model. It is no accident that they could find in medicine a rising tradition of natural philosophy that, since the early seventeenth century, started quantifying the human body by measuring the physiological processes which structure living organisms. Santorio's famous weighing chair is only one perspicuous example among the many early modern attempts to convert the body into a quantifiable being, by measuring it through specific instruments. And while the body reflects a view of the natural world, it tests *in corpore* a new approach to observations and a new way of scientific reasoning, based on instruments and signs rather than on qualitative remarks.

By converting the body into the language of measurement and quantification, early modern medicine treats the body as the border territory where two contrasting concepts of nature and natural science oppose one another: on the one hand, the ancient idea that nature is intrinsically qualitative and intelligent-like, so that it can be understood just within its inner logic, identifying hidden relationships, proportions, and connections in it. On the other hand, the new idea that nature must be examined and anatomised by placing it on the table of artificial ways of reasoning, as signs and numbers are.

Hence, early modern medical quantification of the body provides a pivotal condition for the new epistemological approach of modern science, and it constantly accompanies its evolution in parallel. No quantifiability of natural phenomena could be complete and plausible without the quantification of the body. By measuring the microcosmos of the body, early modern quantification of nature sought to make plausible that mathematics could be applied everywhere in the natural world. On this basis, in the modern age, the qualitative dimensions of natural phenomena are gradually supplanted by their measurable quantitative dimensions, so that, as Isaiah Berlin recalls, 'only the measurable aspects of reality were to be treated as real' (Berlin, 1956, p. 17). As such, the concrete possibility, opened by medicine, of immediately converting the living body into numbers has also contributed to enhancing the idea of *Mathesis* as a metaphysical key for a comprehensive (and often deductive) understanding of the world. This is a pillar of the modern worldview from which even contemporary post-positivistic mathematisation of the world stems. But if it is true that a mathematised science, as well as an algorithmic society, cannot exist without measuring nor without the instruments that facilitate the conversion of the world into numbers, such an apparatus cannot be effective if our natural medium, the body, is not already (and problematically) made homogeneous to the quantification system. This is why early modern medicine, before philosophy or physics, has been responsible for making of such a convertibility of mathematics and reality something obvious.

As is known, over the history of modern philosophy one can find many important instances of such a modern tendency to see mathematics as a universal logic, able to embrace everything. Among the many well-studied cases, two examples would be adamantine. According to John Locke, for instance, the applicability of numbers to 'everything that either doth exist or can be imagined' (Locke, 1979, p. 205) reveals its universal character, founded on its unwavering and unique unity to organise human mind and human thought. Thus, the number 'is that which the mind makes use of in measuring all things that by us are measurable' (Locke, 1979, p. 209). Likewise, Locke's opponent, Gottfried Wilhelm Leibniz developed his infinitesimal calculus with the broad goal of mathematically standardising the mathematical understanding of the transformations that occur in the world. And with his *Machina Arithmetica* (1685), Leibniz intended to empirically materialise a universal method, liable to convert the laws of reason into the laws of calculation. In addition to providing the detection of errors that could affect reason, Leibniz's arithmetic machine aimed to extend calculability beyond the natural limits of the human mind, making of reality something intrinsically predictable and deducible in terms of geometric-mathematical reasoning.[1] At the same time, the Leibnizian arithmetic machine aimed, according to a fully functionalist principle, to free human beings from the arduous task of performing the calculation for themselves. Although manipulated by human workers, the technological imperative was for the machine to free itself from the 'hand' to nurture the 'mind'. Such imperative can be seen as a precursor to the need of designing automated technological means, as in today's digital culture and the burgeoning developments in Artificial Intelligence.

Despite such metaphysical and epistemological outcomes, the idea of nature as intrinsically quantitative and quantifiable remains inherently based on the pillar of the quantifiability of the living body and its processes. To the point that, in the late eighteenth century, one can find interesting cases of a recovery of the ancient idea of the body as a natural unit of measure, now conciliated with the modern conception of measure as intrinsically mathematical and algebraic. It is especially the case of Étienne Bonnot de Condillac, who, in his *La Langue des Calculus* (1798), undertakes a true philosophical panegyric about the scientific virtues of algebra as an exceptional and perfect non-arbitrary symbolic language. One of the uniqueness of his book lies in the relevance that the French author attributes to the relationship between calculation and bodily action. Right in the first chapter, entitled *Du calcul avec les doigts*, Condillac asserts that, originally, calculus refers to a human operation carried out with the fingers, just as language in general has action as its first reference (Condillac, 1877, p. 7).

The 10 fingers of human hands are, therefore, in Candillac's analogical reasoning, the starting point for imagining a series of numerical units and thanks to which it becomes possible to perform linear mathematical operations and represent them for ourselves. Going further in his kinesiological approach, the author states that all forms of calculation can be reduced and explained by means of two opposite movements performed by fingers: the successive opening of the fingers to count (add or multiply) is equivalent to '*numération*' [numbering] and, conversely, the successive closing of the fingers to subtract or divide is '*dénumération*' [de-numbering]. From this analogical point of view, to open the fingers then means

---

[1]Worth noting here, however, that Leibniz was a great defender of the irreducibility of the 'essence of life' to the mechanical model. For him, quantification and mechanisation explain how life happens, but not why (see Leibniz's notion of *vis viva*).

to add, and to close them means to subtract – which is the same as to say that a sensory-motor act supports a mental operation that is specifically mathematical.

The analogue relationship of calculus with the body and the actions performed by it is particularly emphasised when Condillac, in another chapter of *La Langue des Calculus*, sustains that the measurement of space is one of the first tasks that human beings perform. In his words, nature itself has endowed us with an organic measurement faculty, which is why it is only necessary 'to count the steps, the feet, the inches, to be able to imagine several other forms of measurement' (Condillac, 1877, p. 110).[2] Before these formulations, in his famous *Traité des Sensations*, Condillac had already attributed a superlative cognitive function to touch, since, according to him, it is the haptic senses that truly give unity and objectivity to the phenomena apprehended by other sensory modalities. Condillac's sensualism is replete with a mathematical view of nature and beings; indeed, it highlights, above all, the *esprit systématique* that the Enlightenment philosophical thought inscribed both in natural sciences and in the humanities.

However, the core alliance between technology and science established in early modernity reaches a new level with the technological invention of artefacts with integrated mathematical measurement systems – as was the paradigmatic case, for instance, of the invention in the early eighteenth century of the mercury-in-glass thermometer. Soon these artefacts became impregnated with instrumentalist approaches to reality. Equating organisms and quantifiable beings greatly favours biological determinism and anthropological comparison methods anchored in measurement and quantification processes. In the nineteenth century, theories of biological determinism supported several forms of body quantification, such as those of anthropometry, a technical approach to human measurement and classification founded by the French police officer, Alphonse Bertillon, in the 1880s. While craniometry promised a cataloguing and ranking of human races, Cesare Lombroso's criminal anthropology of *l'uomo nato delinquente* tried to locate the genetic and hereditary background of delinquency. At the end of the century, and with Francis Galton's psychometry, further attempts were made to standardise the relationship between body and mental faculties, with the aim of quantifying the alleged intelligence level of each human being.

While scientific research continued to explore new possibilities of quantification and invest in new tools to achieve such goals, some of twentieth century philosophical

---

[2]What springs to mind here is ORLAN's *MesuRages* (1974–1983), a performative artwork in which the French artist uses her body as a unit of measure (ORLAN-corps) [ORLAN-body] to measure public spaces and cultural institutions, including Centre Pompidou in Paris, Saint-Pierre Museum in Lyon and the M KHA in Antwerp. MesuRages is not only about '*mesure*' [measure] but also 'rage', the artist's anger at the dictum of 'man as the measure of all things', as found in the teachings of the ancient architect Vitruvius and illustrated by Leonardo da Vinci in his famous drawing of the Vitruvian man' (see, http://www.reactfeminism.org/nr1/artists/orlan_en.html). Through *MesuRages*, ORLAN ritualistically inscribes the female body onto public spaces and cultural institutions, occupying that which has been historically and exclusively dominated by male power.

thought attempted to break away from quantitative ideals and positivist heritage, showing how the body is irreducible to calculation and measurement techniques. 'Measurability belongs to the thing as *object*', argues Martin Heidegger (2001, p. 98) who also adds that 'measurability means calculability, that is, a view of nature guaranteeing knowledge of how we can, and how we must, count on its processes' (p. 104). For Heidegger, the body is unmeasurable to the extent that it cannot be perceived as a simple object, that is, as something that allows itself to be entirely represented, mediated, and quantified. On the contrary, what makes objects measurable, according to Heidegger, is not only a technologically supported human capacity, but also the very 'thing' dimension of objects.

Regarding the field of medical care, Hans-Georg Gadamer, in *Über die Verborgenheit der Gesundheit*, radicalises the Husserlian phenomenological distinction between the 'living body' (*Leib*) and the 'lifeless body' (*Körper*) – in the latter, the body is considered as merely a physical object – and Heidegger's account of the body's immeasurability, arguing that health cannot be subjected to conventional technical measurement processes. If there is any form of measurement, according to Gadamer, this can only be an internal and subjective measurement, felt through the symbiotic relation of the body with the individual's own states of mind (Gadamer, 1993). The reason is that, for Gadamer, quantitative conventions – like those of scientific measurement techniques – do not cover the true states of somatic equilibrium, which, according to him, obey a kind of natural measure inherent to the body itself and which is not, in turn, translatable by any numerical system. Being sick and feeling sick are, consequently, two different states. Likewise, George Canguilhem (1991) believes that it is the patient's perspective that defines the *experience* of being sick. He argues that

> medicine always exists *de jure*, if not *de facto*, because there are men who feel sick, not because there are doctors to tell men of their illnesses [...] Health is life lived in the silence of the organs. (Canguilhem in Diaz-Bone, 2021, p. 295)

This, in a way, gestures towards the importance of the individual/patient rather than only science and medical expertise in defining what health and sickness are in the first place, a standpoint that is a heart of contemporary movements such as the Quantified Self, biohacking and so-called 'personal science' (Wolf & de Groot, 2020) whose primary aim is to regain individual autonomy and reclaim agency from the clatch of medical expertise and its 'one size fits all' approach.

Canguilhem, and later on Foucault, devoted much effort to scrutinising and unpacking the normativities and assumptions underpinning life sciences and medical understandings of what is healthy, what is normal and what is pathological. Their work, which resonates in recent literature on self-tracking and body quantification, has been instrumental in removing the veil of positivism to uncover the link between discourse and medicine, the effects of social and political forces on science, and the relationship between 'power' and 'knowledge' in the health system. One key lesson to be drawn from their analyses is that no science or technological process is neutral or value free. Every system and every practice, whether social, political, scientific or personal tends to be imbued with a set of norms and values that are derived from various sources and pre-existing rationalities. The quantification of the body is no exception. That is not to say that the individual has no agency in terms of negotiating and appropriating the values and norms of a given practice. But often, consciously or unconsciously, one tends to be 'oriented' towards particular norms or conventions that are not wholly self-generated but originating from external sources and standardised measures – for instance, the recommendation to eat five vegetables or fruits a day and walk 10,000 steps per day which became the baseline for healthy active lifestyle. A similar argument could be made vis-à-vis the design of self-tracking devices and apps, which is mostly decided by technology companies themselves who introduce and embed new standards and categories which determine what is measured and why (Cappel, 2021, p. 240). As Diaz-Bone (2021, p. 305) postulates,

> The categories (and algorithms) have been implemented by technology companies and the resulting categories and data are in many cases neither controlled nor understood by users or adopted to their health practices and their health situation. The underlying measurement conventions are invisible for users and in case the data is transferred to the provider of the app, there is also an informational asymmetry in data analysis and its economical exploitation.

Herein lies one of the challenges and limits of contemporary forms of digital body quantification and self-tracking. Despite the promise of individual autonomy and agency, users are still bound by the design choices of product developers, by existing norms around health and by the market forces of data capitalism. Self-quantification and tracking practices thus sit at the 'fulcrum between self and external control, the objectification of the self, and regulation in accordance with social norms of "health"' (Hille, 2016). This is why building one's quantification and tracking tools has become a major preoccupation for the techno-savvy members of the Quantified Self community who rely on their own technical skills to find ways to circumvent both the medical system as well as the tech industry. However, for the everyday general user, relying on commercial products is not so much a choice but an inevitability.

Moreover, body quantification and tracking technologies have become increasingly intersected with surveillance and control mechanisms, not only within governmental institutions and private organisations but also at the personal, intimate level. We now use biometric fingerprints and facial scans to unlock our smartphones or log into our bank accounts; we use MobilePay to purchase our groceries; fitness trackers, such as Fitbit, to log and analyse daily exercise; period trackers, such as Clue, to manage fertility and menstrual health; voice recognition to interact with virtual assistants such as Amazon's Alexa; contact tracing apps and thermal scanners to detect and contain the spread of coronavirus; and soon, Covid-19 vaccine passports and biometric immunity status apps to access pubs and restaurants, travel across borders, and return to work premises. A very recent survey by YouGov (2021)[3] in the UK revealed that most British people support Covid-19 vaccine passports despite privacy concerns and the potential of such systems to create and exacerbate forms of discrimination, exclusion and inequality. The Covid-19 pandemic has, indeed, normalised surveillance even further and made the quantification and tracking of the body all the more routine.

It is with this background and these issues in mind that this multidisciplinary volume proceeds to tackle the quantification of the body in its various contexts, shedding light on some of the key ontological, ethical, political, and aesthetic issues that arise out of the complex intertwining of bodies and measurements. By bringing together both established and emerging authors working at the intersection of philosophy, sociology, history, psychology, and digital culture, this book provides multi-layered and nuanced analyses of the various facets of quantification and self-tracking practices, offering a critical engagement with the ways these practices are reshaping our relation to health and our bodies. The book is divided into four parts, each of which addresses specific angles and themes, including subjectivity and perception, Cartesian dualism and embodiment, gender and the quantification of the female body, wellbeing and mental health, as well as Artificial Intelligence and prosthetics. By addressing these overarching themes through a variety of theoretical lenses and empirical examples, the book makes a useful and unique contribution to existing literature, highlighting what is at stake in today's ever-growing culture of quantification and tracking.

PART I, Body Quantification and Subjectivity: Philosophical Perspectives, opens with Joaquim Braga's chapter which explores the imaginary of the body underpinning the self-tracking ideology, linking this to relevant philosophical debates. According to Braga, the classic way of understanding the body in Western thought comes from a combination of two complementary approaches: on the one hand, the body is taken as a subject of representation, and on the other, it is considered as an articulation metaphor. Both these notions contribute to seeing the body as an artifact, leading to a constant misunderstanding of it through a 'paradigm of visibility' and through, what Braga calls, 'metaphors of appearance' (the body as a natural semiotic being, a *vera icona*) or 'disappearance' (the mediated body as disembodied and dematerialised). Contemporary body quantification lies, for Braga, in substantial continuity with such misconception of the body and its materiality, which was already preeminent before the rise of wearable technologies (for instance in pre-digital concepts of virtual reality or virtual space). In such a technological imaginary, quantification reinforces a Cartesian model which reduces the body to a mere object of information. In response, Braga exhorts to understand the body as an open and active intersection of possible mediations, and to consider it not just as a passive being or an inscription surface of events (as Foucault himself defined it) but as an autonomous meaning-maker that is irreducible to the mere status of an 'object'. Chapter 2 by Lorenzo De Stefano is dedicated to examining the interplay between self-tracking practices and subjectivity.

---

[3]See, https://yougov.co.uk/topics/politics/articles-reports/2021/04/12/covid-certificates-where-do-public-stand.

It provides philosophical reflections on the cultural phenomenon of the Quantified Self and the extent to which this phenomenon contributes to the making of new subjectivities as well as forms of 'de-subjectivation'. Drawing on Material Engagement Theory, Heidegger's take on the 'question of technology' and Foucault's 'Technologies of the Self', De Stefano highlights how recent techniques and practices of self-tracking have unlocked new ways of self-analysis and introspection which extend and remediate former practices, such as confession and journaling. While such developments are contributing to enhancing our understanding of the self and deepening awareness of the body and its vital functions, they are also encouraging a reductionist perspective that is driven by data and numbers. These developments are, as such, cultivating a 'quantitative aesthetics of individual existence' that is underlined by deeper biopolitical and technocratic phenomena, according to De Stefano. What is at stake, in this sense, is the way self-tracking practices can lead to a de-subjectivation of the user whereby data and apparatuses end up acquiring more power and agency over the life of the subject. Chapter 3 by Alessandro De Cesaris continues the discussion on the forms of subjectivation involved in self-tracking practices, asking what kind of 'self' is being produced through the subject's personal engagement with tracking activities. The focus of this chapter is placed on the extent to which self-tracking practices and quantification devices can be regarded as 'care of the self', in the Foucauldian sense, and how 'design' is the way of thinking that shapes the interaction between users and their devices. Self-tracking, as such, is seen as a product of design, understood as a specific way of conceiving, and organising the interaction between the subject and technical objects. This raises, again, questions around notions of autonomy and empowerment since users, according to De Cesaris' analysis, no longer track themselves per se, but instead, they are tracked by digital devices that act as prosthetic extensions of their bodies, enabling automated quantification. Ultimately, the question becomes whether self-tracking practices can be considered as a form of 'delegated subjectivity' or whether such practices allow the subject to overcome automation and passivity.

PART II, Body Quantification: Historical and Empirical Perspectives, begins with Chapter 4 by Rachael Kent which provides a historical account of health tracking and body quantification in the UK. This chapter aims, in particular, at showing the impact of neoliberal policies on public health and its ideological residues in today's practices of self-management of health. According to Kent, the implementation of the neoliberal policies is responsible for reorganising the very notion of public health and the National Health System established after World War II. The core of such policies can be found in the relocation of responsibility for health from public institutions to individuals themselves, all under the narrative of 'liberating' people from the alleged intrusion of the state. Some of the effects of neoliberalism have been the increasing privatisation of health institutions and the rise of 'healthism', that is, the political discourse of lifestyle correction and health moralism. From this phase, which reached its apex with the Great Recession in 2008, the responsibilisation of individuals for their healthy or non-healthy behaviours comes together with a moralisation of health. The latter identifies a direct link between economic and social factors and self-discipline, dividing the population into healthy or unhealthy social groups. For Kent, this historical path is the premise and the ground for the contemporary techno-utopias of self-quantification and self-management of health, often presented as emancipatory strategies. Such ethos reinforces all the more the ideal of 'private' health, often conflating better healthcare with 'more' healthcare. The current COVID-19 pandemic has strengthened even further the hold of quantification on society, enabling digital surveillance practices and the infrastructure of digital capitalism to consolidate their invasion of people's everyday life, all in the name of health itself. To better understand and appreciate the impact of quantification and self-tracking, it is necessary to engage with the concrete aspects of such phenomena and their material dynamics. Chapter 5 by Btihaj Ajana does precisely that. It analyses body quantification and self-tracking from an often-neglected perspective, the user's direct experience. As Ajana remarks, self-management of wellness, and more broadly the emergence of a 'self-wisdom through numbers', have been approached from many theoretical and academic perspectives in the last decade, most of which descend from well-established conceptual families in Western thought, such as positivism, biopolitics, post-phenomenology, actor-network theory, Marxism, and surveillance studies. Ajana's chapter builds on and extends existing debates by drawing on an original empirical study comprising of an international survey with users of self-tracking technologies. This methodology lets users themselves report their own experiences, and then applies a theoretical analysis to the resulting data. What emerges from Ajana's investigation and analysis is a two-faced experience of digital self-management. On the one hand, especially through gamification, self-tracking displays positive motivational features, encouraging healthier and more active conducts that reflect directly on people's lives. On the other hand, the deployment of tracking technologies often leads to excessive self-monitoring and self-impositions, resulting in performance anxiety, particularly when the user shares her health data through social media and related platforms. Reflecting on the latter, Ajana points out the implicit political danger of today's alliance between capitalism and self-tracking, in particular the anatomo-political risks of current biosocialities, the colonisation of private life through data, and the many issues hidden behind data exchange/sharing or data philanthropy. Chapter 6 by Amanda Karlsson provides further empirical insights by looking at the monitoring of menstrual cycles through smartphone applications. One of the key arguments of the chapter is that self-tracking technologies, developed for 'bodies who menstruate', can promote a uniformity of the female body, equating the control of menstruation with the supposed control of fertile cycles. Taking cue from feminist critique of biological reductionism, Karlsson suggests that gender stereotypes are intrinsic to technological design itself and reinforce normative and reductionist ideas about the female body. But this reductionism and stereotyping are primarily situated in the algorithmic quantification processes of the body. At the level of knowledge production and sharing, there is a greater interweaving of the various materialities that support the relationships of bodies with technology. This constitutes possibilities for expression and emancipation of the female body, no longer restricted to the stereotyped discourse of fertility or, in other words, of the woman's body as a reproductive body. Using several sources of empirical material (interviews and observations carried out between 2017 and 2019), the author raises the hypothesis that the exchange of information and knowledge between women about their bodies can generate a new social movement, a 'techno-feminism', capable of shaking social stigmas and leading to significant cultural transformations. What underlies this change is, above all, the possibility for interaction that the new self-tracking technologies allow, since their users are not limited to keeping quantified information to themselves but share and discuss it among themselves.

PART III, Body Quantification and Mental Health, shifts the focus towards the relationship between quantification and mental health. It begins with Minozzo's chapter which provides useful reflections on the affective dimension of anxiety through a critical engagement with the recent history of its diagnosis and treatment in the context of psychological care. A key argument in Minozzo's contribution relates to the way mainstream psychiatry and the growing wellness industry reduce the subject to the status of the 'dividual', that is to say, a form of alienated ontology that is based on consumption, identification, and endless quantification, through which individuals become data and numbers. 'Dividuality', as Deleuze argues, is also characteristic of the 'society of control' in which we live, and whereby self-surveillance and algorithmic profiling have become a primary form of governance. What transpires out of this dividuation process and in relation to diagnoses and treatments of anxiety and depression, is the loss of the possibility of experiencing a 'subjective truth', according to Minozzo, since the constant pathologising and medicalising of anxiety and the desire to eliminate it, in today's culture, end up depriving the subject from the ability to delve deeper into the root causes of suffering and malaise and the opportunity to learn lessons from such experiences. The ethico-political question thus becomes: 'can the dividual speak?' And, if so, is the clinic ready to listen? The next chapter by Zeena Feldman also considers the issue of mental health but within the broader context of digital culture. Focussing on the increasing use of smartphones in the treatment of anxiety and depression, this chapter provides a very useful mapping of available apps in the UK that are dedicated to mental health and wellbeing, offering critical reflections on the ways these technologies reframe what mental health is in the first place and shift health responsibilities onto the individual. Feldman begins by tracing the key shifts in digital culture with regard to hardware, software, and content evolutions. She then proceeds to develop an analytical framework revolving around four key components, namely the intended audience of mental health apps, their communicative affordances, business model and, finally, therapeutic approach. From here the author develops the concept of *me apps* to account for the increasing individualisation, commercialisation, and desocialisation aspects that are characteristic of the smartphone era. The chapter ends with some reflections on alternative ways of designing technologies of mental health that are oriented towards more collaborative understandings of digital culture and wellbeing.

PART IV, Body Quantification and Smart Machines, considers issues of embodiment, perception, Artificial Intelligence (AI) and smart technologies.

Behind a 'smart machine' there is always a 'smart worker'. This maxim is effectively developed by Phoebe V. Moore, who wants, above all, to show that the working world of 'smart AI trainers' should not be equated with mere digital voyeurism which often implies negative and traumatic experiences, as reported by some of Facebook's moderators. Instead, Moore's chapter considers the wider ontological and ethical issues concerning smart workers in the AI field. It interrogates how intelligence, through textual and image recognition, is depicted and derived, and what kind of embodied labour goes into such AI processes. The main theoretical challenge arising from the consideration of the working world of smart AI trainers comes from the social invisibility to which their work is relegated, resembling, in this sense, the very invisible operations that machines allow and produce. Given this fact, it is necessary, according to Moore, to place the value of work not only in the production, organisation, and manipulation of data, but also in the projection, conscious and unconscious, of human skills onto the smart machines themselves. Many of these skills transcend the domain of the mere quantification of the mental performance of workers and are directly connected with the material conditions that support the cognitive processes of work and the somatic conditions inherent in the bodies and embodied performances of workers. Knowing, in advance, that Artificial Intelligence appropriates these two dimensions – cognitive (mental) and material (manual) –, it is therefore imperative to recognise and protect the rights of such invisible workers and to ensure that the information collected from them is not discriminatory, but can help improve their working conditions, in term of both their psychological welfare and their wage conditions. The next and final chapter in this collection focuses on issues related to the sensory sphere of sensations, bringing together quantitative and qualitative aspects relating to robotic research on the human body. Here the author, Laura Corti, starts with the case of the 'neuroprosthetic hand' to show the theoretical and practical insufficiencies of a purely quantitative approach to the somatic processes inherent to robotic research. If this research considers only the information given by neural signals thereby reducing the touch to the mere manipulation of objects, there is, in qualitative terms and according to Corti, an omission of the subjective dimensions that are present in all perceptual tactile activities. To overcome the gap between information and sensation – still anchored in the Cartesian soul-body dualism – Corti advocates a broadly phenomenological approach, rooted in the Husserlian idea of *Leib* (the living and lived body), in order to respond to those practical concerns of neuro-robotics vis-à-vis the coupling of information with the sensations of objects. Only through such coupling, Corti argues, could a better analysis of the complex relationship between prosthetic technologies and the human body (lived body) be made.

References

Berlin, I. (1956). *The age of enlightenment: The eighteenth century philosophers*. Boston, MA: Houghton Mifflin.

Canguilhem, G. (1991). *The normal and the pathological.* New York, NY: Zone Books.
Cappel, V. (2021). The plurality of daily digital health. The emergence of a new form of health coordination. *Historical Social Research, 46*(1), 230–260.
Condillac, E. B. D. (1877). *La Langue des Calculus.* Paris: Librairie Sandoz et Fischbacher.
Diaz-Bone, R. (2021). Economics of convention meets Canguilhem. *Historical Social Research, 46*(1), 285–311.
Gadamer, H.-G. (1993). *Über die Verborgenheit der Gesundheit: Aufsätze und Vorträge.* Frankfurt am Main: Suhrkamp.
Heidegger, M. (2001). *Zollikon seminars. Protocols – Conversations – Letters* (F. K. Mayr & R. Askay, Trans.). Evanston, IL: Northwestern University Press.
Hille, L. (2016). The quantified self – Ubiquitous control. Retrieved from http://www.digital-development-debates.org/issue-16-food-farming-trend-the-quantified-self-ubiquitous-control.html
Locke, J. (1979). *An essay concerning human understanding,* Edited with a Foreword by Peter H. Nidditch. Oxford: Clarendon Press.
Noji, E., Kappler, K., & Vormbusch, U. (2021). Situating conventions of health: Transformations, inaccuracies, and the limits of measuring in the field of self-tracking. *Historical Social Research, 46*(1), 261–284.
Sysling, F. (2019). Measurement, self-tracking and the history of science: An introduction. *History of Science, 58*(2), 103–116. doi: 10.1177/0073275319865830.
Vitruvius. (1999). *Ten books on architecture.* Translation by Ingrid D. Rowland Commentary and Illustrations by Thomas Noble Howe with additional Commentary by Ingrid D. Rowland and Michael J. Dewar. Cambridge: Cambridge University Press.
Wolf, G. I., & De Groot, M. (2020). A Conceptual Framework for Personal Science', *Frontiers in Computer Science, 2*(21), 1–5.
YouGov. (2021). COVID certificates: where do the public stand? Retrieved from https://yougov.co.uk/topics/politics/articles-reports/2021/04/12/covid-certificateswhere-do-public-stand.

Part I

Body Quantification and Subjectivity: Philosophical Perspectives

Chapter 1

Body, Media and Quantification

Joaquim Braga

Abstract

'What is the meaning of the process of body quantification?' – This is the central question of this chapter. With it, the author intends to question and analyse the way the body relates to new technologies and new technical procedures, and how these depend on the body itself to constitute themselves as mediating cultural forms. To make this enquiry feasible, the author shall critically examine the status of 'object' to which the body has been relegated by the myths of quantification, notably those concerning the universal symbolic character of numbers and measurement techniques. If the body is considered as a mere 'quantified object', then it is unlikely to be distinguished from other objects subjected to the same process. Consequently, it will easily tend to support the imaginary of technological determinism that prevails in our societies. Health trackers for personal use are, today, a good example of how the body is a fundamental element of such imaginary, since the feeling of control that they nurture in their users is also connected with the possibility of sharing information about the body itself. Given all these factors, the author intends to argue that, instead of being a simple quantified object, the body is, for new quantification technologies (namely those related to self-care), a 'medium of the media', insofar as it reinforces the effects of technological mediation processes, and potentialises the increased digital convergence of media. Recognising this means, finally, that the imaginary of quantification and associated techno-myths are also stimulated and reproduced by an extra-discursive somatic level inherent in the empirical use we make of technological devices.

Keywords: Convergence; embodiment; information; mediation; self-care; technology

The Quantification of Bodies in Health: Multidisciplinary Perspectives, 15–28
Copyright © 2022 by Joaquim Braga
Published under an exclusive license by Emerald Publishing Limited
doi:10.1108/978-1-80071-883-820211003

Introduction

The several somatic dimensions involved in mediation and quantification processes – which are the main subjects of this chapter – constitute a theoretical horizon still full of misconceptions and, in many cases, incapable of providing a true epistemic status within the scope of a media theory of such processes. Moreover, in the prevailing discourse on the relationship between medium and body – chiefly anchored in McLuhan's prosthesis-theory – there is a strong anthropomorphic approach that prevents us from glimpsing and exploring possible articulations and links entirely. Allied to this approach are also descriptive frameworks that, in the form of *ekphrasis*, tend to favour more the reification of the individual experiences and the psychic projections of human beings, and less the awareness of the multiple connections that bond the human body to mediation processes. As I want to demonstrate, the lack of a conceptual framework capable of highlighting all these connections not only prevents any critical updating of the concepts used by media theory, but also calls into question analyses of new mediation devices. In addition to that, conceptual misunderstandings tend to obscure the somatic inscriptions that each new medium fosters, as well as their structural effects on the configuration of the medium itself. Considering all these possibilities, I adopt, as a main maxim, the following seminal formulation: in each new mediation artefact there are self-reflexive technological features that, both in the empirical sphere and in the imaginary sphere, restore the place of the body in its own material constitution. Therefore, the purpose of this chapter is twofold: to analyse both the *inscriptions of the body* in technological media and the *representations of the body* prompted by them.

Quantification processes can have multiple objects, organic and inorganic, natural and artificial; but when analysed theoretically, objects tend to lose both the value of their material nature and the value of their symbolic profile. The general tendency is to analyse, above all, the techniques and technological devices that make them possible, as well the main differences that gradually occur among them. We are still, at this theoretical stage, linked to the old paradigm of *mathesis universalis*, reformulated by René Descartes, in his *Règles pour la Direction de l'Esprit*, to support 'a general science that explains everything that it is possible to inquire into concerning order and measure, without applying them to a particular subject-matter' (Descartes, 2003, p. 27).

Consequently, the body as a 'quantified object' is no longer distinguished from all other quantifiable objects. Features that symmetrically describe the body as one more object among many others, and, in the context of a broad technological determinism, as a phenomenon that is unilaterally transformed, distorted, and even dematerialised by measuring techniques and instruments, easily come to light. Theorists of new quantification technologies, such as Deborah Lupton, claim that although

> other aspects of one's everyday life (e.g., work outputs or social encounters) are often recorded as part of producing the quantified self, bodily functions represent a major target of self-tracking activities. (Lupton, 2013, p. 395)

Here it is convenient to ask, first, why *bodily functions* are relevant for the development of the quantification technologies themselves and to question whether the body, at the heart of the quantification processes, should or could be reduced to a simple object status?

Body and Media Theory

For many centuries, the idea of a human body was built through a strong connection with various cultural media. In Western thought, the body was understood according to two main approaches: firstly, as a *representation subject* and, secondly, as an *articulation metaphor*.

In the first case, as a representation subject, the human figure was primarily used to ascertain its expressive potentialities and, simultaneously, through them, those of art itself. Plastic artistic forms, such as sculpture and painting, created and offered us a kind of 'body frame' that covers the pictorial depictions based on human figures. Aesthetic concepts linked to art, such as those of proportion and volume, greatly express the referential value of the body for the configuration and appreciation of all other pictorial elements that can also be symbolised by a picture or a statue. In short, the forms of representation of the body tend to support all other forms of representation of objects in general. In the second approach, as an articulation metaphor, the anatomy of human body came to support the discourse of articulation of 'parts' within the 'whole', extending this logic not only to artistic objects and technological artefacts, but also to several forms of social organisation, political and religious, for instance. In this case, the threshold between body and culture is rather tenuous, because as is evident from the ancient idea of organism – according to which an organ has an instrumental value and a specific function quite like a handmade tool – the notion of body already presupposes a convergence with certain forms of mediation. Common to these two anchors that shape the idea of 'body' is the conception of an expressive contiguity between body and cultural artefacts. Following the ancient conception that the body could render visible certain psychic states and that there is an undeniable transparency between psychic states and their expression, in cultural media there is an intimate analogous link between their own operability and somatic structures, functions and dispositions. The greatest example of this organic unity are the famous words that Socrates, in *Phaedrus*, uses to define the art of discourse in general: 'every discourse ought to be a living creature, having a body of its own and a head and feet' (Plato, 1892, pp. 472–473), in which the parts remain fully articulated with a whole.

The imaginary of pre-digital media is thus anchored in a somatic analogue link, based on the idea of a pre-given and pre-defined body, in which the body itself serves to reinforce the nature-culture binomial. With the emergence of new media – particularly digital media – the suggestive power of the body, although not entirely eliminated, tends to undergo a significant set of changes. The organic metaphor of the parts and the whole is now fully transformed by the active and indispensable involvement of the bodies of users of new media in the several operations provided by them. The body is no longer just a matter of representation;

it also reflects the way in which digital media operates technologically. Thus, if we want to qualify the new metaphor that prevails in the huge theoretical spectrum developed by the studies of new media and new technologies, it may be called the *metaphor of disappearance*.

It is part of the symbolic nature of all metaphors to contain a kind of expressive ecstasy, which allows them to further suggest rather than to properly signify. Although metaphor in general is not, in a narrow sense, a concept, it supports the sense-making processes of concepts, both in their formulation and representation, and, above all, in their unification within a given theory or given theoretical paradigm. This happens to what I call the metaphor of disappearance. In new media theories, such metaphor derives essentially from five assumptions that connect with each other: first, media are extensions of the human body and, therefore, tend to gradually replace the body itself – what starts to be considered an 'extension' becomes, for instance, in Marshall McLuhan's famous prosthetic lexicon, an 'amputation' (McLuhan, 2001, p. 49); second, in impersonal communication at a distance, mediated by digital devices, the invisibility of the interlocutors' body results in a disembodied experience; third, in body depictions operated by digital means, due to the possibility of manipulating pictorial configurations, the old idea of an empirical referent of the body fades and, in its place, the idea of the fragment and of the illusion prevails; fourth, in so-called 'immersion technologies', the viewer-user experiences a kind of somatic dissolution, as there is no clear demarcation line between their body, their artificial representations and those of other multimodal elements that allow the immersion process itself; fifth, and finally, the supposed body disappearance suggests and is suggested by the disappearance of the medium itself, as described, for instance, by Jay David Bolter and Richard Grusin in their book *Remediation: Understanding New Media* (1999).

Through these five assumptions it is possible to see how the metaphor of disappearance intends to replace its precedent – the *metaphor of appearance* – which enlivened the theoretical discourse on pre-digital media and analogical inscription surfaces, such as those of the photographic medium. There is no doubt that, as can be inferred from Roland Barthes' descriptions of photography, the metaphor of appearance has, in its semantic genealogy, an ancestral religious pregnancy, linked to the myth of *vera icona* (Barthes, 1980, pp. 126–133). Through the picture a body appears; in this case the face of Christ, who is the true and faithful visible sign of his existence.

Despite their many and different entailments, the two kinds of metaphors share the same aesthetic paradigm – the paradigm of visibility. *Making the invisible visible* has always been the operative formula associated with the symbolic power of all media. Even if it was deeply rooted within a mythological semantic heritage, it is a formula with a technological import. In the second case, given by the opposite movement of disappearance, the paradigm of visibility is preserved, but with the subtle difference of turning a technological cause into a veritable technological effect. The abovementioned five assumptions are, in fact, anchored in the effects triggered by technological mediation devices and, as such, denote a passive nature of their users. In its eminently religious formulation, as grasped in medieval thought, the invisible never becomes absolutely visible. It never manifests and exhausts itself in a particular and single sensible form – that is, it transcends its material inscription. This discourse, which supports, for instance, the descriptions of religious icons, mitigates the technological import of mediation and its respective core effects.

Consequently, the relevant question that can be inferred from these five assumptions concerns the material nature of media, namely digital media. To be formulated, the metaphor of appearance had to suppress the materiality of the medium. The old metaphysical precept of the subjection of 'matter' to 'form' – as it is formulated in ancient philosophical thought, both in the Platonic theory of ideas and in the Aristotelian theory of the four causes – has shaped, until our days, media studies and a significant part of aesthetics and philosophy of art. The passive role of matter in relation to the active role of form almost always served the expressivist version of the mind's intentionality and its psychical unity.

Such negative conception of the medium's materiality is not, however, overcome by the metaphor of disappearance. On the contrary, the negative approach is here preserved and even seems, in its several types, to sublimate its philosophical legacy. Lev Manovich, in his seminal work on new media, initially raises the following question about digital interfaces: 'What are the relationships between the physical space where the viewer is located, her body, and the screen space?' (Manovich, 2001, pp. 94–95). According to Manovich, unlike the pre-digital screen, where there is a clear contrast between observer and medium, in the digital universe this contrast no longer holds. The author gives the example of the so-called 'virtual reality' (VR) to vindicate the belief on the screen disappearance: 'with VR, the screen disappears altogether', namely, as he reiterates,

> The virtual space, previously confined to a painting or a movie screen, now completely encompasses the real space. Frontality, rectangular surface, difference in scale is all gone. The screen has vanished. (Manovich, 2001, p. 97)

Yet, as he adds, such disappearance is initially caused by the sensory-motor operations of the viewer-user: 'to look up in virtual space, one has to look up in physical space'. In this mediation context, 'The spectator is no longer chained, immobilized, anesthetized by the apparatus that serves her ready-made images; now she has to work, to speak, in order to see' (Manovich, 2001, p. 109). Despite such performative dimension, however, Manovich finds in VR technology an unsurpassed 'paradox', by the fact that 'it requires the viewer to move in order to see an image and at the same time physically ties her to a machine' (Manovich, 2001, p. 110).

The emergence and development of immersion technologies allow us, in accordance with the multi-sensory experiences they induce, to find a major source of descriptions related to techno-fantasies. Unlike those of the past, which are based in purely speculative, utopian and dystopian literary scenarios, these descriptions have empirical features given by users' experiences. Digital materiality is not autonomous, substantial, but rather derived from the user's performative effects on the medium. Therefore, we cannot conceive of the materiality of new media according to the same assumptions as pre-digital media since the latter have almost always been explained through the epistemological possibilities and boundaries of the subject-object relationship. With the emergence of digital technologies, materiality itself came to acquire a new ontological status, whose nature is no longer determined under the paradigm of mere observation. In general, the materiality of the digital medium is traced by a continuous exchange between the technological dispositions of the medium and the sensory-motor dispositions of the viewer-user. In other words, it is not the Cartesian materiality of the extension of bodies – the *res extensa*, given *in* and *by* space – that is at stake, but a deep, temporal phenomenon. One of the great transformations carried out by digitality is precisely that materiality can only be intuited through the temporal order of operations made possible by the medium; it is, consequently, an operative materiality, devoid of an autonomous ontological substrate.

Nevertheless, we must follow the principle that the materiality of a medium does not match that of the objects of our cognitive environment. First, because it is in close articulation with the possibilities of meaning offered by the medium, even if this fact gives it, at a perceptive level, a certain degree of sensible discretion. There are media which display a discrete material nature – such as those used by scientific knowledge – unlike others whose materiality is exponential and an integral part of their symbolic value, as is the case with works of art. Thus, mediation processes are inscribed in the perception of their material elements, sometimes enhancing them, sometimes weakening them, just as the nature of such elements influences *ab initio* mediation itself.

In the particular case of digital media, their materiality should not be confined or reduced to that of the screen. Doing so without considering all the other material dimensions that support said media, gives rise to strong misunderstandings that compromise any theoretical scrutiny. From a comparative point of view, we can, as Lev Manovich does, draw an evolutionary line between the cinematic screen and the computer screen and find important convergence and divergence points. However, in both cases, materiality is not restricted to the screen. This is well illustrated by digital media in that they bring into play several and unusual material implications that intersect with each other and bear the signs of their user's bodies. Indeed, when we speak of digital materiality, we must describe it as a *shared materiality*. Digital materiality does not resemble the materiality of traditional media – it requires performance, it requires touch, it requires body contact. This means that it is a relational materiality, built by the interactions between users and devices, and, like the information contents each device can provide, it can also be to a certain degree manipulated and changed. To truly understand this conception, we must set aside the inaccurate idea that a medium is a mere object of our perception. Not being comparable to the objects of our cognitive environment, the materiality of each medium is intrinsically connected with mediation processes and, in this narrow sense, does not always acquire the same sensible expression.

Techno-myths and Quantification

The metaphor of bodily disappearance is the outcome of an unwavering bond between media and technology, reinforced, above all, by techno-fantasies – those utopian and dystopian descriptions emerging from literature, advertising, politics, and philosophy itself. The scientific enquiry of the body's nature, as well as the development of medical and therapeutic practices, inevitably implied the destruction of certain beliefs which, to a significant extent, had originated from cultural mediation forms. However, nothing can lead us to claim that others have not replaced such beliefs, mostly through the emergence of new technological artefacts. An example of this is the Cartesian archetype of *res extensa*, whose theoretical profile cannot be thought without the analogical link between machine and organism. Descartes drew from the technological inventions of his time, such as the hydraulic automata, the mechanistic model to be applied to bodies' motor functions and anatomical structures. Georges Canguilhem points out in his lecture, *Machine et organism*, that the mechanistic model is one-dimensional, once it imposes an autonomous technological reality on the study of the body. Thus, 'the relationship between machine and organism has generally been studied in only one way'; in most cases, 'the organism has been explained on the basis of a preconceived idea of the structure and functioning of the machine' and, for this reason, 'only rarely have the structure and function of the organism been used to make the construction of the machine itself more understandable' (Canguilhem, 1992, p. 45).

Certainly, science and technology, in tight connection, pursue together a universalisation purpose. The body represents, for both, a primordial source of dissemination of their precepts, discoveries and inventions. Technical-scientific knowledge has in the body its great pervasive expression, since it is also through it that the results, it can achieve, become more visible and understandable. This fact is so established that one can hardly imagine the connection between the two domains – between science and technology – without the pivotal inclusion of the human body.

Now, a *quantified body* is one of the possible expressions of a *Cartesian body*; it easily becomes a machine-like body, in which all its structures, functions and operations are measurable and thus also comparable to each other and to all other bodies. Hereupon, numbers govern the relationship among the media implicated in processes of body quantification. For Theodore Porter, for instance, quantification is based on an economy of scientific communication, which, in turn, allows its acceptance and the consequent dissemination of the scientific research outcomes. He defines it as 'a form of rhetoric that is especially effective for diffusing research findings to other laboratories, languages, countries and continents'; since 'mathematics is a highly structured language' – that is, 'a language of rules' – in those cases where 'a reasoning process can be made computable, we can be confident that we are dealing with something that has been universalized' (Porter, 1992, p. 644). The relevant word here is *trust*. As Porter reiterates in this regard, 'reliance on numbers and quantitative manipulation minimizes the need for intimate knowledge and personal trust', just as there is a perfect link between quantification and communication capable of producing 'knowledge independent of the particular people who make it' (Porter, 1995, p. IX). Otherwise stated, the issue of trust in numbers lies in the belief that the decisions they themselves support 'has at least the appearance of being fair and impersonal', and, since scientific objectivity demands neutrality, quantification processes are 'a way of making decisions without seeming to decide' (Porter, 1995, p. 8). Under this light, myths of quantification tend precisely to stem from beliefs in the magical power of numbers, in the universal language of mathematics, in the alleged affective neutrality of numbers and mathematics within the measurement and comparison processes. They are, in short, myths of 'disembodiment', which in turn easily converge with the widespread myth of technological neutrality.

We must always bear in mind that in any creation of techno-myths there is a double principle that expresses the unlimited desire to overturn the constraints imposed by technological devices. Firstly, technological fantasies take advantage of the spectrum of possibilities hanging out of the invention and emergence of artefacts; secondly, such fantasies, integrating the same possibilities into a futuristic scenario, distinct from the everyday use of artefacts, turn technology itself into a self-contained reality capable of self-reproduction and without human intervention at all.

Quantification and Information

The phenomenon of quantification is also part of the scope of the social imaginary promoted and developed by technology over time. For a long time now, the close link between information techniques and quantification processes served as a basis to the new demands of science, as well as to new forms of mass communication. The very idea of 'knowledge' is today, more than ever, inseparable from such link. In the last decade of the nineteenth century, J. McKeen Cattell made the paradigmatic claim that 'modern knowledge and ways of thought seem to depend more and more on quantity and measurement' and, consequently, as the author illustrates, 'we no longer speak of the boundless sea and the innumerable host of the Argives. We ask, how many? how much?'. Such symbolic effects of quantification on linguistic expression also reveal that 'the line between science and everyday knowledge is, indeed, continually shifting', to the point that the 'methods of measurement and their more important results take their place in the widening circles of common knowledge and daily life' (Cattell, 1893, p. 317).

As in the case of linguistic expression, mentioned by Cattell, some of the most evident effects of the quantification processes are reflected, in turn, in the way information means are thought. One such example is suggested by the application of mathematical models to communication processes. Claude Shannon and Warren Weaver reduced the idea of a *mathematical theory of communication* to the concept of information, especially to the quantitative determination of the contents exchanged, through a mediation channel, between a sender and a receiver. It was enough for that, according to their mathematical models, to abstract the contents from the 'noise' that intervenes in each communication exchange process

(Shannon & Weaver, 1998, pp. 65–80). Both authors also start from a unimodal view of mediation, centred, solely and exclusively, on a single medium, be it visual or purely auditory. Just as information theory does not positively include semantic issues related to communication exchange, so the relationships between different media – the multimodal horizon of communication – are not considered. There is no doubt that information theory, thus conceived, is heir to the great theoretical postulates of linguistics and semiotics. Both theoretical areas, deeply developed and promoted in the two last centuries, are fundamentally tied to the informative content that each sign, according to its representation modes, can convey. Here, the versatile nature of representation prevails, but almost always to the detriment of its material inscription and the multimodal relations that it can often imply.

Now, one of the key features of quantitative information has to do with the possibilities of its reproduction. Regardless of the medium that, for the first time, provides a particular informational matter, the related content only truly becomes a *fact of information* when several distinct media can reproduce it. Information in general generates and propagates itself through a transcendent effect over the nature of the medium associated with it. Paradoxically, however, it is because of such an effect that it manages to impose a linear convergence among media, to the point that unsurpassed material and symbolic differences cease to exist among them. Accordingly, Steffen Mau asserts in his book, *The Metric Society,* that

> The numerical description of the world relies on the fact that information can be lifted out of the medium in which it is embedded, yet still be related back to it at any time;

moreover, quantitative information 'can be combined with other information in various ways and readily reused', thus increasing the possibility 'to link more and more data' and to give rise to 'a world of comparability in which hitherto barely connected or wholly unconnected 'islands' are brought into a relationship with each other' (Mau, 2019, p. 14). Such a world of comparability engendered by quantification processes and the medial convergence they allow should also be, for instance, thought of according to the geometrical possibilities of the two-dimensional inscription surfaces. The depiction of Vitruvian man, as Leonardo da Vinci shaped it, epitomises, precisely, a figurative convergence of the body with the picture, but through a geometric nexus conceived by the circle and the square. Therefore, graphical two-dimensionality combined with geometry is an incessant source of quantitative information – or, in the words of Bruno Latour, 'You cannot measure the sun, but you can measure a photograph of the sun with a ruler' (Latour, 1990, p. 46).

It is now important to ask what then, according to this theoretical background, will be the relevance of the body to the double convergence among media and between them and the body itself.

In order not to give the body a plain object status, only comprehensible under the broad spectrum of causal relationships, it is necessary to conceive it as condition and possibility of our symbolic constructions and interactions. Ernst Cassirer, in his *Philosophie der symbolischen Formen*, anchored the formation of symbolic inscriptions to the expressive coupling of body and soul. According to Cassirer, such relationship presents itself as the first *Vorbild* (prototype) and *Musterbild* (model) of a symbolic relation (Cassirer, 1994, p. 117), and, without it, it would be difficult to understand all sense-making processes that each symbolic form allows, as well as the material and sensible elements of their multiple inscriptions.

Taking this into account, we cannot conceive the human body as a mere object of information, among many others. Following this precept, on the contrary, would give it a passive epistemological nature, whose main theoretical extension is announced in contemporary utopian and dystopian narratives related to its alleged complete disappearance. Nor can we conceive of the body only as an inscription surface, as Michel Foucault generally did. Not revealing himself in a purely phenomenological approach, in which the body appears to be stripped of its historical-social configurations, Foucault tried to conceive power relations in accordance with their somatic inscriptions. For the French author, the body is the 'inscription surface of events' (*surface d'inscription des événements*) *par excellence*, namely those related to punitive and disciplinary processes that weave social order and normative discourses; therefore, even more assertively, Foucault applies his genealogical method to the 'articulation of the body with history', in order 'to show a body totally imprinted by history and the ways of history's destruction of the body' (Foucault, 1971, p. 143). Foucault tends to consider such articulation, consequently, as a one-way process, in which history vigorously prevails over the body. Quite the reverse – and taking into account Cassirer's archetypal model – the body is not only a surface, but, *ab initio*, the possibility factor of any inscription surface.

Information and Self-care

There is a *spontaneous sense of activity* that is imposed on what we grasp from the body and through the body, despite being susceptible to changes and transformations by social and cultural developments. Even in those cases where the body is intervened upon by medical care, the body remains irreducible to a mere object status. The technical-scientific pressure exerted on the human body (as with the case of so-called health trackers for personal use) demonstrates very well the need *to give sense* to quantification through its somatic inscription. The subtle alliance between number and rhythm – as had been intuited, albeit in a mystical-mathematical approach, by Pythagorean thought – is not at all unimportant for understanding the effects caused by use of body trackers in general terms. Numbers seem to more accurately reflect the users' feelings of such devices when applied to the body and the auscultation of its physiological dynamics. Nevertheless, here what is in operation is the principle that these sensations are already the result of an interaction process between human being and machine, not existing outside it, but within it. Furthermore, in combination with these technological developments and the personal use of self-tracking tools, there is a kind of communicative pressure, whose main function is to arouse interest in sharing information and, through this, enable comparisons between the data obtained by their users. This sharing of information, in addition to reinforcing the body's involvement in communication processes, greatly increases the feeling of control over it.

The theoretical issues raised by novel personal care technologies are mainly centred on the relationship between the search for information and the privileged self-perception of the body. Within the same analytical scope, Luciano Floridi proposes, in the processes of 'dephysicalization and typification of individuals' (Floridi, 2014, p. 75), two main phenomena that articulate the body with new digital health technologies. The first is called 'the transparent body' and concerns the way in which technological devices – for example, wearable smart devices used in monitoring sports activities – make 'our bodies more usefully and pleasantly transparent to ourselves'; the second is called 'the shared body' and designates the typification of the body according to certain information transmission parameters, which naturally implies biological comparisons between my body and the bodies of others, such as those made through genetic characterization (Floridi, 2014, pp. 75–77). Sharing these informative contents can, however, bring up some problems to the 'health' of users of technological devices. Although devices may increase positive feelings – such as 'less loneliness, more hope, easier spreading of best practices, more prevention, and better planning' – the uncontrolled use of these devices can lead to the fallacious judgement of 'everybody does it', to the point of the belief in 'normality in numbers' be able to arouse an abrupt transition from 'medicalization to the socialization of unhealthy choices or habits' (Floridi, 2014, p. 77). Metaphorically illustrating this effect, Floridi tells us that, potentially, 'If I can join a group that endorses nail-biting, I may end up thinking it is not an impulse control disorder that needs treatment' (Floridi, 2014, p. 77). In general, as Floridi adds, the transparency and the sharing of information about the body is linked to the following three growing trends: 'a democratization of health information, an increasing availability of user-generated contents that are health-related, and a socialization of health conditions'; if the result of 'democratization' comes from the increase in the generation and accessibility of information to an unlimited number of individuals, 'socialization', in turn, puts at stake the active role of patients themselves in the production and sharing of health information (Floridi, 2014, pp. 77–78).

The sociological formulations on the effects of self-tracking tools, such as those proposed by Floridi, are, nevertheless, still insufficient to substantiate all possible personal and interpersonal relationships that their users establish with the technological means involved. Such relations, which greatly foster the increase of information and its social sharing, are not only aroused by mere mental representations. They are, indeed, *embodied relations* and must already be situated at the level of a high performative bound of the user's body with the contents that the self-care media enhance. Yet, as far as this is concerned, we must always bear in mind that not all users' sensory-motor dispositions operatively converge with the technological dispositions of the digital medium. The case of touch digital devices is a good illustration of this. Finger somatic capacities, while touching a screen that triggers a set of mediation operations, are not entirely actualized; most of its sensory skills are inhibited. For instance, the user does not feel the roughness of the surface or the motor resistance it may offer. There is, so to speak, a deep divergence between motor skills and sensory skills. Many media thinkers, supported in part by Maurice Merleau-Ponty's body phenomenology, advocate the notion of an alleged techno-biological convergence of the body with the digital machines, in virtue of a total coupling of the eye with the hand. Inversely, such implicit divergence must be understood as a major 'resistance' effect of the digital medium's materiality, which, in this case, refers and expresses to what I have already called *shared materiality* between user and medium.

Indeed, according to what I have argued above, one of the *sui generis* features of digital interfaces is the relationship established between the user's operations and the representation contents provided by the medium itself. The two dimensions are not indifferent to each other. On the contrary, they feed on each other to suggest and create the illusion of a perfect functional convergence. But what does this mean? That the representation contents – such as the graphic and quantitative inscription on the depiction of human bodies – replicate, in a purely mimetic way, the viewer's feeling of himself/herself and, as a machine user, of his/her own body?

At first, there is, in fact, a symmetrical bond between use and observation, the meaning of which comes from the manipulation possibilities that each medium provides. The machine users can configure, size, select, add, and delete the multi-modal information that suits them best as observers; they may, by way of example, forge their picture, to the point where their portrait seems younger than they really are. Most digital interfaces lend themselves to such purpose – to the expressive coupling of operations with representations. Secondly, the bond between use and observation acquires a distinct status. It is no longer a matter of converging the use of the medium with its inscription possibilities, but rather of reversing the logic of its use. Finally, we come into the realm of the stereotyped nature of representations, whether of the figure of the human body or even of other living beings. Contrary to what could be expected, it seems to be a consensual fact that digital media have reproduced many contents that, in one way or another, had been relegated by traditional media to the background, like certain stereotypical views related to sexuality and human gender. In the world of advertising, for instance, pictorial contents in newspapers, magazines and television have increasingly come to include both the female body and the male body. In the present-day sphere of digital media, on the contrary, the female voice is the predominant voice in the services of the so-called 'intelligent virtual assistants', such as those of voice-guided navigation.

What are the reasons that lead to such massive return of stereotypes? We can list several: from the apparent communicative need to multiply information objects, to the weakening of the temporal distance among those same objects. However, that is just one side of the coin. We will also have to consider what might be the manipulative effects that the medium allows and causes on the user, and include another side linked to the reproduction of stereotypes. It belongs to the nature of stereotypes to introduce into our time consciousness a wide bridge between past and future, unable to be undone by the present – in other words, *what has been is what will always be.* The impossibility of change characterizes the idea of stereotype – and it is hereupon that its peculiar meaning-making process serves well the digital medium; it works as a kind of counterbalance to digital manipulation, by mitigating the operative and symmetrical effects of the coupling of the use (user) with the observation (observer). The user lends, so to speak, his/her body or parts of it to the machine, so that the medium itself can be workable and controlled. At the same time, in the strict domain of representation, stereotypes are in charge of revealing and reproducing perfect, untouchable, and healthy bodies, full of virility and sensuality.

Final Remarks

If self-care practices supported by new technological means of quantification have an enormous potential for massification, it is because, first of all, they 'appear' to reduce the complexity of mediation processes and give the body a prominent place in the overcoming of such complexity. From a strictly theoretical point of view, the reduction of complexity can only be fully understood, having as a basic premise the idea that each user of a technological self-care device employs, simultaneously, in his/her day-to-day, other media to obtain and generate information. In these two acts of seeking and generating information, there are often more uncertainties than certainties, more reactions than responses. That is why, too, the *return to the care of one's own body*, mediated by quantification processes, works as a powerful way for new media users to recover or mitigate this lost balance in the vast universe of communication channels and information networks. The feeling of certainty, induced by the information on personal physical well-being and the possibility of it being controlled daily, seems to restore and actualise, in a certain way, the trust in the technological universe.

In summary, the meaning we give to reality includes an active mediation of the body. From the moment when the body also becomes an object of quantification, all other quantified and quantifiable phenomena take on exponential meaning – their suitability and acceptability as objects of quantification is to some extent reinforced and tends to cease to be put in question. The more necessary the convergence of media becomes, the greater the involvement of the body. The body is, in this strict sense, a *medium of the media*. Several processes and forms of mediation are inscribed in and through the body, the most visible effects of which are revealed in the way a new medium reuses the operative conditions and functions of the preceding ones. Since the body is neither passive nor unresponsive to all these processes and forms, it can generate in itself a somatic memory of mediation. We also owe to this somatic memory the possibilities of articulation of media and technology, as well as the convergence links that support these possibilities. Learning to 'count on fingers' is perhaps the oldest and best illustration of such phenomenon.

References

Barthes, R. (1980). *La chambre claire. Note sur la photographie.* Paris: Gallimard/Seuil.
Bolter, J. D., & Grusin, R. (1999). *Remediation: Understanding new media.* Cambridge, MA: The MIT Press.
Canguilhem, G. (1992). Machine and organism (M. Cohen and R. Cherry, Trans.). In J. Crary & S. Kwinter (Eds.), *Incorporations* (pp. 44–69). New York, NY: Zone Books.
Cassirer, E. (1994). *Philosophie der symbolischen Formen, Dritter Teil: Phänomenologie der Erkenntnis.* Darmstadt: Wissenschaftliche Buchgesellschaft.
Cattell, J. M. (1893). Mental measurement. *The Philosophical Review, 2*(3), 316–332.
Descartes, R. (2003). *Règles pour la Direction de l'Esprit.* Trad. et notes de J. Sirven. Paris: Vrin.
Floridi, L. (2014). *The fourth revolution: How the infosphere is reshaping human reality.* Oxford: Oxford University Press.
Foucault, M. (1971). Nietzsche, la généalogie, l'histoire. In D. Defert, F. Ewald., & J. Lagrange (Eds.), *Dits et Écrits* (Vol. 2, 1970–1975, pp. 136–156). Paris: Gallimard.
Latour, B. (1990). Drawing things together. In M. Lynch & S. Woolgar (Eds.), *Representation in scientific practice* (pp. 19–68). London: The MIT Press.
Lupton, D. (2013). Quantifying the body: Monitoring and measuring health in the age of mHealth technologies. *Critical Public Health, 23*(4), 393–403.
Manovich, L. (2001). *The language of new media.* Cambridge, MA: The MIT Press.
Mau, S. (2019). *The metric society: On the quantification of the social* (S. Howe, Trans.). Cambridge: Polity Press.
McLuhan, M. (2001). *Understanding media: The extensions of man.* London: Routledge.
Plato. (1892). Phaedrus. In *The dialogues of Plato* (Vol. I, 3rd ed., pp. 391–490) (B. Jowett, Trans.). London: Oxford University Press.
Porter, T. M. (1992). Quantification and the accounting ideal in science. *Social Studies of Science, 22*(4), 633–651.
Porter, T. M. (1995). *Trust in numbers: The pursuit of objectivity in science and public life.* Princeton, NJ: Princeton University Press.
Shannon, C., & Weaver, W. (1998). *The mathematical theory of communication.* Chicago, IL: University of Illinois Press.

Chapter 2

I Quantify, Therefore I Am: Quantified Self Between Hermeneutics of Self and Transparency

Lorenzo De Stefano

Abstract

This chapter explores to what extent the Quantified Self, and in general the self-tracking culture, could be considered as a 'technology of the self': hermeneutical apparatuses generating new processes of subjectivation. Quantified Self, described by Wolf as a 'self-consciousness through numbers' (Wolf, 2010), refers both to the cultural phenomenon of self-tracking with devices and to a community of creators and users of self-tracking technologies. In this context, the author considers mainly the first aspect of this phenomenon and examines how its uses are diffused throughout the social mainstream. The author begins with the author's own personal experience using self-tracking devices, then the author considers the phenomenon of self-tracking in relation to its historical context described by Floridi as the era of the '4th Revolution' (Floridi, 2014). The second part of the chapter deals with the theoretical framework. The author discusses the Quantified Self from the perspective of the Material Engagement Theory (Malafouris, 2013) in order to outline the genealogical and anthropological perspectives of the relationship between man and technology. The author concludes that man and technology have always had a biunivocal relation; man shapes technologies that shape man, both materially and cognitively. In the final part of the essay and through the lens of Foucault's and Agamben's theories, the author discusses the Quantified Self as a 'technology of self' to underline the ambiguous nature of the phenomenon and its social and biopolitical implication in the age of transparency (Han, 2015) and surveillance capitalism (Zuboff, 2019).

Keywords: Quantified Self; material engagement theory; Big Data; transparency; self-tracking; surveillance

The Quantification of Bodies in Health: Multidisciplinary Perspectives, 29–48
Copyright © 2022 by Lorenzo De Stefano
Published under an exclusive license by Emerald Publishing Limited
doi:10.1108/978-1-80071-883-820211004

Introduction: The Critical Case

I woke up early this morning. I checked my smart watch: I slept 8 hours and 11 minutes, consisting of 3 hours and 5 minutes of light sleep, 2 hours in the Rapid Eye Movement Sleep (REM) phase, and 3 hours and 6 minutes of deep sleep. The app monitoring my general health says that it is a strong result and my average sleep over the last week has been 7 hours and 50 minutes, which is average for a person of my age. I checked my heartbeat as well; my minimum is 40 beats-per-minute and the average during the day is 50 beats-per-minute. I have what is known as a bradycardic heart – my average resting beats-per-minute is lower than the norm and gives me a unique advantage in preventing fatigue in sports like cycling and running. Currently, I am training intensively for an amateur cycling race and today I will train for 6 hours on a mountain route to help me reach good physical shape. After a healthy and abundant breakfast, I am ready to ride. I clip into my pedals and switch my Garmin on; it is a very important tool, since I can download the route and read the data that my wearable devices – a powermeter, a speed sensor, a cadence sensor, and a heart rate sensor – collect. Tracking my training is crucial to improve performance: I am able to follow the schedule the trainer gave me, manage my energy during an intense ride, know when to eat and drink, keep track of how many kilometres remain, and visualise the general ascent of the lap. At the end of the training, I download all the data collected – calories consumed, the route, total distance, average speed, heart rate zones, power zones, and cadence – onto a few apps on my phone, including Strava – an online social network for sporting people, and Training Peaks – an app where athletes can upload and monitor their training plans.

This allows me to have a general picture of my training sessions and to compare my performance with previous ones, so that I can monitor my improvements and reach my monthly goals. Since I began to monitor my training, I have seen improvement in both my form and overall performances compared to previous years. For example, my anaerobic threshold is higher: I have a general functional-threshold-power of 310 watts and my neuromuscular power peak is around 1,100 watts. When I am off the bike, I monitor the quality of my sleep, my heartbeat, my blood oxygen levels and calories consumption all thanks to my smartwatch. All my main physiological parameters are constantly monitored and datafied.

The devices I am using allow the development of a detailed knowledge of my body, they are powerful hermeneutical machines; when I started cycling in the early 2000s, this was impossible. At the time, these types of devices were available only to high-level professional athletes. Today, with a relatively small investment, anyone can buy one. In using these devices, my training has become more effective, more interesting, and safer. My body and my technical knowledge have also been improved by these technologies. I am more transparent with myself and more conscious of my limits, strengths, and weaknesses. This allows me to train more intentionally. I have become mentally stronger, too. All this would not have been possible without devices and data. The Internet of Things made it possible for the so-called 'personal science' and the self-tracking practices to thrive. If we consider the subject not as a fixed entity, but rather a dialectical process, we can argue that the relationship with technological devices enhances the subject's self-knowledge and his understanding of the world. Without knowing or planning it, I have become a regular and enthusiastic participant in the self-tracking culture.

The pioneer of this relatively new cultural habit is the Quantified Self movement. The term Quantified Self does not simply indicate a certain kind of technological device, it is rather a philosophy, or better an *ethos*, a personal disposition to *lifelogging* and to self-tracking through numbers. The first meeting of the Quantified Self community was held in October 2003 in California and the first article on Quantified Self was published by Gary Wolf in 2010. Since then, the participants of the Quantified Self movement have met frequently and in growing numbers. At first, these meetings focussed mainly on self-tracking projects by individuals that addressed three fundamental questions: What Did You Do? How Did You Do It? What Did You Learn? (Wolf & De Groot, 2020). By 2019, the network of Quantified Self had grown to 110 Meetup groups in 30 countries.

At the beginning, the movement included only 'geeks' obsessed with technology and devices. However, it soon became a full-blown trend in western countries thanks to the development of new technological devices and trackers such as smartphones, smartwatches, and countless apps, and, above all, the development of cloud technology and the advent of Big Data. Quantified Self practices have become common in a large part of the population and basically indicate nowadays a certain predisposition to analyse our life through numbers in order to gain knowledge. According to Wolf, four things have changed when compared to the beginning of Quantified Self (Wolf & De Groot, 2020):

- Electronic sensors got smaller, more accurate
- People started to wear powerful computing tools
- Social media made it seem normal and desirable to share everything, and therefore those who do not are labelled as weird or suspicious
- The advent of a general superintelligence called the Cloud.

Quantified Self, and in general the self-tracking practices, have thus become a major and mainstream cultural phenomenon of the digital era.

The Hyperhistorical Background

It is argued that the advent of the new digital Information and Communication Technologies (ICTs) and Big Data has enabled a democratisation of platforms, applications, and technologies as never seen before. It is impossible to comprehend the phenomena of lifelogging and Quantified Self without considering this technical and historical background or without considering that we have entered a new era: the era of dataism (Harari, 2016).

Luciano Floridi coined the term 4th Revolution to indicate the current hyperhistorical era driven by ICTs, in which the being is essentially converted into data and information, forming a new 'meta-world' called 'infosphere'. In his work, *The 4th Revolution*, Floridi states that 'thanks to the new ICTs we have entered the *age of zettabyte*' (Floridi, 2014, p. 13), an era in which almost everything humanity makes is potentially convertible into bytes. According to Moore's Law, the number of transistors on integrated circuits doubles every two years, enabling, at the same time, a growing capacity for processing data and the decreasing cost of computational power. In Floridi's opinion, this has determined a *caesura* in history: we have entered the era of hyperhistory where human society has become vitally dependent on ICTs and information to the point that we can affirm that data is the oil of the twenty-first century. Today, every innovation has gone 'from being ICT-related to ICT-dependent' (Floridi, 2014, p. 6).

In history, there have been several societies where ICTs played a key role. ICTs record and transmit information, but these past societies depended mainly on other kinds of technologies concerning primarily resources and energy. In hyperhistory, ICTs manage, and extract information autonomously as human societies are becoming increasingly dependent on them and on information as a fundamental resource in order to flourish. ICT devices – the self-tracking devices belonging to this category – are constantly working to keep us afloat, extracting and organising this enormous stream of data. This naturally affects our anthropological condition, since man is always the dialectical product of the relationship with his technologies (Hide & Malafouris, 2018). The new ICTs are environmental forces, alethiological and hermeneutical machines which affect:

- our self-conception (who we are)
- our mutual interactions (how we socialise)
- our conception of reality (our metaphysics)
- our interactions with reality (our agency).

This has huge ethical, legal, and political relevance, especially connected to the problem of privacy and transparency, leading to at least four major transformations, according to Floridi (2015, p. 2):

(a) the blurring of the distinction between reality and virtuality
(b) the blurring of the distinction between human, machine, and nature
(c) the reversal from information scarcity to information abundance
(d) the shift from the primacy of stand-alone things, properties, and binary relations, to the primacy of interactions, processes, and networks.

In this chapter, I will focus only on a few of the above aspects in relation to the phenomenon of self-tracking. What is certain is that we have entered a new era where the human being is obligated to share his environment with technological beings able to produce knowledge (*episteme*) and truth (*aletheia*). Generation X and Y are the last that experienced the difference between offline analogic life and the online environment. Nowadays, we increasingly live in a hybrid dimension that our smartphones and digital devices have created. Our profile, location, biometric data, and preferences are constantly being monitored by our devices, whether we like it or not (Ajana, 2018). In the Quantified Self philosophy, the monitoring is often requested and accepted. Floridi calls this new dimension *onlife* (Floridi, 2015, p. 7). I will discuss the risks of this hyperconnected era later.

Our environment is now populated by a variety of organic and artificial entities, some partly artificial and partly human. 'Inforg' is the name of this new being. It is an 'informational agent' of whom *principium individuationis* does not lie on a substrate or a substance but on a 'function': the capacity to interact and to produce information. Since the information is shared, the inforgs can operate with them freely, creating a new informational network of connected entities. We are constantly uploading and delegating our memory, decisions, tasks, and activities like the management of our houses, our bank accounts and so on to an inforg.

We can even positively understand ourselves as an inforg among inforgs since our Being-in-the-World in the infosphere is a being in a stream of information. Our temporal and spatial 'being there or here' is always potentially monitored by the location services of the smartphones. This does not mean that smartphones and wearable devices have made us cyborgs turning us into a Sterlac performance, nor that in a foreseeable future we are going to be replaced by artificial superintelligence. It has more to do with the integration with our devices, with the removal or the reduction of interfaces and media, such as screens and keyboards, to have a more direct interaction and communication with them. The fact that we dialogue with our phones and devices means that we somehow share a common dialogical-informational nature which does not obliterate the differences. This involves a new, non-Cartesian perspective which considers the devices as an autonomous agent rather than an extension of the subject's mind.

Inforgs also are not a DNA modified post-human man with bodily integrated artificial prosthesis. In short, the term inforg does not indicate a futuristic-fictional hybrid creature, but simply the fact that we interact with other informational beings such as the mobile devices for lifelogging: we understand ourselves as informational organisms among others (Floridi, 2014, p. 98). But if we are just our information, or better if we are individuated only by the capacity of producing information and by the quantitative value of this information, the subject is suffering a sort of de-individualisation; our 'soul' has become electrical (Ippolita, 2016). The quantification of our body and performance is an important feature which leads to the reduction of man into inforg through the collection and extraction of data from our daily practices.

Quantified Self is a specific phenomenon of this new hyperhistorical era which implies, from a theoretical perspective, an ontological turn: the reduction of the human into a stream of information. From a sociological perspective, this fetish for quantification and numbers is the defining trait of modern managers obsessed by optimisation of productivity, which is, of course, an epiphenomenon of technocratic capitalism. There is, however, a difference: while in an economic environment the monitoring is always projected towards a specific goal or result, for many self-trackers the goal can be unknown at the very moment data are collected. Potentially, there are answers to questions they have not even asked yet.

In one of his masterworks, *The Question Concerning Technology,* the German philosopher Martin Heidegger bonded the perspectives underlining how functionality and efficiency are the fundamental characteristics of modern technology as the last *destinal* phase of western metaphysics; according to its essence, technology has the characteristic of setting-upon in the sense of a 'challenging forth':

> That challenging happens in that the energy concealed in nature is unlocked, what is unlocked is transformed, what is transformed is stored up, what is stored up is, in turn, distributed, and what is distributed is switched about ever anew. Unlocking, transforming, storing, distributing, and switching about are ways of revealing. Regulating and securing even become the chief characteristics of the challenging revealing. (Heidegger, 1977, p. 17)

Unlocking, storing, transforming, and switching are just the operations that our body-devices do as well. For example, the extraction of our biometric data in an ICT-dependent society contributes to the unlocking of nature and of our body as part of it. Our bodies and habits are revealed and stored up as a computable quantity like a stream of data. In this sense, our body is 'at hand': it stands here just so it may be on call for further tasking, it stands at our disposal as 'standing reserve' *(Bestand)*. As such, the subject, intended as a union of body and soul, feelings, biometric and physiological performances, has become something orderable and understandable in the way of 'standing reserve'. This can be more evident if we consider what Wolf (2010) indicates as a categorical imperative of the Quantified Self:

- Monitoring
- Measuring
- Recording

To:

- Self-improvement
- Self-discovery
- Self-awareness
- Self-knowledge.

There is a strong convergence between what Heidegger indicates as technology's revealing character and the promises of the Quantified Self. Trackers focussed on health, trackers recording mental states indicating personal fulfilment, trackers trying to motivate us and prescribe a training regime fitted to our body type, competitive goals strengths and weaknesses, seem, at first sight, to be able to uncover our dormant potential. In this respect, the philosopher of technology Günther Anders highlighted in his work, *Die Antiquiertheit des Menschen* (Anders, 1954), how in the technological era 'a mean is not just a mean'; self-trackers are not just devices but revealing agents, they are able to prescribe actions and lifestyles: they unlock a new perspective on the world and on ourselves, on the power structures of our society in which world and man are turned into measurable quantity. In this sense, we are hybridised with devices and hybridised is also our self-understanding.

In this sense, self-tracking devices are not solely an instrument of optimisation and monitoring, but also of discovery: they are alethiological machines since they disclose (*alethein*) the being in the way of the essence of technology. They are hermeneutical tools insofar as they produce a new representation of reality. Self-tracking devices disclose a new perception of the self. In this regard, the American philosopher, Don Idhe, underlined how technologies provide representation, understanding and interpretation (Idhe, 1990); we gain a new access to and understanding of the body and its performances through the interpretation of data. Technology in this case also mediates the perception of the performance and the exercise in a dialectical way. When the subject reads, measures, and monitors the data, it becomes aware of its performance, it recognises itself and its datafied efforts, gaining a new level of experience. In this way, technology is incorporated in the human body and mind (Kristensen & Prigge, 2018; Verbeek, 2008).

The human–technology relation constitutes a *continuum* where it is not clearly possible to define where the body starts and technology ends. Devices are experienced as extensions of our human body, mediating our perceptions and actions. The body and the world are experienced in a mediated way. However, what is at stake is not a new kind of 'cyborg hybrid intentionality' as Verbeek pointed out (Verbeek, 2008). Rather, self-tracking devices, as technologies, reveal a fundamental anthropological character of technology in its relation to human body and mind, an aspect we shall examine in the next section.

Quantified Self and Material Engagement Theory

Man and technology are co-constituted (Renfrew, 2008) – technology shapes us as much as we shape technologies. To understand the meaning of the Quantified Self phenomenon, its philosophy, and its power to generate a new form of subjectivity, it is important to consider its genealogy as a particular case of technical mediation. To do that, I refer to one of the latest theoretical developments within cognitive archaeology and anthropology, namely, Material Engagement Theory. 'Material Engagement Theory takes this metaplastic recursive relationship between brains, bodies and things as the main analytical unit for the study of human thought processes' (Malafouris, 2019, p. 2).

Since early prehistory, humans have been shaping and reinventing themselves and their ecosystem through technical artefacts and through the skills and knowledge developed by using them (Malafouris, 2013). Material Engagement Theory focusses on the technical mediation, asserting that making and fabricating have a foundational role in man's evolution. This theory assumes a relational ontology, according to which subject and object are not separate entities but an integrated system; this means that the Cartesian paradigm of the duality between *res cogitans* and *res extensa* is integrally refused by this perspective, since cognition is always an embodiment, and the body is in a dialectical relation with the artefact. Technics are not just mental or physical features. Human–technology relations are not representational but constitute embodiment relations (Idhe & Malafouris, 2019).

This is true both for the prehistoric lithic industry and for contemporary phenomena such as ICTs and self-tracking devices. The limit where our self ends and the rest of the world begins is therefore blurred. This is evident if we consider the Quantified Self philosophy; according to it, the emotions and even the inner psychological and physiological states can be recorded and objectivated on a device or on a screen. These recordings and monitoring activities dialectically affect our emotions, our performances, and the perception we have of ourselves. Every artefact, in the ontological sense, is an extension of our body-mind-world integrated system. Material Engagement Theory states that the human mind is ecologic because it is always 'outside'. As such, setting the boundaries under which an activity falls inside or outside is always difficult if we reject the traditional cartesian distinction between mental and physical being. This binary logic falls in real-life situations where the process of thinking, making, and doing are connected as a part of a dynamic material ecology. Humans think by constructing signs and by leaving memory traces, in a process that Malafouris calls 'creative thinking': 'Humans become through a saturated, situated engagement of thinking and feeling with things and form-generating materials' (Malafouris, 2014, p. 144). This process is the core of our biological and social evolution from the primitive lithic industry to the latest digital cultures. This is evident in the shaping of a material tool, such as a lithe, but can also be recognised in contemporary phenomenon such as self-tracking: the signs and the artefacts that man produces objectifying his intelligence are not a mere reflection of it, rather intelligence is enacted through them proceeding along signs and material artefacts.

For that reason, the evolution of the human mind must be paired with the evolution of its traces and technologies: the making of a stone tool or the making of an app. The objectivation of thought through language and of data through a self-tracking device are not just products of thinking, but rather a way of thinking. When we look at a tool, we do not simply relate to an externalised form or skill, but also to the possibility of a certain experience and relation with things and the world. Tools 'bring forth and constrain organism's possibilities for action, imagination and communication' (Malafouris, 2019, p. 3). Therefore, mind is not a brain centred feature or a product of a subject's intentionality. It has no a priori location or place of origin inside the head, it is always outside in the world. Human thought (*nous*) is then *hylonoetic,* it always involves the stuff (*hyle*) of the outside world. Not just the lines we draw on paper, the tools we shape, but also the imaginary forms and projects, along with the books we read and the data we collect allow us to become self-conscious beings, since we, as humans, inhabit the space where the brain, body, culture, matter, and technology conflate. Cognitive life must be considered in a broader sense as an integrated body-mind ecology. The material ecology and the cognitive ecology that substantiate our being-in-the-World are in fact inseparable, especially in our contemporary digital era. Malafouris concludes that mind-stuff do not have a specific location or set properties, since they equally pertain to brains, body, and things: a neural activation pattern, a manipulating movement, a sign written on a piece of paper, a chipped stone, are all mind-stuff. The anthropologist calls this ontological gathering of mind and stuff *thing-ing,* instead of thinking. It describes better the activity of human mind that thinks primarily with and through things.

Thing-ing is not a psychological process of internalisation and representation of things, by which they are constituted as objects for a subject, rather it is an act of consciousness. With the notion of *thing-ing* the accent falls on process ontology and ecologies (Baetson, 1979; Ingold, 2012) rather than on the description of a single decontextualised object, as in the orthodox phenomenological approach. In this *hylonoetic* context, it does not make any sense to consider isolated identities. For that reason, Material Engagement Theory is opposed to both the cartesian point of view and to a cognitivist approach. This notion helps us to understand not just what a thing is, but mainly how things come to be and what is their specificity and their life history. Thinking and *thing-ing* are inseparable and this opens new possibilities for exploring the relationship between mind and things, and how they are connected to each other.

Therefore, we can conclude that things have a cognitive relevance and a cognitive life for what they do. Things play a key role in integrating and coordinating on neural, physical, cultural, and evolutionary processes. According to Malafouris, things 'through their physical persistence, they help us to move across the scales of time and to construct bridges between temporal phenomena that operate at different experimental level' (Malafouris, 2019, p. 8). They work by constructing biographies through joint participation in cultural practices in ways that escape temporal and spatial limits and the limits of a subject's experience. They are non-biological stuff that pairs with organic biological entities. It is now evident how this theory is crucial to the aim of the essay insofar as it offers the anthropological and ontological background to the concept of inforg and to the understanding of lifelogging practices and how and to what extent they produce a new kind of subjectivity.

Material artefacts such as computers, smartphones and digital devices like the trackers widely used in Quantified Self practices, are embodied prosthesis of our body as well. Just like a lithic artefact, they are non-biological extension of our biological existence. In this regard, in early 1900, Paul Alsberg stated that tools and artefacts, at once, deactivate and enhance our bodily functions (Alsberg, 1922). Through this dialectic between deactivation and enhancement, which directly affects our physiological and biological constitution, technics edifies an ecology that is material, cognitive, and embodied (Idhe, 2009). For this reason, the evolution process is not just a biological event, rather human and things are inseparably linked and co-constituted (Malafouris, 2016). This understanding of technology, which Material Engagement Theory shares with Postphenomenology (Idhe & Malafouris, 2018), is anti-essentialist and genealogical. This corrects Heidegger's approach, which regards technology as a *destinal* trait of the history of Being, considering technology as the fulcrum of human becoming, to the point that there is no man without technology. Technology is a universal anthropological feature rather than a product of western metaphysics, and, as such, it is beyond good and evil. Therefore, there is no specific 'era of technology' since every era is a technological era. Additionally, the concept of a cyborg also does not exist because man and technologies has always been hybridised.

To understand a specific trait of an era and the anthropological dimension of man in a specific time, our attention must be turned to technologies and artefacts; it is valid for prehistoric societies as well as for the contemporary informational society as described by Floridi. From the point of view of the co-evolution of people and things, the dualism between nature and culture makes no sense at all, since our nature is to make artefacts and our nature is defined, through this making, by artefacts. Adapting Heidegger's conception to the Material Engagement

Theory, it could be affirmed that the *Dasein* is the only being whose essence is his existence conceived as technological project. The kind of mind that we have, our self-understanding, our understanding of the world and even our cultural values can be revealed by the history of tool-related behaviour.

Heidegger was right when he stated that technology is a way of unconcealing (Heidegger, 1977, pp. 3–35), but he misinterpreted the character of technology as an event in the history of Being. Technology is rather an anthropologic universal feature of human and technical mediation, which discloses new paths beyond natural selection. Evolution is not a unidirectional adaptive process between organism and environment. Organism and environment, nature, and artifice, pre-exist their relational ontological constitution: organism is always a being-in-the-world, and the world exists only in its totality of relation. This relation cannot be configured as dualism between natural and artificial sphere. 'Material Engagement Theory reacts against the opposition between a "natural" sphere of human speciation and a "cultural" realm of "technological" change' (Idhe & Malafouris, 2019, p. 203). This implies that the informational society, the inforgs, the AI, the Quantified Self are historical manifestations of the technologically centred human behaviour; insofar they are technologies, they could be regarded as 'ecological forces' configuring our niche and shaping our subjectivity. They are part of a unique cognitive process which, following Malafouris, I identified in terms of the notion of *thing-ing*. For that reason, I conclude that the Quantified Self is a cultural movement that has a lot to do with the anthropological origin of technology. It is an epiphenomenon of mind–things relationship in the era of the digital revolution, where the material world is not constituted anymore by lythes, but by digital machines, information, and data. This also means that there is nothing intrinsically good or bad in technological development *per se*, but it must be studied and understood to liberate human creative energies and to turn technology into an instrument of emancipation and generalised progress: a hermeneutical instrument of self-consciousness instead of alienation.

Quantified Self as 'Technology of the Self'

This leads us to consider technology under a wider perspective. The *hypermoral* character of technology implies that, in order to understand its historical-situated dimension and its power of shaping mind and subjectivity, we must understand the power relations that lie behind it as well. As Michel Foucault pointed out, power manifests itself through accepted forms of 'knowledge' (e.g. scientific understanding, school discipline, prison surveillance) and 'truth', since knowledge and truth are products as well:

> We must cease once and for all to describe the effects of power in negative terms: it 'excludes', it 'represses', it 'censors', it 'abstracts', it 'masks', it 'conceals.' In fact, power produces; it produces reality; it produces domains of objects and rituals of truth. The individual and the knowledge that may be gained of him belong to this production. (Foucault, 1991, p. 194)

Technology could be considered a system of power concerning knowledge, self-knowledge, and dominion. According to Foucault, power, just like art and technology, has before any ethical implication a *poietic* nature: it produces knowledge and individualities. This theoretical standpoint, I think matches perfectly the extra-moral sense of technology described by Material Engagement Theory and it is useful in understanding, theoretically and ethically, the phenomenon of Quantified Self. The creative nature of power is also a major source of social discipline and conformity. From this perspective, technologies can be a huge tool of control and standardisation depending on the contextual power relations. In the present case of Quantified Self, for example, technologies can extend the biopolitical control over the body by prescribing which physical condition is acceptable. For example, which health parameters are required to be met so as to obtain health insurance, which psychological conditions and emotional tones are socially acceptable, and so on. They can also reproduce gender differences and inequalities. Added to this, it is important to note that most of the platforms where our biometric data are stored, collected, and organised are owed by private corporations. Therefore, we give our data for free without knowing who will read, analyse, and use them. Electronic trackers are often presented as being emotionally and morally neutral. But beyond this cold objectivity of the machine, social constrains lie hidden, rendering these technologies as powerful instruments of conformism. Since, as we stated in the previous section, technology shapes and integrates with the subject; electronic trackers are producers of a new kind of subjectivity. As is known, Foucault in *Technology of the Self* distinguishes four types of technologies:

> (1) technologies of production, which permit us to produce, transform, or manipulate things; (2) technologies of sign systems, which permit us to use signs, meanings, symbols, or signification; (3) technologies of power, which determine the conduct of individuals and submit them to certain ends or domination, an objectivising of the subject; (4) technologies of the self, which permit individuals to effect by their own means or with the help of others a certain number of operations on their own bodies and souls, thoughts, conduct, and way of being, so as to transform themselves in order to attain a certain state of happiness, purity, wisdom, perfection, or immortality. (Foucault, 1988, p. 18)

From this point of view, Foucault seems to share with Material Engagement Theory, the Actor Nework Theory and Postphenomenology: the idea that subjectivity is not something given once and for all, a metaphysical being situated beyond the flux of becoming, but it is the result of a relationship, in this case with a *dispositif* (in English, apparatus) of power. It is a relational entity rather than a substance, or better: a same individual (substance) could be the place of multiple processes of subjectivation: e.g. one can be a musician, a Facebook user, a writer and so on. This proliferation of processes of subjectivation is due to the proliferation of technological apparatuses. Giorgio Agamben in *What is an Apparatus?* gives his personal definition of apparatuses extending the meaning of Foucault's technical term:

I shall call an apparatus literally anything that has in some way the capacity to capture, orient, determine, intercept, model, control, or secure the gestures, behaviours, opinions or discourses of living beings. Not only, therefore prisons, mad houses, the Panopticon, schools, confession, factories, disciplines, juridical measures and so forth (whose connection with power is in a certain sense evident), but also the pen, writing, literature, philosophy, agriculture, cigarettes, navigation, computers, cellular telephones and-why not-language itself, which is perhaps the most ancient of apparatuses – one in which thousands and thousands of years ago a primate inadvertently let himself be captured, probably without realising the consequences that he was about to face. To recapitulate, we have then two great classes: living beings (or substances) and apparatuses. And between these two, as a third class, subjects. I call a subject that which results from the relation and so to speak from the relentless fight between living beings and apparatuses. (Agamben, 2009, p. 14)

For Agamben too, the subject is then a product of the relationship between a biological form and a non-biological component. In this respect, in the Quantified Self manifesto published by Wolf on Wired in 2009 entitled *Know Thyself: Tracking Every Facet of Life, from Sleep to Mood to Pain 24/7/365*, the author reflects on how the development of self-trackers and smartphones produces new forms of knowledge about ourselves, and in the words of Agamben and Foucault, new forms of subjectivation derived from a dialectic relationship with artefacts. On the other hand, these technologies undock and re-orient the medical and physiological knowledge from the hand of medical specialists to everyday users. Numbers are no longer cold entities but help us in the everyday management of our existence: self-knowing through numbers means at one time self-becoming through numbers and self-caring through numbers. As Wolf admits, in the history of man there were several technologies addressed to self-knowledge, the most well-known is undoubtedly *gnothi seauton* of Delphic Oracle (Wolf, 2009).

Quantified Self is then a form of self-care. Self-care and self-cure are deeply analysed in Foucault speculation. In his abovementioned course *Technology of the Self*, Foucault discusses Plato's *Alcibiades*, distinguishing two moments in which self-knowledge is articulated: (1) what is the self; (2) what is the care of oneself (*Epimeleia heautou-cura sui*). For a long time, the question of the subject was articulated according to the *gnoti seauton* of the Delphic Oracle. It was the founding expression of the relationship between subject and truth. Often, in ancient Greek texts, the Greek precept appears coupled with *epimeleia heautou*; the coupling is rather a subordination of the self-knowledge to the care of the self (Foucault, 2005, p. 4). *Gnoti seauton* is a modality of the general framework of the *epimeleia heaoutou*, a concrete application of the general rule. It is evident in Plato's *Alcibiades* that Socrates is the person associated with the imperative of 'caring about yourself'.

What is of greater importance in relation to the problem of Quantified Self is the historical sedimentation of the caring of the self, of which the object of this study is the last technological evolution. According to Foucault, *epimeleia heautou* indicates a certain way of being/behaving in the world and to relating to others. It is an attitude towards self, others, and the world. It is connected to meditation (*melete*). Self-caring is an activity exercised on the self by the self; it is an action that implies a responsibility for oneself and through which the subject produces himself and seeks to transform and purify himself. To this category belongs a vast series of practices adopted in Western culture, such as 'spiritual exercises' (Hadot, 1995), meditation, memorisation, examination of conscience that defines a certain way of being through forms of reflection. These practices are apparatuses which play a key role in the history of subjectivity.

In Greek culture, the knowing of the self, that is, of the dynamic action of the soul, was always connected to the performing of the right political action in the context of the *polis*; the care of the self defines the place of man in his community. The self is therefore the soul (*psyche*), the capacity of acting and enduring. The soul is *dynamis*, and as stated before, mind and intellect always become. The care of the self is the rational management and harmonisation of reason, spirit, and appetite (*logos, thymos*, and *eros*) (Plato, 2002). These practices of self-knowledge and of self-cure evolve throughout history in relation to the political context. In the Hellenistic period and in the Roman era, the inner private dimension replaces the political one. The care of the self is therefore identified as knowing/caring about one's inner self, as a continuous monitoring of emotions and states through diaries (Marcus Aurelius) or letters (Epicurus, Seneca).

What is most important to underline is that, at this point, self-care practices are not confined anymore to the pedagogical education of students but accompany man throughout his entire existence. Moreover, the Platonic pedagogical attitude has been replaced by the medical model, as for example in Epicurus *tetrapharmakos*. From then on, the care of the self became identified as a health issue: philosophy is 'medicine of the soul'. This approach has been translated in Christian confession, where the health of the penitent soul is dependent from an outer imperative: the conformity to the Word of the Lord and to his Commandments. The way Christianity requires truth from individuals is a 'duty to know who he is, that is, to try to know what is happening inside him, to acknowledge faults, to recognise temptations, to locate desires [...] the truth obligations of faith and the self are linked together' (Foucault, 1988, p. 40).

In two conferences he held at Dartmouth College in 1980, Foucault discussed two Christian practices, *exomológēsis* and *exagoreusis*. The former consists in recognising oneself as sinner and in confessing sins to a cleric in order to do penance. This is a status that involves self-punishment and self-revelation: to prove suffering and to show shame is the way the punishment is accomplished (*publicatio sui*). Here, medical, juridical, and martyrdom models are used by Christian authors, such as Tertullian, to describe the ways punishment is actualised: 'one must show one's wounds in order to be cured', 'one always appeases one's judge by confessing faults', and 'self-revelation is at the same time self-destruction', respectively. In *exomologesis*, truth about self is overlaid by 'violent rupture and dissociation' that are 'symbolic, ritual, and theatrical' (Foucault, 1988, p. 43). *Exagoreusis* instead is a practice of the fourth century which has its roots in Stoics ethics. This technology of the self concerns self-sacrifice as the sacrifice of the will. An example is the monk's *ethos* in which the self is constituted through obedience and contemplation of God. It is a renouncement of the world in search of the mystical ecstasy. It operates on the present and entails the scrutinising of thoughts and eliminating the ones that divert form God. Foucault distinguishes three types of this kind of verbalised self-examination:

- The Cartesian involving self and reality
- The Senecan involving self and rules
- The Christian that discloses the inner self the deciphering of inner thoughts.

Christian examination requires an outer moral (and ontological) criteria to discriminate between good and bad. It is, therefore, based on 'verbalization'. According to Foucault,

> there is only one way: to tell all thoughts to our director, to be obedient to our master in all things, to engage in a permanent verbalisation of all our thoughts. (Foucault, 1988, p. 47)

There is then a hermeneutic relation between monk and master and monk and his inner self. On the other hand, the desire of verbalisation makes everything that could not be expressed and confessed a sin. This 'unmentionable' is where the sin resides. *Exomologesis* and *exagoreusis* both require the renunciation of the self in order to have his disclosure. Such technologies are a way of disclosure and production of subjectivity. In the former, like in the martyrdom case, we assist to the killing of the self ascetically, in the latter the purification is obtained through verbalisation and permanent obedience to an external will.

In modern age, the technology of self, based on verbalisation, survived in a secularised form and has been reinserted in different contexts by human science in order to create positively a 'new self' (Foucault, 1988, p. 49) – the most common example is Freudian psychoanalysis. In the digital era, blogs, Facebook, and other social media fulfil this role through the verbalisation of our everyday experience shared with millions of users. What has changed is the conception of truth and the power relations in which technologies of the self exist.

This Foucauldian excursus is preparatory to focus on the role of Quantified Self as a technology of the self. For all intents, Quantified Self seems then to fit the pattern of technology of self since it delivers.

- A new idea of truth
- A new production of subjectivity
- A precise notion of care
- A new political dimension/a new kind of society.

In the following section, I will specifically discuss these four points.

Truth, Subject, Cure, and Transparency

The idea of truth that lies behind Quantified Self culture is, as I tried to demonstrate before, a form of post-positivism where the precision of data and numbers are the main epistemological criterion. Truth is identified in the accuracy of quantification. Numerical data processed by algorithms represents the highest expression of truth and objectivity. This data-fetishism defines the Quantified Self culture as an epiphenomenon of the era of the 4th Revolution (Floridi, 2014). Everything around us is converted into data, including the food we eat, the steps we make, the percentage of oxygen in our blood, the quantity and quality of sleep. Our cars collect our data, the same goes for our phones and watches. Social networks and platforms like Amazon and Google (the so-called GAFA) monitor every interaction we make on the Web and collect them in order to 'profile' us. It seems that the data extracted through our everyday activities, which contribute to form our worldly experience, via our devices and internet interactions, represent the contemporary form of the verbalised confession described by Foucault.

Every time we 'accept' terms and conditions of a certain app, every time we declare our understanding of privacy policies on a website or on a social network, we agree to confess our habits, lifestyle, passions, beliefs, and tastes to an invisible entity. Of course, the Quantified Self is not the only way of extracting data, but it is a paradigmatic example since, in this case, the confession is mostly on a voluntary basis. The case is paradigmatic since it reveals also how platform capitalism and the new totalitarianism of surveillance act through data. The datafication of our lives is the last form of reification of man that started with industrial revolutions, and which entails the reduction of man and society to a behavioural mechanism prefigured in Wiener's cybernetics (Wiener, 1961) and Skinner Behaviourism (see Zuboff, 2019, pp. 391–430). As I suggested before, the transformation of subject into informational organism (inforg), enabled by these new technologies of the self, realises the synthesis between the natural and the machinic, with the potential integration into a theory or function (the algorithms) designed to guide, discipline, and regulate this organism.

Once quantified, data become a precious instrument of optimisation and narration of the self: they reveal behaviours and preferences and convey a certain image of truth. This produces a new kind of subjectivity. The datafication process is a double-faced phenomenon. As Foucault stated, this is typical of every power relation, since on the one hand, power is a productive and creative force that opens new possibilities, and on the other hand, it allows control, standardisation, and exploitation. Data help us gain a better understanding of our bodies and a healthier life regime, and as product of technologies they contribute to shaping our mind and behaviour as a new kind of material knowledge and material engagement. They are an important resource for medical and scientific research, too (Lupton, 2016). But, at the same time, they can be easily turned into an instrument of control and political propaganda as demonstrated by the scandals of Prism and Cambridge Analytica (Lupton, 2016, pp. 114–136). The role of an external moral agent, which in the *exagoreusis* described by Foucault, was played by the master of the monk or by the world of the Lord itself, is today played by the imperative of efficiency of techno-capitalism (Zuboff, 2019). It is easy to understand, then, how the data can be the technology through which mass conformity is realised, just like in the past the believer was conformed by the theological apparatus.

The modern subject has become a flux of data in its hybridisation with digital technologies; dataism realises the modern Galileian-Cartesian dream to reduce the being in numeric predictable and calculable quantity. Even the soul, the *res cogitans,* has become to a certain extent calculable and transparent. The subject as a product of Quantified Self culture turns into a reified product of the every-day confession practices on devices and platforms. In synthesis, Quantified Self culture aims, indeed, to convert our feelings, behaviours, habits, moods, as well as our physiology and genetics into objectively detectable quantity: I quantify, therefore I am. This new hybrid creature, that I defined following Floridi as 'the inforg', is a 'node' of Internet of Things network, since the reduction to 'informational being' completes the hybridisation between man and machines, between our cognitive and physiological structure and our devices.

Internet of Things and ambient intelligence share the same goal with Quantified Self in terms of creating networked products and spaces, such as beds with sleep trackers or devices which track the energy consumption of the house and so on. They edify our onlife experience, where man is ontologically close to machine and even obsolete compared to it. Machines have become alethiological entities that make decisions autonomously, that store our data and memory, and set our vital standards, to the point that it is impossible to decide whether machines are our prosthesis or we the organic prosthesis of machines. Now it is particularly evident what Material Engagement Theory points out: our gestures are completely externalised and delegated to machines; our function increasingly exonerated in the technological mediation. This mediation has an ontological and anthropological feedback regarding the construction of subject.

Therefore, in the Quantified Self era, the subject is, on the one hand, determined and constructed through the numeric reflection of itself, which constitutes a new form of self-consciousness. On the other hand, data are the viaticum of biopolitical power which act subliminally. The recent scandals of Prism and Cambridge Analytica demonstrate how datafication is implicated in power relations and forms of digital control. The 'transparency society' described by Byung-Chul Han and Shoshana Zuboff works exactly through data control. In fact, the data we extract and upload on platforms such as Strava, Facebook, and Google, on our computers and mobile devices, as Jaron Lanier pointed out (Lanier, 2011), are property of the owner of the platform. In this way, the GAFA capable to harvest and store Big Data become the authentic instance of power in our era; this attests a transfer of sovereignty from national state and international organisations to the main actors of platform capitalism, that are private organisations operating internationally and on which states, and populations do not have any control.

This represents the major technological risk of our era. Things have been changing partially thanks to the increasing awareness raised by Cambridge Analytica scandal. In the EU, for example, the General Data Protection Regulation (GDPR) implemented in May 2018, represents a concrete effort to limit the power of Internet companies, but it is not enough. The digital panopticon described by Han (Han, 2015) cannot be limited by single national laws, insofar as it appears to be a direct consequence of digital technologies and of the structure of power of so-called platform capitalism. It is evident, then, how the Quantified Self and the lifelogging practices could realise a voluntary and non-coercive subjection of individuals to the so-called society of transparency.

Transparency is the new ideology of technocratic totalitarianism, which tends to replace politics with administration. It is the way technology discloses our world and, at one time, a modus of truth – what Heidegger calls unconcealment – affecting the public and private spheres. This process engages the narcissism of the contemporary subject, described by Lasch (Lasch, 1979), among others, in the following way: the neoliberal society of performance and optimisation, whose anthropological paradigm is the self-made man, has imposed since the 1960s a complete transvaluation of values. The self-made man, as we argued before, is a product of apparatuses and technologies, which encourage self-optimisation. Self-tracking practices appeal to the narcissism of the contemporary subject, to his craving for exposition and optimisation: we are proud of our data, of our digital profiles, of our performances. We make charts and seek exposition 24/7. But behind this façade, the checkmate of the modern subject is accomplished.

In conclusion, the culture of self-tracking, on the one hand, promotes a better knowledge of ourselves in our integrated dialectical relationship with technology. On the other hand, it shows the artificial nature of the subject and the way it is at the mercy of external powers. This means that the self-made man has never been truly self-made, but he is a result of the apparatuses he uses and in which he lives. He is a product of his products, often a slave of his technological devices. At a closer look, the apparatuses with which we have to deal in this phase of techno-capitalism act no longer as producers of subjectivity but lead to a process that Agamben calls 'desubjectivation' (Agamben, 2009). The apparatus is a machine producing subjectivations and, at the same time, it acts as a machine of governance. Clearly every subjectivation has desubjectivation as the other side of the coin, as an implicit dialectical moment; it implies the relationship with alterity. As we saw before, the penitent self is individuated through the confession that implies the Other as the referent of the dialogical technic. In the Material Engagement Theory, the alterity is represented by things and the stuff. In the era of techno-capitalism, this dialectic involving alterity gives rise to a new subject only in a larval or spectral form. According to Agamben,

> he who let himself be captured by the 'cellular telephone' apparatus – whatever the intensity of the desire that has driven him – cannot acquire a new subjectivity, but only a number through which he can eventually be controlled. (Agamben, 2009, p. 21)

From this perspective, if we consider technology not *per se*, but rather in relation to power apparatuses we must conclude that it is not a neutral force anymore, and therefore, its ontology must be paired with an ethic of responsibility based on a genealogical perspective.

If a certain process of subjectivation (or, in this case, desubjectivation) corresponds to every apparatus, then it is impossible for the subject of an apparatus *sic et simplicter* to use it 'in the right way'. Those who continue to promote similar arguments are, for their part, the product of the media apparatus in which they are captured' (Agamben, 2009, p. 21). Here lies the triumph of economy and the eclipse of politics which presuppose the existence of subjects and identities. Techno-governmental machines have no use for the subject and identity but needs neutral 'consumers' to augment profit. The more we individuate ourselves through consumption, the more our identity is deindividualized. In this frame, self-tracking technologies, as biometric and anthropometrical apparatuses, cooperate with this biopolitical surveillance power; the more apparatuses invade every field of life, as in the case of Quantified Self, ambient intelligence, internet of things and AI, the more government and private companies acquire an ever more elusive power over people. To this desubjectivation corresponds then the a-teleological perpetration of the providential governmental machine that techno-capitalism is. The era of Big Data or the so-called dataism is a complex and double-faced phenomenon. In one way, it is certainly a scientific and epistemic revolution. In another sense, it is a mask of power structures that leads the subject to his desubjectivation and the world to catastrophe. As such, the most complicated duty for philosophical and scientific thought is to figure out if this process can be reversible and influenceable, or whether, inasmuch as subjectivity is a product of technology and apparatuses, there is no possible alternative to this model since every alternative arises from the same power structure. This is precisely a question of whether the new digital technologies and movements like the Quantified Self could produce a new type of subjectivity that can in a certain way resist the apparatuses, or if resistance has to necessarily pass through a refusal of the current technological era. From an ontological standpoint, it means to understand the ontological direction of the relationship between subject and apparatuses. The theological model of Agamben which, to a certain extent, is shared by Heidegger and Foucault, considers the subject as an accident: modus of power. The single subjectivity in every possible declination is just a result of a fight between living beings and apparatuses (Agamben, 2009, p. 14). In this theoretical frame, the subject has no leeway.

Conclusions

An integral refusal of the digital society is not possible at least on large scale – Floridi was right when he stated that our lives are permanently *onlife* and a large part of our existence takes place in this hybrid dimension – we need then to understand whether the subject of this post-industrial digital era is doomed to desubjectivation or if digital technologies give birth to a new kind of subjectivity. In this chapter I argued, assuming the standpoint of Material Engagement Theory, that every culture has a distinctive material and technological trait, that technology and material culture always inform the mind, that consciousness is always outside objectified in stuff, things, and artefacts. Digital cultures, to which Quantified Self belongs, are the contemporary expression of this fundamental ontological and anthropological nexus between mind and things, between man and technology. This relationship can produce new knowledge and practices but, as Foucault stated, also new risks insofar as technology as apparatus is, at one time, a dispositive of power, that is, a dispositive of truth and dominion.

Quantified Self and self-tracking practices are then an ambiguous phenomenon both on a theoretical and political perspective: they provide a new level of self-knowledge and disclose new perspectives for medicine, biology and for self-care. At the same time, they could be a powerful instrument of control and dominion. Harmonising these two dimensions is not an easy task, especially because digital devices are nowadays an indispensable part of our daily lives and a specific cultural characteristic of digital era; the idea of progress and technological development do not include reversals, but at the most, new adaptations. Since it is not possible to escape from the digital era and, overall, it is not even desirable, we have a desperate need of active biopolitics. The fact that these technologies of the self lead to a better understanding of our selves could show a way in this regard.

Material Engagement Theory, in fact, states that if it is true that we are shaped by technologies, it is also true that we shape technologies and apparatuses, which means that technology is an answer to a vital need of the technological animal: the *homo faber*. Life, intended both as *zoe* (the characteristic of all living beings) and *bios* (a collective, qualified life in a *polis*), is the subject and the object of this technological practices. At a closer look, even Agamben stated that the subject is the result of an interaction where one of the two poles is the living being. Life in its immediacy emerges also in the lifelogging practices of Quantified self, although in a technologically mediated form, as something to be preserved and improved. Life is, then, the field of conflict where what is at stake is the subjection of the subject to apparatuses. What we need is therefore a change of direction, a 'turn' which reverses the hierarchy between life and apparatus in the production of the subject. If in our era technology and apparatuses are the formal features disciplining life, a new process of subjectivation can be produced only if life, and its ineradicable root of freedom, becomes the centre, the criterion, and the regulating principle of apparatuses.

References

Agamben, G. (2009). *What is an apparatus? And other essays*. Stanford: Stanford University Press.
Ajana, B. (Eds.) (2018). *Self-tracking. Empirical and philosophical investigations*. London: Palgrave Macmillan.
Alsberg, P. (1922). *Das Menschheitsrätsel: Versuch einer prinzipiellen Lösung*. Dresden: Sibyllen-Verlag.
Anders, G. (1954). *Die Aantiquiertheit des Menschen*. München: Beck Verlag.
Baetson, G. (1979). *Mind and nature: A necessary unity*. New York, NY: Bantam Books.
Floridi, L. (2014). *The 4th Revolution: How the infosphere is reshaping human reality*. Oxford: Oxford University Press.
Floridi, L. (Ed.) (2015). *The Onlife manifesto, being human in a hyperconnected era*. London: Springer.
Foucault, M. (1991). *Discipline and punish: The birth of a prison*. London: Penguin.
Foucault, M. (1998). *The history of sexuality: The will to knowledge*. London: Penguin.
Foucault, M. (2005). *The Hermeneutics of the Subject, Lectures at the College de France 1981–1982*. London: Palgrave Macmillan.
Hadot, P. (1995). *Philosophy as a way of life. Spiritual exercises from Socrates to Foucault*. Oxford: Blackwell Publishers.
Han, B.-C. (2015). *The transparency society*. Stanford: Stanford University Press.

Harari, Y. N. (2016). *Yuval Noah Harari on big data, Google and the end of free will.* Retrieved from https://www.ft.com/content/50bb4830-6a4c-11e6-ae5b-a7cc5dd5a28c

Heidegger, M. (1977). *The question of technology and other essays.* London: Garland Publishing.

Idhe, D. (1990). *Technology and the lifeworld: From Garden to earth.* Bloomington: Indiana University Press.

Ihde, D. (2009). *Postphenomenology and Technoscience: The Peking University lectures.* New York, NY: State University of New York Press.

Ihde, D., & Malafouris, L. (2019). Homo faber revisited: Postphenomenology and material engagement theory. *Philosophy & Technology, 32*(2), 195–214.

Ingold, T. (2012). Toward an ecology of materials. *Annual Review of Anthropology, 41*(1), 427–442.

Ippolita, (2016). *Anime elettiche. Riti e miti social.* Milan: Jaca Book.

Kristensen, D. B., & Prigge, C. (2018). Human/technology association in self-tracking. In B. Ajana (Eds.), *Self-tracking. Empirical and philosophical investigations.* London: Palgrave Macmillan.

Lanier, J. (2011). *You are not a gadget. A manifesto.* New York, NY: Penguin.

Lasch, C. (1979). *The Culture of Narcissism: American Life in an age of diminishing expectations.* New York, NY: W.W: Norton.

Lupton, D. (2016). *The quantified self.* Cambridge: Polity Press.

Malafouris, L. (2013). *How things shape the mind: A theory of material engagement.* Cambridge: The MIT Press.

Malafouris, L. (2014). Creative thinging: The feeling of and for clay. *Pragmatics and Cognition, 22*(1), 140–158.

Malafouris, L. (2016). On human becoming and incompleteness: A material engagement approach to the study of embodiment in evolution and culture. In G. Etzelmüller & C. Tewes (Eds.), *Embodiment in evolution and culture* (pp. 289–305). Tübingen: Mohr Siebeck.

Malafouris, L. (2019). Mind and material engagement. *Phenomenology and the Cognitive Sciences, 18*, 1–17.

Morozov, E. (2013). *To save everything, click here: The Folly of Technological Solutionism.* Chester: Public Affairs.

Plato, (2002). *Phaedrus. A new translation by Robin Waterfield.* New York: Oxford University Press.

Renfrew, A. C. (2008). *Prehistory: The making of the human mind.* New York, NY: Modern Library.

Verbeek P.-P. (2008). Cyborg intentionality: Rethinking the phenomenology of human-technology relations. *Phenomenology and the Cognitive Sciences, 7*(3), 387–395.

Wiener, N. (1961). *Cybernetics or control and communication in the animal and the machine.* Cambridge: The MIT Press.

Wolf, G. I. (2009). *Know Thyself: Tracking Every Facet of Life, from Sleep to Mood to Pain, 24/7/365.* Retrieved from https://www.wired.com/2009/06/lbnp-knowthyself/

Wolf, G. I. (2010). *The data-driven life.* The New York Times, 28 April. Retrieved from https://www.nytimes.com/2010/05/02/magazine/02self-measurement-t.html.

Wolf, G. I. (2011). *Our Three Prime Questions.* Retrieved from https://quantifiedself.com/blog/our-three-prime-questions/

Wolf, G. I., & De Groot, M. (2020). *A Conceptual Framework for Personal Science.* Retrieved from https://doi.org/10.3389/fcomp.2020.00021

Zuboff, S. (2019). *The age of surveillance capitalism. The fight for a human future at the new fronteer of power.* New York, NY: Public Affairs.

Chapter 3

Quantified Care: Self-Tracking as a Technology of the Subject

Alessandro De Cesaris

Abstract

The debate concerning the Quantified-Self Movement (QS) has been extremely polarised. As Tamar Sharon has pointed out, each aspect of the lifestyle promoted by Gary Wolf and Kevin Kelly has provoked opposite reactions, generating a debate that revolves around some basic conceptual dichotomies: empowerment versus surveillance, self-awareness versus reductionism, and personalised healthcare versus disintegration of public assistance (Sharon, 2017). The aim of this chapter is to provide a critique of QS, namely an assessment of its limits and its (technological and social) conditions of possibility. In particular, the author's analysis will focus on the relationship between technology and subjectivity, and its main theoretical framework will be Michel Foucault's research on the notion of 'care for the self' (Foucault, 1986, 2005). Quantification is an essential and unescapable aspect of our present technological environment. The devices that make our *onlife* (Floridi, 2014) possible are connected with a complex technological system made of GPSs, satellites, computers, and networks. Health is no longer managed through a distinct set of practices within the limits of a well-defined space (the hospital or the ambulatory), but it rather becomes a dataset integrated into a system where all aspects of life (health, law, leisure, work, social relations) are treated and managed simultaneously. This technological condition implies a new form of cognitive and practical delegation (Ippolita, 2016; Morozov, 2013), which makes the very notion of '*self*-tracking' at least problematic. Individuals do not track themselves anymore: on the contrary, they are tracked by prosthetic extensions of their own bodies. This, however, does not mean that they do nothing. Our digital devices require a specific set of practices, a determinate way of life. The author will argue that these practices are the product of design, understood as a specific way of conceiving and organising the interaction between subject and technical object (Flusser, 1999). Through our technological environment, design

The Quantification of Bodies in Health: Multidisciplinary Perspectives, 49–67
Copyright © 2022 by Alessandro De Cesaris
Published under an exclusive license by Emerald Publishing Limited
doi:10.1108/978-1-80071-883-820211005

reshapes the social and political function of bodies, their interaction and the set of practices connected to them (Bratton, 2015; Dyer, 2016; Vial, 2014). Automated quantification is an aspect of our designed user experience. As such, this chapter discusses design as a key element to understand the role of quantification in our digital *milieu*. It analyses the QS movement as a specific way of responding to our new technological condition. The main research question will be the following: is QS to be regarded as a simple acceptance of a new form of delegated – and thus alienated – subjectivity, or is it a kind of practice that allows the subject to overcome his passivity, and to take part in the process through which quantification is designed and managed? Is it possible to understand QS as a *technology of the self* (Foucault, 1988, 2005)?

Keywords: Quantification; self-tracking; subjectivity; care; Michel Foucault; technology of the self

Introduction

In this chapter, I will try to investigate the notion of 'self-tracking' from the point of view of the philosophy of technology. As widely known, self-tracking is the fundamental idea at the basis of the Quantified-Self Movement (henceforth QS), a community originally founded by Gary Wolf and Kevin Kelly, whose members adopt a lifestyle based on the massive use of technology in order to generate and elaborate information about their bodies. As Kevin Kelly (2007) writes in the blog of the QS official webpage, being a self-tracker can involve several different activities: chemical body load monitoring, personal genome sequencing, lifelogging, self-experimentation, researching about one's own legal rights and duties, behavioural monitoring, location tracking, digitising body info, medical self-diagnosis and much more. While QS can be viewed as a radical way to implement self-tracking in our lives, practices recognisable as forms of 'self-tracking' are becoming increasingly widespread and common in our society.

The debate concerning the QS – and self-tracking in general – has been extremely polarised. As Tamar Sharon (2017) has pointed out, each aspect of the lifestyle originally promoted by Gary Wolf and Kevin Kelly has provoked opposite reactions, generating a heated discussion that revolves around some basic conceptual dichotomies: empowerment versus surveillance, self-awareness versus reductionism, and personalised healthcare versus disintegration of public assistance. The question is very complex and involves many different levels of analysis, which are distinct but, at the same time, closely intertwined: the political issues about biometrics and governance (Ajana, 2013); the role played by self-tracking devices in the evolution of working conditions and marketing strategies (Ajana, 2013, pp. 121–133; Moore, 2018); the relationship between information technologies and tracking power (Koopman, 2019; Neff & Nafus, 2016), as well as the social and cultural transformations generated by the phenomenon (Selke, 2016);

finally, the general question concerning self-tracking as a practice, and its consequences for our notions of identity and self (Ajana, 2018; Lupton, 2016). Of course, it is impossible to deal with any of these questions without at least taking into consideration all the others. Nevertheless, I will try to avoid discussing the strictly political, economic, and social aspects of the issue, and to focus on some ground theoretical issues concerning self-tracking.

In particular, I will try to provide an analysis of self-tracking as a practice embedded in a very specific technological environment. My aim is to show the technological conditions of possibility and limits of what we call self-tracking today, and to determine the specific character of 'digital self-tracking' in the general context of self-tracking practices throughout history. To do so, it will be necessary to give equal attention to the elements of continuity and of discontinuity. On one side, I will describe self-tracking as a step in the multimillennial history of self-care practices; on the other side, I will show what aspects of self-tracking – as we conceive it today – cannot be reduced to traditional self-care practices.

I will use Michel Foucault's notion of 'technology of the self' as a theoretical framework. Foucault's work has been referred to several times in the debate concerning self-tracking, and by way of understanding biometrics as a new stage of biopolitics. Here, instead, I focus on Foucault's interest in ancient ethics and on his understanding of the relationship between technology and subjectivity. I will argue that self-tracking can be understood as a transformative practice of the self, but also that this practice – as a form of subjectivation – is structurally shaped by a certain way to conceive and engineer the interaction between subject and devices. As we will see, my thesis is that design is the way of thinking that best shapes this interaction.

Therefore, the present chapter will be structured as follows: in the first part, I will start by sketching the basic theoretical issues I would like to address with reference to the notion of 'self-tracking'. Here I will focus in particular on the question of autonomy, which has been at the centre of the discussion concerning self-tracking devices. In the second part, I will use Foucault's notion of 'technology of the self' in order to show the connection between self-tracking and subjectivity. Finally, in the third and last part I will show why we need to speak about design in order to identify the specific aspect of self-tracking as we understand it today: here I will propose using the term 'metatechnology' to describe the role of design in the development of hypermodern subjectivity.

Foucault and Technology: Devices, Practices and Autonomy

The polarisation internal to the debate about self-tracking technologies is an expression of the classic opposition between technophobes and techno-enthusiasts. This opposition is not contingent, but structural, and has to do with the paradoxical features of media themselves: it is in the very nature of what is in-between to escape any simple form of evaluation. Far from being something we can judge from the outside, media are the very condition of possibility of our expressive and judgemental faculties. There can be no 'neutral' approach to technology because it is impossible for us to detach ourselves from it and to objectify it. Since its beginning, media theory has focussed very much on this ambivalence in our relationship with technology. By treating media as extensions of our bodies, media theorists also keep reflecting on Marshall McLuhan's famous motto: every extension is at the same time a self-amputation (McLuhan, 1964, p. 42). This statement does not simply mean that each technology has 'pros and cons'. It rather means that every technology shapes the domain of the possible: it determines what we can or cannot do.

Now, the main issue when dealing with the so-called 'self-tracking' technologies is precisely the interpretation of the notion of 'self'. The relevance of the debate about the significance of self-tracking in our culture consists precisely in the fact that, trying to assess the meaning of technology for human life, it summons some of the most fundamental issues philosophy has faced since Plato. In this sense, the disagreement in the academic and public debate is not just about the 'value' of self-tracking, namely about whether it is 'good' or 'bad' for society and for individuals, or whether it 'works' or not. On the contrary, the opposition is based on the structural possibility to understand self-tracking in two completely different ways, which both focus on the notion of 'autonomy' of the subject. To explain this structural ambivalence, though, it will be necessary to clarify some basic conceptual features of the notion of 'technology', in particular the relationship between the material-objective and the ethical-subjective aspect. In other words, it will be necessary to explain the relation between 'technology' as a device or a set of devices, and 'technology' as a practice.

The question of autonomy is pivotal in the whole philosophical debate about the essence of modernity. Even though I am not going to focus on it I would like to start from a famous text, Immanuel Kant's *An Answer to the Question 'What is Enlightenment?'*:

> The motto of enlightenment is therefore: *Sapere aude!* [Dare to be wise!] Have courage to use your *own* understanding! Laziness and cowardice are the reasons why such a large proportion of men, even when nature has long emancipated them from alien guidance (*naturaliter maiorennes*), nevertheless gladly remain immature for life. For the same reasons, it is all too easy for others to set themselves up as their guardians. It is so convenient to be immature! If I have a book to have understanding in place of me, a spiritual adviser to have a conscience for me, a doctor to judge my diet for me, and so on, I need not make any efforts at all. I need not think, so long as I can pay; others will soon enough take the tiresome job over for me. (Kant, 1989 [1784], p. 54)

What is striking about this passage is that the problem of reason is not considered from a theoretical, but rather from a practical point of view. Kant is not speaking about the limits of reason or the question of knowledge: the focus is on the use – better: the public use – of reason, namely a set of practices, whose exercise can help us distinguish between mature and immature human beings. In other words, here Kant is talking about the relationship between a certain kind of practices and autonomy as a basic value for human beings in general.

Now, the question of autonomy has been a key topic for Western philosophy of technology since its beginning. Plato's critique of writing in the *Phaedrus* can be interpreted as a critique of how the delegation of memory to an external device – what Plato calls 'trust' or 'confidence' (*pistis*) – makes us subject to that device itself (*Phaedrus*, 275a2-6). Those who confide in external devices in order to remember are no longer autonomous: this is, at first glance, the position expressed in the dialogue.

We will come back to Plato, but first let us analyse further Kant's quote. It is very interesting to see how, based on this passage, one can draw two completely opposite interpretations of the significance of self-tracking. According to the first, self-tracking is a step forward in the pursuit of what Kant describes as 'adulthood'. The self-tracker is an adult because, to use Kant's words, she does not have 'a doctor to judge her diet for her': she makes her own diet, with the help of the devices that extend and enhance her body and her cognition. Self-tracking allows a form of *disintermediation*, thanks to which the subject finally becomes fully autonomous and capable of doing by himself all that is required in order to live in society, instead of confiding in experts. Finally, self-tracking allows a new form of *transparency* of the subject to himself: we finally 'know ourselves through numbers', as QS expressly promises. Information itself is transparent, because it is finally expressed in a clear and simple form – namely through a set of quantitative values.

Following this interpretation, autonomy, disintermediation, and transparency are the three key features that make self-tracking a way to live as adults. And yet, a completely different interpretation is also possible. According to it, self-tracking devices are precisely what adulthood is *not* about. Just like in Plato's critique of writing, using tracking devices is a way of delegating to an artefact an activity that should be executed by us. In this way, it is possible to reply to the first interpretation by subverting its three core statements. First, the self-tracking subject is no longer autonomous because he needs something external in order to know himself. He is no longer the subject, but the object of the measurement. Ironically, there is no 'self' in self-tracking, and the name associated with the phenomenon betrays the ideological attempt to conceal a very simple truth: thanks to our devices, we stop being subjects. Secondly, far from being a form of disintermediation, self-tracking devices provide a form of *hypermediation*, namely a form of mediation so radical that it does not even appear as such. Finally, this new form of mediation is everything but transparent: beyond the interface we interact with, the actual functioning of the device remains completely hidden. Not only do we not take the measurements, but we also ignore the process through which the measurement itself is taken.

This polarisation is the root of many other opposite evaluations of the outcomes of self-tracking – security versus surveillance, personalisation of care versus blurring of the medical institution as such and so on. The very core of this contraposition can be traced back to the difference between externalisation and internalisation: are these devices to be treated like extensions of ourselves, and so as improvements of our skills, or are they ways to stop thinking about a task?

Now, as I pointed out in the introduction, the possibility of interpreting a technological phenomenon in two completely opposite ways is not contingent, but structural. A first thing to remark, in fact, is that these two interpretations are based on two different approaches to technology: in the first case, self-tracking is viewed as a *practice*; in the second case, self-tracking is viewed as an operation granted by a certain kind of *devices*.

The first view of technology, which I would call 'practice-based', is more directly linked with the original meaning of the word '*techne*' in Greek culture: *techne* is primarily a specific kind of knowledge, what we would call 'competence'. *Technai* are practices grounded on a certain know-how, the practical expression of a competence. The second view of technology, which we could describe as 'device-based', progressively acquired importance in the history of Science and Technology Studies, as well as in the history of Philosophy of Technology as a whole.

Both understandings of technology are implicitly present in Kant's quoted passage. On one side, the reference to doctors and spiritual advisers evokes the question of competence; on the other side, it is quite telling that Kant uses the example of a medium, or better, *the* medium of the modern era – the printed book – to illustrate the dangers connected to the use of external devices.

In this context, I can finally justify my choice to use Michel Foucault's notion of 'technology of the self' as a theoretical framework. It has been argued whether it is possible to consider Foucault as a proper 'philosopher of technology'[1] (Clarizio, 2013, p. 57; Dorrestijn, 2012; Gerrie, 2003). For those who focus on Foucault as a theorist of power relations and institutions, it is possible to argue that he 'does not focus often on technology' (Feenberg, 2002, p. 68), and yet, that his analysis of the panopticon and his view of the relationship between power, knowledge and institution can be used as a model to 'deduce' Foucault's critical theory of technology. While this is of course true, and it would be wrong to envision a gap between an 'early' Foucault focussed on power and institutions, and a 'late' Foucault more interested to the so-called 'technologies of the self', it should also be underlined that Foucault's philosophy of technology is in no way 'implicit'. On the contrary, it is developed with an explicit stress on the importance of understanding what we mean when we speak about 'technology'.

Now, we could see Foucault's work as the most important practice-based approach to technology in the philosophical debate of the last few decades. Not only does Foucault expressly refer to the ancient meaning of the word 'techne' as 'practical rationality governed by a conscious goal' (Foucault, 1984, p. 255); in his late work, Foucault also develops the notion of 'technology' in order to provide a deeper and more extensive account of the relations between power, knowledge, infrastructures, and subjects (Foucault, 1988, p. 18). In this framework, technology is never understood as a 'thing'.[2]

---

[1]The literature about Foucault's philosophy of technology does not always take under consideration the late works and seminars of the French philosopher, namely the ones where Foucault expressly develops a systematic approach to the Greek notion of *techne* and shapes his own use of the term 'technology'. Gerrie (2003), for instance, stops at the late Seventies in his analysis of Foucault's approach to media.

[2]It is striking, in this sense, that Gerrie argues that Foucault 'may have felt more comfortable confining the term "technology" to artifacts' (Gerrie, 2003, p. 72).

Nevertheless, in Foucault's discourse, there is a very close interplay between the two aforementioned dimensions. Steven Dorrestijn refers to them as the 'technical determination of power relation' and the 'training of technically mediated routines' (Dorrestijn, 2012, pp. 229–230). These two expressions name the two sides of the very close relationship between media and practices: on one side, every power structure requires a material infrastructure in order to function; on the other side, every material device requires some sort of training in order to be integrated in its user's existential or professional practice. One could dare to say that practices without material media are empty, and material media without practices are blind.

This means, of course, that the history of concrete practices cannot be considered as something separated from the history of technological media. At the same time, as Emanuele Clarizio points out, this complex history of practices and material infrastructures is viewed by Foucault not much as a question about knowledge and truth, but rather as an ethical problem. Foucault's interest is to show how the analysis of these technologies allows us to determine concrete historical processes of subjectivation (Clarizio, 2013). In this way, Foucault's notion of 'technologies of the self' shares at least two basic assumptions with Marshall McLuhan's media theory.

The first assumption is that there is no 'neutral' subject before its interaction with a technological milieu. Subjectivity is never something given, but it is the result of a process, and this process must be analysed taking under consideration not only the – static – set of devices that constitute the social space, but also the – dynamic – *ethos* that the subject needs to develop in order to live in that environment.

The second assumption, which can be traced back to the teachings of Georges Canguilhem on the nature of normativity, is that media are normatively charged. This means that Foucault, just like Simondon (Clarizio, 2013) rejects any 'instrumental' view of technology, according to which any instrument is neither good nor bad in itself, but only according to its use. It is easy to show that this is a consequence of the first assumption, because such a perspective on technology implies some sort of separation between instrument and behaviour.

Foucault's approach can be very useful to approach the question of autonomy I sketched at the beginning of the chapter. It is well known that Foucault was not fond of the notion of autonomy and used the term quite seldom in his works – even though one of the occurrences takes place precisely in his commentary to Kant's text on Enlightenment (Cremonesi, Irrera, Lorenzini, & Tazzioli, 2016, p. 1). Nevertheless, it is precisely this suspicion that helps us in this case, as it allows us to show that the dichotomy between autonomy and subjection – or, in other words, between internalisation and externalisation – does not hold.

Let us go back to Plato's *Phaedrus* and the critique of external memory. A reading that simply condemns technological supports for memory would not do justice to the complexity of the dialogue. Any unilateral judgement about the relationship between media and practices overlooks their interplay. Sure, one way to see it is that our practices and skills are fashioned and modified by our external prostheses. At the same time, though, the significance and social role of media is co-determined by the practices we associate with them. Let us take, as an example, Plato's distinction between *hypomnesis* and *anamnesis*. *Hypomnesis* – a word thoroughly studied by Foucault that, in the Greek language also refers to the *blocknote* – is the mere recording of something, an external prosthesis of human memory. Stiegler calls it externalised, passive memory (Stiegler, 2016). *Anamnesis*, on the contrary, is the active process of remembrance. Now, that between *hypomnesis* and *anamnesis* is not an alternative. As the rest of the dialogue shows, when Socrates comes to speak about the difference between good and bad writing practices (277e–278a), there is a way to record our memories (*hypomnemata*) in a way that is functional to *anamnesis*. In other words: there is a way to use our devices in order to make them functional to a practice, and not to let them replace it. Education (*paideia*) is the process through which we learn how to do just that: how to avoid the danger of our memory instead of enhancing it.

That of full autonomy is therefore a myth, but not because it is our destiny to be slaves. On the contrary, it is impossible to conceive the subject outside of the many relations it entertains with the environment, with others and with itself: all those relations, including self-relations, are mediated by practices and devices (Clarizio, 2013).

In this first part I have gathered some basic principles: that media and practices cannot be analysed separately; that technological mediations are inherently normative; that subjectivation is the process through which the interplay of media and practices produces a certain – historically specific – way of being a subject.

Before proceeding with the analysis, I am going to state very briefly some of the points I will develop with reference to self-tracking. First, self-tracking – in general – can be interpreted as a complex way to develop subjectivity in a given technological milieu. It is what Foucault calls a practice of care of the self (*souci de soi*).

Secondly, as a particular stage in the history of self-care practices, self-tracking can be regarded as the form taken by the care of the self in the age of digital technologies. Here, we will have to avoid two mistakes: interpreting self-care practices as a mere epiphenomenon of how digital media are shaped; and understanding media as mere gadgets for an independent practice.

Finally, I will try to show in what sense the way in which self-tracking as a practice interacts with self-tracking devices is shaped by a metatechnology, namely a very specific form of conceiving the relation between humans and technology, something that shapes our media and, at the same time, the way we use them. This metatechnology is design, and the set of practices it implements in our social environment determines a new form of subjectivation: that of the user.

Self-tracking as a Stage in the History of Self-care

I have already tried to show how self-tracking can be regarded at the same time as a practice and as the extension of the subject through a certain set of devices. Before proceeding further, I would like to point out that this intertwine of device- and practice-based approach is particularly necessary in the case of self-tracking devices. Strictly speaking, in fact, the notion of 'self-tracking device' as a particular kind of device, today, has a meaning only if we refer it to a particular way to use that device. Sure, there are devices which are exclusively designed to extract and process data about ourselves, but these technologies do not cover the whole domain of what we refer to as 'self-tracking devices', and limiting our analysis to them would force us to ignore many aspects of what we call 'self-tracking' as a social practice.

If we only focus on the material aspect, namely on the technology that constitutes our artificial environment in contemporary society, the distinction between self-tracking and other devices is extremely difficult: all digital media today are self-tracking devices, at least in the sense that they 'track the self'. Every digital device has a readable memory. Every device connected to the internet produces metadata. My computer, my phone, my credit card, my social ID, my internet browser, my car, in some cases my fridge, my oven, my house are all self-tracking devices. The evolution of digital culture is strictly connected with what Luciano Floridi has called 'the fourth Revolution', namely the revolution brought about by information technologies. But information technologies are structurally designed to translate analogue data into digital data, and to store these data in order to be able to perform all kinds of operations with them.

It is also very important to remark that such data are not only quantitative, but also qualitative. My digital environment constantly tracks what I watch, what I buy, where I am, with whom I speak. This tracking is also not limited to the domain of health, but rather invests all aspects of life: my social relationship, my desires, my financial condition, my legal status, my political orientation, my conversations.

This tracking isn't only pervasive, but ineluctable: it cannot be avoided, it is a structural element of how our technology works. There is, of course, the possibility of managing the storage and distribution of data in order to grant some rights, like a certain degree of privacy. For this reason, the political struggle about data ownership and protection is a pivotal one. Nevertheless, in principle the efficiency of digital devices is directly proportional to their ability to store and process data which are archived or extracted from the environment through sensors. Aside from the political and economic interests that shape technology in a certain way, there are some *a priori* conditions of possibility for technology itself which cannot be avoided: technology is the domain of what is possible, but the character of any given technology sketches the boundaries of what we can and cannot do with it.

The traditional opposition between devices and practices is overcome when we start reflecting on devices themselves as practical agents. Contemporary philosophy has been increasingly dealing with the 'agency' of artefacts, with their ability to behave as quasi-subjects with respect to the environment (Latour, 2005). In fact, the polarised opposition between autonomy and heteronomy, mentioned in relation to the two possible interpretations of self-tracking, makes even less sense in this technological context. An absolute separation between 'self-tracking' and 'tracking by others' is only possible in an environment that keeps subject and artefacts completely separated. The distinction between the user and the digital environment she lives in, however, is based on constant interaction: the user's world is a world of interfaces (Bratton, 2015; De Cesaris, 2020) in which all devices are interconnected and every individual artefact works thanks to a very complex infrastructure. I can keep track of myself because I accept to share my information about myself, but at the same time, what allows me to share data is the fact that they are already structured according to some practical needs, for instance the desire to follow a diet or to save money. Right now, of course, I am using the expression 'self-tracking' in a very broad sense: people track themselves when they check how much money they have, see where they are on a map, or check a chat log to remember what they said to some friend a while ago. In this very broad sense, self-tracking is a constitutive aspect of digitalised societies, a practice that structures the very way we interact with our digital environment and with each other.

Now, if we want to identify self-tracking as it is specifically meant by movements such as QS, it still does not seem sufficient to refer to a set of devices – or apps – which are explicitly created for a particular kind of data collection and processing. In this way, in fact, the focus would be on the major efficiency and processing power of these devices with respect to other traditional self-tracking practices. Digital self-tracking would only be a faster way of doing something that we already did before: taking note of our expenses in order to spend less, or writing what we eat and weighing ourselves in order to become fitter. But – as QS's co-founder Gary Wolf expressly points out, such practices are not just about 'getting better results': 'Self-tracking [...] isn't really a tool of optimization but of discovery' (Neff & Nafus, 2016, p. 33). To fully disclose the specific nature of this attempt at self-discovery, we should consider it in the history of practices connected with self-knowledge and self-development. Once we have identified QS as a social practice, the focus on the specific features of digital media can help us identify its distinctive elements with respect to pre-digital practices.

I would like to argue that self-tracking must be regarded as a practice of care of the self. As mentioned, this notion was developed by Michel Foucault in his studies on the history of sexuality, and it has been perfected in his researches on ancient ethics. In particular, the 1981–1982 lectures on the *Hermeneutics of the Subject* at the Collège de France develop the notion of *epimeleia eautou* and show how it corresponds to a certain way to shape individual subjectivity in a social context. This notion of *epimeleia eautou* is expressly connected with that of 'technology of the self', which Foucault would use more and more frequently in his later writings (Foucault, 2005, p. 46).

A precise definition of what Foucault meant with the term 'technology of the self' is very important, in this case, because it allows us to distinguish between the general influence of Information and Communication Technologies (ICTs) on the processes of identity generation in contemporary society, and the specific way self-tracking can be regarded as a conscious practice in our culture. For instance, in his ground-breaking book *The 4th Revolution*, Luciano Floridi expressly speaks about ICTs as powerful 'technologies of the self' (Floridi, 2014, p. 59). However, according to Floridi, personal identity is shaped by ICTs through two passages:

> Change the social conditions in which you live, modify the network of relations and the flows of information you enjoy, reshape the nature and scope of the constraints and affordances that regulate your presentation of yourself to the world and indirectly to yourself, and then your social self may be radically updated, feeding back into your self-conception, which ends up shaping your personal identity. (Floridi, 2014, pp. 60–61)

Personal identity is shaped through two mediations, that of our social life and of our self-conception. In this way, ICTs are 'technologies of the self' in a very different sense than the one introduced by Foucault. First, this term refers to conscious, voluntary practices, and not to the side-effect of our unaware technological habits. Secondly, as we will see, there is a social component to the technological practices of the self, but these practices are expressly focussed on the subject. Floridi's 'broad' use of Foucault's terminology is useful to clarify the difference between two different ways to consider self-tracking in the context of digital media: in the first sense, as we just saw, self-tracking is a constitutive aspect of how ICTs reshape our social environment, producing new habits and new social practices. In a second and more specific sense, however, self-tracking is a conscious practice performed by the subject. It is a practice of care of the self of which QS represents a radicalised version, but that is very present in our society in its less extreme, socially more acceptable forms.

To analyse self-tracking as a practice of care of the self, we have to consider what Foucault identifies as the key features of this kind of practice. According to Foucault, the care of the self is based on three fundamental elements:

> First, the theme of a general standpoint, of a certain way of considering things, of behaving in the world, undertaking actions, and having relations with other people. The *epimeleia heautou* is an attitude towards the self, others, and the world. (Foucault, 2005, p. 10)

Self, others, world: the care of the self is a technology that regulates the interaction between subjects and their environment. As we will see, these three domains would become the object of three disciplines strictly connected to the care of the self: dietetics, erotics and economics. Now, contemporary self-tracking practices do express a general attitude, since they are not only a way to keep track of ourselves, but they also collect and promote data about our surroundings and those who are close to us. In other words, self-tracking practices promote a very specific attitude towards ourselves, the world, and others, since they offer a new way of considering things as *data*, and a new way of interacting with them through *digital interfaces*. It is important to remark that this has nothing to do with what Noal Yuvah Harari has called *Dataism*, a world-vision connected to the idea that everything is made up of digital data. Self-tracking is a *practical attitude*, in which that of data is the implicit form we give to everything we enter in contact with. In the same way, digital interfaces are the symbolic form we are progressively interiorising in our way to deal with everything, from our own private life to the public sphere: when Alexander R. Galloway insists on considering them not from an ontological, but rather from an ethical point of view, he is stressing precisely that interfaces are a way of *doing* rather than simply a way of *being* (Galloway, 2012).

The second constitutive feature of the care of the self is the peculiar orientation of this way of being:

> Second, the *epimeleia heautou* is also a certain form of attention, of looking. Being concerned about oneself implies that we look

away from the outside to 'oneself'. The care of the self implies a certain way of attending to what we think and what takes place in our thought. The word *epimeleia* is related to *melethe*, which means both exercise and meditation. (Foucault, 2005, pp. 10–11)

As Foucault remarks, this attitude is not simply *introspective*: taking care of oneself does not simply mean getting back to one's own interiority. There is no opposition between knowledge of the self and knowledge of what is external: '"converting to the self" is still a way of knowing nature' (Foucault, 2005, p. 259). Converting to the self has nothing to do with the exploration of the soul's inner secrets (the Christian *arcana conscientiae*). It is a form of thoughtfulness that spiritualises the subject's gaze on the world, and allows him to determine his place in it while at the same time suspending his immediate immersion in it. From this standpoint, Wolf's claim that QS is a form of self-discovery seems to go in this direction: The Self-Quantifier is a knower, he is not a shut-in, secluded in his own private space, but an explorer that takes some time of his life to exercise a precise way of looking at the world – through data.

Finally, it is significant that the notion of care (*epimeleia*) does not refer to some form of contemplative attitude, but rather to a very concrete set of practices:

Third, the notion of *epimeleia* does not merely designate this general attitude or this form of attention turned on the self. The *epimeleia* also always designates a number of actions exercised on the self by the self, actions by which one takes responsibility for oneself, and by which one changes, purifies, transforms, and transfigures oneself.

In this sense, the subject's theoretical stance towards itself is to be considered as a particular practice, in other words as a particular way of behaving. This also clarifies how a practice of care of the self is a practice of 'subjectivation'. It produces a 'self', a certain way of being of the subject, thanks to the subject's personal engagement in a certain form of activity. We will see in the next chapter what particular form of subjectivation is produced by the self-tracking subject.

Now, these key features are important in order to confirm *whether* self-tracking can be regarded as a form of self-care practice: they are still not sufficient to determine *what kind* of self-care practice it is, namely what kind of subjectivation it implies. As we will see in the next section, in order to operate this determination, it is necessary to consider the interplay between practices and devices. As we have seen, the analysis of this interaction is not always a focus in Foucault's philosophy of technology, but some steps in this direction can be found in his work. I will now emphasise them in order to complete this analysis of self-tracking as a practice in the context of digital media.

The Features of Self-tracking as a Practice

Reading Plato's *Alcibiades*, Foucault emphasises how the care of the self does not coincide with the care for our body, our belongings, or our loved ones. The time we dedicate to the care of ourselves is not 'free time' or 'leisure time': it is a precise practice. This also implies that the practice of care of the self is not incompatible with medicine, but it is still something quite different. Let us go back to Kant's quote: the aim is not to make ourselves 'autonomous' and avoid recurring to the counsel of the medic or to the wisdom of the judge, or to stop using books in order to remember things. The aim is to give a new meaning to the way we interact with these forms of intermediation. To use Kant's terms, the 'public use of reason' does not put in any danger our obedience to the judge, but it changes our way to deal with legal bureaucracy.

In his lectures on the *Hermeneutics of the subject*, Foucault points out a remarkable aspect. The 'self' does not coincide with the body, our belongings, or our beloved ones, but rather is 'the soul'. He argues that the soul is the 'subject of action', and especially the subject of the 'kresthai', namely the subject that uses the body, manages its belongings, and communicates with others. The cure of the self is a way for the subject to use a certain number of instruments, primarily the 'archi-instrument' that is the body. In Plato's first dialogues, the body is somehow considered as the 'first medium' we have at our disposal, an idea that we will find throughout the history of Western culture and that will be expressed in the most radical way in Hegel's anthropology. This element is of great importance, as we will see, because it allows us to clarify something about the difference I would like to introduce between technology and metatechnology. For now, however, it is fundamental because it helps describe a major shift in the way self-tracking works as a technology of the self.

In the second volume of his *History of Sexuality*, Foucault analyses the structure of self-care practices by identifying four different factors: the ethical substance, the mode of subjection, the ethical work, and the *telos*.[3] This theoretical framework is what allows him, for instance, to differentiate between the ethical practices of the Classic Greek Age and those of late antiquity, or early Christian practices like *exagoreusis* and *exomologesis* (Foucault, 1988, pp. 41–49). Let us try and analyse self-tracking according to these factors.

According to Foucault, the ethical substance is the 'prime material of moral conduct' (Foucault, 1990, p. 26), namely that part of the subject that is exposed to a need for ethical change. In an interview, Foucault clarifies how in modern society the ethical substance consists of feelings, whereas it was intention for Kant, and desire for Christian thought (Foucault, 1984, p. 352). In our digital society, the ethical substance is somehow 'externalised' and refers no longer to some inner faculty of the soul, but instead to the subject as a whole, as it is turned into *data*. Of course, only what pertains to the body, or to the devices which extend it, can be turned into data. In this way, the ethical substance in our contemporary society consists of *data* themselves, namely all forms of expression of the 'subject of action' inasmuch they are collected and stored. It must be clarified that, even though data collection only pertains to concrete actions, and therefore

---

[3]As Steven Dorrestijn remarks, Gilles Deleuze was probably the first to identify the model of this structure in Aristotle's theory of the four causes (Dorrestijn, 2012).

what actually happens in a body or in a device, this does not mean that these data only concern 'material' aspects of the subject's life. Desires, intentions, beliefs, thoughts can be collected and stored in the form of data, as long as they are *expressed* in some way (i.e. through a wish list on a commercial website).

The second aspect is the mode of subjection. Foucault defines it as 'the way in which the individual establishes his relation to the rule and recognizes himself as obliged to put it into practice' (Foucault, 1990, p. 27). Divine law, natural law, rational rules, or an aesthetic imperative are all possible modes of subjection (Foucault, 1984, p. 353). Now, in the case of self-tracking – even in its most radical applications, for instance Quantified Self – we could point out the same thing that has been broadly remarked about post-modern or hypermodern society: a passage from a society of moral obligations to a society of leisure (Lipovetsky, 2005), or from a disciplinary society to a society of performance (Han, 2015, p. 11). The gamified experience of the individual is no longer based on a direct obligation. Instead, there is some kind of *soft imperative* based on the 'can' rather than the 'ought'. Even the motto of QS, 'self-knowledge through numbers', does not express an imperative comparable to the Greek 'know thyself'. Here the appeal to quantity is secondary. What is important is that the motto seems to express a different kind of imperative, an invitation that could be translated as follows: 'Know yourself through numbers, because you can, because it's fun!'

The third element is the ethical work, namely the actual set of practices performed by the individual in order to manipulate the ethical substance – and therefore shape himself. Now, this ethical work always consists in the use of a certain medium, at least of that proto-medium that is the body. As known, Foucault analysed extensively two medium-based forms of ethical work, both linked to writing: the use of notebooks (*hypomnemata*) to keep track of one's own actions and thoughts, and communication via correspondence. This analysis takes place, in particular, in the lectures of 1981–1982 and in a small essay titled *Self-Writing* (Foucault, 1997, pp. 207–222), in which writing about the self and writing of the self are expressly intertwined.

When Foucault describes the evolution of the notion of care of the self in late antiquity, he shows that the practice is conceived as a self-examination like the unravelling of a written page (Foucault, 2005, pp. 162–163). This changes many things: for instance, the domains of medicine, economics and communication are no longer excluded, but are the very field where the care of the self is exercised. Foucault expressly writes that it is irrelevant whether the reference is to an actual book or to a metaphorical book of memory. This does not mean that the reference to a technology like the book is irrelevant. On the contrary, it means that, once writing has been internalised as a technology, it operates on the subject even when the subject does not actually use it. What Foucault describes is the passage from an oral form of self-care – the master, the mentor – to a form of self-care typical of a society that has finally interiorised the private use of writing.

In the case of digital self-tracking, there is a big difference between the close circle of the members of QS, or those who practice self-tracking in a radical way, and those who still engage in it as a conscious practice, but simply confide in what the market offers to them. This difference can be expressed as the opposition between an active and a passive relation with design: a radical self-tracker designs his own devices, takes part in the ideation and construction of the devices necessary for the practice; on the contrary, an ordinary self-tracker relies on apps and devices which are designed by someone else, and standardised for all users. Given this opposition, the role design plays in the configuration of the relationship between user and device allows us to recognize some common features. In both cases the core element of the ethical work is the interaction with an interface. I will focus on design in the conclusion, since – as we will see – it is a pivotal element in this analysis.

Finally, there is the *telos* of the ethical work, namely the final aim of the practice of care of the self. The tranquillity of the self, the self-mastery, or the detachment of the self from the world are all examples of such a *telos*. In the case of self-tracking, usually the explicit aim is some sort of minimal and specific self-improvement: weight loss, more regular sleep, better use of personal finances. For QS, the general aim is the perfect transparency of the subject to herself: through data analysis, we are finally able to *really* know ourselves. I would like to argue that behind both objectives lies a more radical and general aim: the extension – we could call it integration, or displacement – of the self through devices. In the case of the ancient technologies of the self, the *hypomnema* is just an instrument: I use it not as an extension, but as a means to an end that still relies on myself. The subject aims at changing himself through media, but he keeps the distinction between his own subjectivity and the devices helping him change it. On the contrary, the user of digital self-tracking devices embraces them as a part of herself, *interacting* with them in a constant exchange. Her aim is to reach complete integration with her technological environment, a point in which her technological extensions are part of her own agency, have normative effects on her and actively take part in the shaping of her choices, desires and needs.

Self-tracking Users: Design and Subjectivation

In his analysis of the *epimeleia eautou*, Foucault points out that 'the care of the self is actually something that always has to go through the relationship to someone else who is the master' (Foucault, 2005, p. 58). In particular,

> The master is the person who cares about the subject's care for himself, and who finds in his love for his disciple the possibility of caring for the disciple's care for himself. (p. 59)

This expression is particularly useful for me because it reveals the metatechnological aspect of the care of the self.

I define 'metatechnology' as a 'technology of technology', namely as a form of technology whose aim is to mediate between the subject and his technological environment. The care of the self involves the relationship between the individual and her environment at the most basic level, as a subject dealing with himself, the world, and others: it is not a private practice, but rather a strictly intersubjective and 'social' one.

Hence a history of metatechnologies of self-care. This means that the history of self-care is not only a history of practices and devices, but also a history of the ways in which the interaction between subjects, practices and devices has been integrated in the social sphere. We have seen that an example of oral technology is the master. Education (*paideia*) is a general form of metatechnology for the care of the self. With the invention of printing came bureaucracy, made up of institutions devoted to the regulation and coordination of the care of the citizen for herself. Foucault's research about the origins of medical institutions, but also Ivan Illich's or Fritjof Capra's criticism of institutionalised medicine, can be read as studies on a particular metatechnological configuration of Western society. And as said, Kant's considerations on enlightenment are also the product of a typographic age, when judges, books, and medics were parts of institutions (publishing, the state, public health).

My conclusion is that the most powerful and specific form of metatechnology in our era is not an institution like bureaucracy or school, as in the past, but design. Since this is not the focus of this chapter, I will only stress a few points. First, design is a metatechnology because it does not directly invest 'technology' in itself but is rather a way to coordinate the relationship between the subject and technology. It is not strictly a practice, but a way to shape practices. There is a very close connection between the birth of design and the growing use of the word 'interface', one of the key concepts of the so-called 'digital turn' (Floridi, 2014, pp. 34–39). In his study on the notion of interface, Branden Hookway remarks that interfaces are not technologies in themselves, but forms of relation with technology (Hookway, 2014, p. IX).

If we understand it in this way, then we should add an element to Foucault's quadrilateral theoretical framework: the metatechnological element is a core factor in the determination of how a practice of care of the self shapes the subject. In the context of self-tracking devices, design is the metatechnological feature that guides and shapes our way to take care of ourselves: they are the result of a specific way of imagining our relationship to technology (there is not always some 'new' technology *stricto sensu* being implemented in these devices).

We have seen that the notion of self-tracking can be understood in three different ways: in a very broad sense, as a general feature of our relationship with digital media; in a more proper sense, as a *light* practice enacted by a part of the population; in a strict sense, as a *strong* practice that defines the lifestyle of a community (such as QS). While only the latter sense is perfectly identifiable with what Foucault named 'technologies of the self', I maintain that this notion is useful in order to understand how these practices affect subjects, even when they do not correspond to a proper 'ethical conduct'. In particular, I would like to highlight that, in this framework, the five features I identified – data as ethical substance, leisure as mode of subjection, interface interaction as ethical work, integration with the technological environment as *telos*, design as metatechnology – still apply to all three cases.

Now, in this analysis of the form of subjectivity of the 'self-tracker', my claim is that the general kind of subjectivity produced by design as a metatechnology, of which the 'self-tracker' in only a special sub-category, already has a name, a name we find everywhere: *user*. The 'userification' of society is not a neutral operation, it involves an entire way to conceive the interaction of users with themselves, with others and with their environment. A general analysis of the metatechnological features of today's technological environment would imply an investigation of the specific way in which design configures the interaction between subject and device. My final point is that the specific character of design is a radical separation between technology and metatechnology. This means, for instance, that self-tracking as a practice of subjectivation is based, today, on digital media, but does not require any kind of technological competence. In other words, the main consequence of design as a metatechnology is the radical separation between users and experts.

This idea is expressed, for instance, by Bernard Stiegler's notion of 'proletarianization'. With this term, Stiegler addresses a curious paradox of our era: the focus on the notion of 'cognitive capitalism', that is, the great many efforts put into the technological enhancement of knowledge, has made us completely unable to master the processes that lead to knowledge. We have lost our 'savoir faire' and our 'savoir vivre' when it comes to knowledge, because we no longer master the means for the production of that knowledge (Stiegler, 2016). Going back to the opposition between radical self-trackers designing their own devices – who are experts – and ordinary self-trackers – who are just users – it could be argued that, in a way, the kind of relationship we build with our digital devices can be regarded as a form of de-subjectivation, or – better – as the process through which our practices create a form of passive subjectivity.

Many paradoxes of our era, our obsession for transparency, but also some populistic forms of enthusiasm for the idea of 'immediacy' are determined by our experience of a world shaped by infographics, interfaces, technologies with no learning curve and so on. Many advocate for radical solutions: everyone should learn how to code, for instance, or data property should be completely reorganised. In my opinion, the dangers connected to the use of self-tracking devices must be regarded as a design problem. The question I would like to ask is the following: how should we design these devices in order to improve their ability to engage the subject in a practice of active care of the self?

In this context, an important element is that this question does not address a technological problem. Nothing prevents us from creating different user experiences. The point is to understand why we choose not to do so, and I believe, with Jaron Lanier, that the answer lies in the connection between design as a metatechnology and a specific business model (Lanier, 2010, 2018).

For these reasons, I think it is pivotal to consider self-tracking not only as the rigidly codified practice of a close community (QS), but also as a general aspect of our everyday interaction with digital media. The notion of metatechnology is useful to identify the different possible relationships between devices and practices, to show that the relationship between the 'technical determination of power relation' and the 'training of technically mediated routines' is not a given. Only here, far from the simple polarisation between opposite abstract positions – autonomy or dependency, subject or object, practice, or device – can we find the field for an actual political struggle.

References

Ajana, B. (Ed.) (2013). *Governing through biometrics. The biopolitics of identity*. New York, NY: Palgrave MacMillan.

Ajana, B. (Ed.) (2018). *Self-tracking. Empirical and philosophical investigations*. New York, NY: Palgrave MacMillan.

Bratton, B. (2015). *The stack. Software and sovereignty*. Cambridge, MA: MIT Press.

Clarizio, E. (2013). Assoggettamento e soggettivazione. *Tecnica e tecniche. Noema*, *4*(1), 51–60.

Cremonesi, L., Irrera, O., Lorenzini, D., & Tazzioli, M. (2016). Rethinking autonomy between subjection and subjectivation. In L. Cremonesi, O. Irrera, D. Lorenzini, & M. Tazzioli (Eds.), *Foucault, and the making of subjects* (pp. 1–10). London: Rowman & Littlefield.

De Cesaris, A. (2020). Morphologie des interfaces. Le design comme métatechnique. In R. Olcèse (Ed.), *L'art tout contre la machine* (pp. 187–200). Paris: Hermann.

Dorrestijn, S. (2012). Technical mediation and subjectivation. Tracing and extending Foucault's philosophy of technology. *Philosophy and Technology*, *25*, 221–241.

Dyer, J. (2016). Quantified Bodies: A Design Practice. *Digital Culture & Society, 2*(1), 161–168.

Feenberg, A. (2002). *Transforming technology. A critical theory revisited*. Oxford: Oxford University Press.

Floridi, L. (2014). *The 4th revolution. How the infosphere is reshaping human reality*. Oxford: Oxford University Press.

Flusser, V. (1999). *The Shape of Things. A Philosophy of Design* (A. Mathews, Trans.). London: Reaktion Books.

Foucault, M. (1984). *The Foucault's reader* (P. Rabinow, Ed.). New York, NY: Pantheon Books.

Foucault, M. (1986). *The Care of the Self. Volume 3 of the History of Sexuality* (R. Hurley, Trans.). New York: Vintage Books.

Foucault, M. (1988). *Technologies of the Self*. In Martin & al., 16–50.

Foucault, M. (1990). *The use of pleasure* (R. Hurley, Trans.). New York, NY: Vintage Books.

Foucault, M. (1997). *Ethics. Subjectivity and truth* (R. Hurley, Trans.). New York, NY: The New Press.

Foucault, M. (2005). *The Hermeneutics of the Subject. Lectures at the Collège de France 1981–1982* (G. Burchell, Trans.). New York, NY: Palgrave MacMillan.

Galloway, A. (2012). *The Interface Effect*. Boston - New York: Polity Press.

Gerrie, J. (2003). Was Foucault a philosopher of technology? *Techné, 7*(2), 66–73.

Han, B.-C. (2015). *The Burnout Society (2010)*. Stanford, CA: Stanford University Press.

Hookway, B. (2014). *Interface*. Cambridge, MA: MIT Press.

Ippolita (2016). *Anime elettriche. Riti e miti social*. Milan: Jaca Book.

Kant, I. (1989). *Political writings* (B. Nisbet, Trans.). Cambridge, MA: Cambridge University Press.

Kelly, K. (2007, October 5). What is the quantified self? Retrieved from https://www.webcitation.org/66TEY49wv?url=http://quantifiedself.com/2007/page/3/

Koopman, C. (2019). *How we became our data. A genealogy of the informational person*. Chicago, IL: The University of Chicago Press.

Lanier, J. (2010). *You are not a gadget. A manifesto*. New York, NY: Alfred A. Knopf.

Lanier, J. (2018). *Ten arguments for deleting your social media accounts right now*. New York, NY: Henry Holt.

Latour, B. (2005). *Reassembling the social. An introduction to actor-network theory*. Oxford: Oxford University Press.

Lipovetsky, G. (2005). *Hypermodern Times (2004)*. New York, NY: Polity Press.

Lupton, D. (2016). *The quantified-self. A sociology of self-tracking*. New York, NY: Polity Press.

Martin, L., Gutman, H., & Hutton, P. (1988). *Technologies of the self. A Seminar with Michel Foucault.* Amherst: The University of Massachusetts Press.

McLuhan, M. (1964). *Understanding media. The extensions of man.* New York, NY: McGraw-Hill.

Moore, Ph.V. (2018). *The Quantified Self in Precarity. Work, Technology and What Counts.* London - New York: Routledge.

Neff, G., & Nafus, D. (2016). *Self-tracking.* Cambridge, MA: MIT Press.

Selke, S. (Ed.) (2016). *Lifelogging. Digital self-tracking and lifelogging – Between disruptive technology and cultural transformation.* Boston, MA: Springer.

Sharon, T. (2017). Self-tracking for health and the quantified self: Re-articulating autonomy, solidarity and authenticity in an age of personalized healthcare. *Philosophy and Technology, 30*(1), 93–121.

Stiegler, B. (2016). *Anamnesis & Hypomnesis.* Retrieved from http://arsindustrialis.org/anamnesis-and-hypomnesis. Accessed on November 10, 2020.

Vial, S. (2014). *Court traité du design.* Paris: PUF.

Part II

Body Quantification: Historical and Empirical Perspectives

Chapter 4

From the UK Welfare State to Digital Self-Care: Historical Context of Tracking Public Health and Quantifying Bodies

Rachael Kent

Abstract

This chapter provides a historical contextualisation of health tracking and public health communication from the post-World War Two development of the welfare state, through the birth of neoliberalism, until today's individualising practices of digital health tracking and quantification of bodies. Through an examination of these three phases of public health quantification of bodies, encompassing the socio-economic, cultural and political shifts since 1948, combined with the development and wide adoption of digital health and self-quantifying technologies, this chapter traces the changing landscape and the dramatic implications this has had for shifting who is responsible for maintaining 'good' health. This chapter illustrates how neoliberal free market principles have reigned over UK public health discourse for many decades, seeing health as no longer binary to illness, but as a practice of individual self-quantification and self-care. In turn, the chapter explores how the quantification and health tracking of bodies has become a dominant discourse in public health promotion, as well as individual citizenship and patient practices. This discourse still exists pervasively as we move into the digital society of the 2020s, through the Covid-19 pandemic and beyond; with public health strategies internationally promoting the use of digital health tools in our everyday, further positioning citizens as entrepreneurial subjects, adopting extensive technological measures in an attempt to measure and 'optimise' health, normalising the everyday quantification of bodies.

Keywords: Health tracking; digital health; quantified self; public health; welfare state; neoliberalism; Covid-19

The Quantification of Bodies in Health: Multidisciplinary Perspectives, 71–92
Copyright © 2022 by Rachael Kent
Published under an exclusive license by Emerald Publishing Limited
doi:10.1108/978-1-80071-883-820211007

Introduction: The Three Phases of Health Tracking and Quantification of Bodies

This chapter provides a historical contextualisation of health tracking and public health communication from the post-World War Two development of the welfare state, through the birth of neoliberalism, until today's individualising practices of digital health tracking and quantification of bodies. Through an examination of these three phases of public health quantification of bodies, encompassing the socio-economic, cultural and political shifts since 1948, combined with the development and wide adoption of digital health and self-quantifying technologies, this chapter traces the changing landscape and the dramatic implications this has had for shifting who is responsible for maintaining 'good' health. In turn, we explore how the quantification and health tracking of bodies has become a normalised discourse in public health promotion, as well as individual citizenship and patient practices.

This chapter illustrates how free market principles have reigned over UK public health discourse for many decades, seeing health as no longer binary to illness, but as a practice of individual self-quantification and self-care. This discourse still exists pervasively as we move into the digital society of the 2020s, with international public health strategies promoting the use of digital health technologies, thus positioning citizens as entrepreneurial subjects, adopting extensive technological measures in an attempt to measure and 'optimise' health, this, in turn is normalising the everyday quantification of bodies. After examining the quantification strategies of the food and consumer goods rationing of World War Two, phase one explores how the UK's public health strategies presented the state as the guarantor of the health of their populations. In turn, the UK welfare state was born. This first section of the chapter discusses how the British National Health Service (Rivett, 2021) was developed in 1948 as guarantor of the health of the population, and in turn, doctors were conceived as the gatekeepers of medical information and guidance.

The second phase, the 'birth of neoliberalism' describes the dramatic public health promotion and policy shifts from the 1960s onwards until the global recession of 2008. These shifts included a move away from the inclusive welfare state towards promoting individualised health management. The dominance of neoliberal rationalities over public health were further cemented during the economic and unemployment crises of the 1970s and 1980s (Harvey, 2005), putting the economy before the needs of its people (Brown, 2006), and prioritising open, competitive and unregulated markets. This process created a shift from the classic liberal values of the welfare state as a supporter and facilitator of public health, towards neoliberal practices, which included the privatisation of public institutions and the self, and the promotion of individualised health management and health tracking. These health responsibilisation practices were promoted in the wake of social unrest, and a shift from classic to neoliberal political rationalities. The cultural and political shifts towards neoliberalism, in turn led to a form of health promotion on the part of both the state and commercial business, which was characterised by practices of 'healthism' (Crawford, 1980). These practices presented lifestyle correction via discourses of 'individual responsibility' and measuring the body (Leichter, 1997). In the 1990s, UK public health marked a return to social epidemiological acknowledgements of the socio-economic impacts of health and disease upon people's livelihoods.

The third and final phase of the quantification of bodies has evolved since the global recession and financial crash of 2008, with its accompanying global austerity, increasing privatisation of public health services, and in turn, the pervasive promotion and adoption of health technologies, as a direct impact of our current digital society, which reaches its culmination to date with Covid-19 contact tracing apps. The novel coronavirus now globally known as Covid-19 was first identified in December 2019, and quickly grew into a global pandemic affecting at least 223 countries, with 89,048,345 confirmed cases and sadly 1,930,265 confirmed deaths worldwide (World Health Organization, 12January 2021). As of 12 January 2021, the UK has had 3,118,518 total cases of Covid-19, with 81,960 total deaths (BBC News, 12 January 2021), and the country is currently in its third national lockdown. The UK government have attempted to manage the wide spread of Covid-19 through NHS public health initiatives such as 'Test and Trace' (testing for Covid-19 through home testing or walk-in sites), and the NHS Covid-19 App (NHS, 2021) which provides users with contact tracing services, local area alerts, and geo-tagging venue check-ins. Similar technological initiatives have been developed around the world in attempt to reduce the spread of Covid-19, further expanding the bounds of what digital health means to citizens and state, and how the tracking and quantification of bodies is increasingly normalised in a digital society responding to a global pandemic. To give an indication of how pervasive the digital health market has become, the commercial market alone was valued at $106 billion in 2019 and is projected to grow to a global market value of $605 billion by 2025 (Statistica, 2021), which will have dramatic implications for health management globally, especially given these statistics are projected prior to Covid-19. This third part of the chapter illustrates the return to individualised health responsibilisation practices of self-care, further enabled by health tracking and consumer devices and health promotion strategies advocated through the political structures of neoliberal societies. The final sections of the chapter, framed through the context of digital society and the Covid-19 pandemic, explores the limitations and challenges that tracking health and quantifying bodies generate for its users, citizens and patients, now and for the future.

Phase 1: The UK Welfare State

The information technology revolution of the twentieth century made it possible to govern individuals and cities through a variety of surveillance methods (Townsend, 2013). These practices of measuring populations are 'entangled with the practices of measuring and disciplining bodies' (Nafus & Sherman, 2012, p. 4). This production of authority and the disciplining of populations and various bodies are exercised through, for example, the UK national census, which identifies population size and demographics. This distancing between the measured and the measurer was enabled through 'merchants' early accounting techniques, turned into vast and elaborate tools of state control' (Nafus & Sherman, 2014, p. 2). This also led to the Big Data ideologies of cataloguing, systematisation, quantification and making useful knowledge about the world (Nafus & Sherman, 2014). Taking Lyon's (2003, p. 20) definition of surveillance as a system which

> obtains personal and group data in order to classify people and populations according to varying criteria, to determine who should be targeted for special treatment, suspicion, eligibility, inclusion, access, and so on,

we can begin to understand how tracking health and quantifying bodies exists both inside and outside of healthcare and health management domains. The technological developments and scientific rationality of the twentieth century enabled the legitimation of commerce by the business class, which further increased the distance between the measured and the measurer (Poovey, 1998).

Similarly, until the twentieth century, little was known about the nutrients of food and its impact upon the health of individuals (Mozaffarian, Rosenberg & Uauy, 2018). Most research into dietary impact on health centred around reductive notions of amounts of food or a specific diet being associated with good or poor health. By the mid-twentieth century, increasing knowledge about the complexities of the quantification of nutritional needs became more secure, with the development of descriptions of nutrient groups as a template for dietary planning (Mozaffarian et al., 2018). Prior to World War Two, 'free' trade across the British Empire had diversely fed the United Kingdom (Lang et al., 2001). During the earlier stages of World War Two, food security could not be promised, which in time forced decision-makers to turn towards such planning in the development of the Recommended Dietary Allowances as a quantification strategy for food and consumer goods rationing. The 1942 Beveridge Report developed the foundations of the institutions of the welfare state through five targeted areas of government actions: 'Want, Disease, Ignorance, Squalor, and Idleness' (Anderson & Gilllan, 2001, p. 14). Challenges centred around agreed ways to 'connect biological needs for nutrients with economic and social policy indicators' (Lang, Barling, & Caraher, 2001, p. 73), which without reliable measures of food security, nutritional science would not begin to develop fully until the 1970s and 1980s (Lang et al., 2001). This led to a food revolution after World War Two, which transformed how food was grown, processed, distributed and cooked (Goodman & Redclift, 2001), and in turn led to a new wave of food governance, centred on the creation of new national food agencies, and new trade bodies changing world food trade rules (Lang et al., 2001).

With the establishment of the NHS in 1948 as one key institution of the welfare state, the state became responsible for population health and well-being; it became 'both orchestrator and guarantor of the well-being of society and those who inhabited it' (Rose, 2007, p. 91). Before the birth of the NHS, 'patients had perforce been consumers – their economic purchasing power (or lack of it) had been critical in defining their relationship with healthcare providers' (Anderson & Gillam, 2001, p. 14). The birth of the NHS changed this relationship for patients, repositioning citizens not as consumers but as part of a healthcare system which invoked feelings of inclusion, unity and support. Demand management came in the form of prescription pricing charges to moderate patient choices rather than seeking to enable consumer freedoms (Anderson & Gillam, 2001). This new welfare state was not designed with consideration of specific individual needs but as a tool for social transformation. Doctors and medical staff in the National Health Service were seen as purveyors of 'medical prestige' and health expertise in the eyes of the public (Seale, 2003). This relationship was extremely paternalistic, in that clinical expertise was conceived as a powerful role, not questioned by passive and unknowing patients (Anderson & Gillam, 2001). The movement for health reform at this time adopted a broad view, accepting social determinants of health as influential in the causation and containment of disease. In turn, public perceptions of the NHS, its clinical expertise and all-encompassing responsibility, positioned its institutional role as the safeguarder of UK public health.

Phase 2: The Birth of Neoliberalism

Shifting Public Health Perspectives from the 1960s to 1980s

Perspectives on health promotion and public health, however, began to change in line with the social movements of the 1960s and 1970s, when social justice and issues of inequality came more to the forefront of social consciousness (Brandt & Rozin, 1997). These cultural movements became part of a rebellion against 'the establishment' and British society's imposed social 'norms' and responsibilities. In turn, a new discourse concerned with resistance to institutional state power circulated throughout British culture. The radical left argued for freedom of 'governance' (Rose, 2007). This in turn led to the development of a new ideological approach within state support, and an advanced right-libertarian government (Brandt & Rozin, 1997). The socio-economic, cultural and political shifts towards neoliberalism in the 1970s and 1980s prioritised de-regulation; competitive and open markets liberated from state control (Brenner & Theodore, 2002). This 'liberalisation' was not concerned with a cultural liberation, but with liberating the government from historically embedded responsibilities and institutional concerns related to preventing social inequalities. Neoliberal political rationalities over public health were further cemented during the economic and unemployment crises of the 1970s and early 1980s (Harvey, 2005). As Prime Minister from 1979 to 1990, Margaret Thatcher's conservative government fiercely argued that current Keynesian principles of social spending and welfare (Hardt & Negri, 2001) were no longer able to serve the UK economy as it had post war (Callaghan, 1975). To reverse this decline, the Conservative Party sought to resuscitate economic liberalism through dominating political and social spheres by market concerns, through the outsourcing and privatisation of state institutions (Brown, 2006). The state wanted to disentangle itself from economic and social activity and mounted a view of itself as an enabler rather than a tool for intervention in economic and social affairs (Crouch, 2011; Davies, 2015, 2016; Harvey, 2005). For example, The Black Report (1980) identified that ill-health and death are unequally distributed in the UK. These findings highlighted that social inequalities had been widening rather than diminishing since the birth of the National Health Service in 1948 (Grey, 1982). This was not due to failings within the NHS itself, but rather to social inequalities influencing health (income, education, housing, diet, employment, and conditions at work) (Gray, 1982). The Black Report was virtually disregarded by the then Secretary of State for Social Services, Patrick Jenkin, with the Thatcher government reframing the achievement of 'good health' through a libertarian discourse of individual 'choice' (Grey, 1982). In turn, free market principles of 'neoliberalism' and individualisation were encouraged, 'freeing' the citizen from the 'dead hand' of the state (Harvey, 2005).

This new type of liberalism, what we now define as neoliberalism, differed from state interests in that it assumed that human bodies and behaviour should be governed in the interests of the society, but society as a realm separate to the state (Rose, 2007). This distanced responsibility was achieved by 'devolving those quasi-autonomous entities that would be governed by distance [...] and other technologies that were both autonomising and responsibilising' (Rose, 2007, p. 1). These economic crises, political shifts and cultural movements initiated the drawing of a distinction between state and society. One particular impact was the redistribution of the hierarchy between doctors and patients, from paternal to be focussed on a more ethical imperative (Anderson & Gillam, 2001). This fragmentation between social and political consensus and the welfare state left the NHS exposed, and in turn the paternalism of the clinician–patient relationship was challenged. Rather than conceiving of the NHS as the safe guarder of public health, public health promotion and citizenship practices were orientated towards citizens becoming managers of their own healthcare provision through the discourse of individual choice.

Alongside these shifts, the development of clinical research and nutritional science in the 1970s and 1980s led to a shift in social and cultural values which prioritised quantifying nutrition, health, and the body, which in turn contributed to a state and media encouraged global 'health' agenda and 'fitness movement' (take for example, Weight Watchers). The development of clinical research and nutritional science during this time (Brandt, 1997; Mennel, 1992) was also associated with an increase in British press coverage of 'health issues' (Williams & Miller, 1998). A heightened awareness of the science of 'health' developed, which reconsidered its social impact, rather than just focussing on 'bad' food consumption in relation to the development of ill health. This rise in nutritional knowledge and health sciences, led to the development of the self-help movement and political priorities shifted towards the needs of the individual rather than the rights of the whole society (Anderson & Gillam, 2001). This social 'liberation' and drive for freedom problematically further encouraged the birth of political neoliberalism, which advocates that the self must be governed individually, not solely in the interests of the state, but for individuals and society as a whole. The neoliberal subject was born: a self-responsibilising, entrepreneurial individual 'freed' from state governance, who in turn embodies the self-regulatory 'government of the soul' (Rose, 1999, p. 11), to maintain and manage individual 'health'. This ideological push by right-libertarians for the 'creation of freedom' was integral to neoliberal strategies of 'governance of the self' or biopolitical 'governance of the soul' (Foucault, 1979, 1997; Rose, 1999).

The new public health discourse of the 1970s and 1980s operated under neoliberal values of putting the economy before the needs of its people (Brown, 2006). Yet, this liberation from state intrusion involves 'coercive, disciplinary forms of state intervention in order to impose market rule upon all aspects of social life' (Aguirre, Eick, & Reese, 2006, p. 1). This process created a shift from classic liberal values of the welfare state as a supporter and facilitator of public health, towards neoliberal practices of the privatisation of public institutions and the self, and the promotion of individualisation and self-care (Crouch, 2011; Davies, 2015, 2016; Harvey, 2005). Within the advanced (neo) liberal government, 'subjects obliged to be free were required to conduct themselves responsibly to account for their own lives' (Rose, 2007, p. 90). The new, distanced means of regulating ensured that responsibility for enforcing institutional structures within business and public behaviours encouraged an 'individualising culture' in contemporary Britain. In turn, public health shifted from a state responsibility towards an individualised responsibility of 'health' (Hey, 2005). This legitimised governmental inaction and ensured the circulation of a political discourse, which re-configured the human being as 'cast in terms of market rationality' (Brown, 2003, p. 9). In this context, the citizen was situated as no longer under care of the state in the prevention of social inequalities, but as a subject to be consumed and profited from.

'Healthism'

Within the UK, the public health promotion strategies of the 1970s and 1980s were concerned with discourses of lifestyle correction and health moralism, privileging what was determined 'good health' over other priorities in life, without taking into consideration the socio-cultural and economic influence upon illness and disease. This contributed to a state and media encouraged 'health' agenda within Britain (King & Watson, 2005), and further encouraged the 'fitness movement', which refers to the boom in physical exercise in the 1970s and 1980s (Brandt & Rozin, 1997). This meant that 'fitness' became integrated into the lifestyles of the British public. Crawford (1980) theorised this development as 'healthism', which discursively prioritises the maintenance of good 'health', over all other aspects of lifestyle. Good living, in 'healthism', is dependent upon individuals making healthy choices (Crawford, 1980, p. 378) and becoming entrepreneurial subjects seeking out the best self-care for health. We see here how such a restructuring and dismantling of social and economic spheres 'figures and produces citizens as individual entrepreneurs and consumers whose moral autonomy is measured by their capacity for "self-care"' (Brown, 2006, p. 694). Through the concept of neoliberal 'governmentality' (Foucault, 1979, 1997b, p. 67), the regulatory activity of both the self and external influences was advocated by healthcare policy and the media, shaping public beliefs and behaviours towards individual regulation and self-maintenance. This 'privileging' of 'good' health and lifestyle choice with inherent victim-blaming inclinations despite socio-economic determinations of disease in medicine was central to these health promotion activities (Lupton, 2013). Sufferers and 'victims' of ill health and disease, therefore, would be positioned by healthcare promotion and policy as being irresponsible, and would subsequently be blamed for poor health management. This discourse argued that whether you are dealing with chronic disease or minor ailment you are responsible for managing that on a day-to-day basis (Lorig & Holman, 2003). A refusal to engage in healthy behaviours or to actively manage ill health, according to Lorig and Holman (2003, p. 1) reflects a poor 'management style':

> Unless one is totally ignorant of healthful behaviors it is impossible not to manage one's health. The only question is how one manages. The issue of self-management is especially important for those with chronic disease, where only the patient can be responsible for his or her day-to-day care over the length of the illness. For most of these people, self-management is a lifetime task.

'Good' health and a healthy body were no longer simply considered in opposition to ill health but were demonstrative of economic and social factors and self-discipline, thus embedding ill health within a moral discourse. To further extend Lorig and Holman's (2003) argument; it is not just sufferers of chronic conditions but the everyday layperson, who now embody this dominant discourse. Health self-management, when not enacted effectively, becomes tied to personal blame (and shame) over lack of personal responsibility and poor health management. Unlike classic liberalism, this extends to individual behaviour, whereby neoliberalism ensures individual conduct is discursively prescribed for citizens to 'enact' behaviours in a consumerist capitalist state (Brown, 2005). This social change was further cemented through increasing lay understanding of nutritional science, which led to concrete conclusions about individual diet and exercise and their relationship to the prevention of disease and cancer. In essence, the broader public via the state encouraged the media's agenda towards 'healthism'. In turn, citizens increasingly understood how individual choices around food and fitness would impact their health, and it became their responsibility to self-manage their self-knowledge, as opposed to relying upon the NHS as gatekeepers of clinical health information.

New public health campaigns in the 1990s had a renewed focus on social epidemiology, which identifies how social groups, taken as a whole, could be considered 'healthy' or 'unhealthy' (Raphael, 2008). Public health policy at this time was centred on moving away from individual responsibilities, to identifying the social determinants of health (Raphael, 2008). This notion that the social and economic conditions in which people live are expressed within their bodies was seen to identify 'intimate links between our bodies and the body politic' (Krieger, 2001, p. 693). Under a neoliberal political rationality, the social epidemiology public health discourse placed social groupings as:

> part of the government of the self in neoliberal contexts, thus drawing attention away from the role of state agencies in supporting health promotions and alleviating the reasons for people's ill health. (Lupton, 2013e, p. 4)

Social epidemiological findings and subsequent social discourses ensured that the public understood ill health and disease as being associated with socio-economic disadvantage.

Phase 3: From the 2008 Global Recession to the Digital Society of 2021

The global financial crisis of 2008 and subsequent austerity measures meant that the priority of the British government was to govern health through the individual actions of citizens (De Vogli, 2011), with the goal to achieve better health outcomes through lower health costs (Dentzer, 2013). This prompted questions related to how to allocate resources more fairly and efficiently, further focussing on individualised practices as solutions to these shortages. The question thus emerged as to whether personal responsibility should be used as a criterion or a way to determine access or rationing of health care resources (Buyx & Prainsack, 2012). This question was considered to redefine the 'relationship between the state as the guarantor of the health and well-being of its citizens and the state as the promoter of markets and consumerism' (Tritter, 2009, p. 279). Health promotion strategies that prioritise patient's individual decision-making positions these patients are strategists and managers of their own healthcare provisions. Since 2008, these neoliberal rationalities have been more pervasive than ever (Crouch, 2011). Many governments' role in addressing public health issues, in particular the living conditions of those 'at risk' from ill health and disease, is now focussed upon marketing campaigns which promote behaviour change and seeking medical solutions to broader public health problems (Lupton, 2013). This individual governance and health maximisation can be identified through an international and even global approach to such neoliberal governmental health policy. Earlier sections of this chapter have explored the changing institutional structures that have impacted upon public health promotion strategies and practices, notably shifting public notions of 'health' from state support to individually managed. This next section will explore the final phase: the development and rise in the adoption of digital health technologies within the current digital society.

Digital Self-Care and Quantification of Bodies

In the neoliberal political systems that currently dominate many developed countries (such as the United States, the UK, Australia, New Zealand, and Canada), the politically active approach towards public health tends to be disregarded, with preference for a focus on individual personal responsibility for managing health behaviours, regardless of lifestyle factors (Ayo, 2011; Crouch, 2011; Davies, 2015, 2016; Lupton, 2013; Raphael, 2011). Such developments mean that governments are driving citizen engagement with digital technologies as a part of individual health responsibility and self-care (Oudshoorn, 2011). Such technologies for patient and citizen engagement with and management of their health are defined as 'digital health', which refers to 'the use of information and communications technologies in medicine and other health professions to manage illnesses and health risks and to promote wellness' (Ronquillo, Meyers, & Korvek, 2020, n.p.). Governments promote engagement with digital health technologies as improving access to healthcare, improving care quality, and providing a more 'personalised healthcare' experience, which in turn attempts to lower the cost of healthcare for public and private healthcare providers (Ronquillo et al., 2020). Digital health promotion, through digital self-care, can be identified as the latest stage in this enactment of health promotion ideology and health practices since the birth of the NHS.

Public health campaigns advocate the use of digital health technologies by promoting their possibilities for maintaining and monitoring individual health (Swan, 2012a; Topol, 2012). The new active consumer of health is now expected to take personal responsibility for maintaining individual care of the self. Non-commodified public spheres, like healthcare, are being replaced by commercial systems through the adoption of digital health devices (Swan, 2012a), which serve to monitor and encourage self-regulatory monitoring behaviours. Digital health is also an umbrella term for the use of wearable and self-tracking technologies (Fitbit or Strava, or MapMyRun), mobile devices in health management (Apple Health Application), telehealth and telemedicine (NHS Digital, TECS from england.nhs.uk/tecs/), and using a variety of digital platforms (AI Chatbots, Babylon Health), and even social media (such as Instagram) to follow 'health guidance', or even perform 'healthy identities' (Kent, 2018, 2020). Such technologies are celebrated as 'revolutionising' healthcare and promise to optimise individual health through reflexive self-regulatory practices (Kent, 2018). Such practices illuminate Davies' (2015, p. 42) recognition that 'reconfiguring institutions to resemble markets is a hallmark of neoliberal government'. There are, however, problematic issues with using digital tools to manage health, due to app and wearable inaccuracies, their reductive nature and oversimplification of the human body, as well as the addictive and compulsive practices that they can encourage. Some of these issues will be further unpacked later in this chapter.

Digital Health Tracking and the Neoliberal Quantified Self

Digital health tracking then, is a practice which refers to capturing information and (often quantifiable, but also qualitative) data about the body, in an attempt to manage and often improve individual health. Usually, this is achieved through using digital tracking wearables or tools like Fitbits or health apps, but it can also be achieved through sharing content about one's health-related behaviours (data, fitness, food, and related lifestyle) on social media, through the construction of a 'health self' (Kent, 2018, p. 65). These health tracking data can come in the form of numerical data, graphs, geo-location mapping, and statistics, as well as other often photographic representations of the human body (muddy trainers depicting running in the countryside), food (foodporn), gym and fitness selfies, or exercise equipment and spaces (landscapes or a home yoga studio) (Kent, 2020a). Tracking health digitally has now become a pervasive everyday tool for citizens and patients, for those dealing with specific ill-health issues, for those managing health, or those who wish to improve their health, fitness and/or diet. We can now capture increasingly greater amounts of data on many aspects of our bodies and health, including geo-location, emotion, as well as physical function, which can then be analysed and shared (Swan, 2012b). As Ajana (2017, p. 1) highlights:

> life in the 21st Century is witnessing an intensive infiltration of networked wireless technologies and digital mobile devices. Individuals and societies are becoming increasingly reliant on algorithms and data to manage all aspects of everyday activities.

These new types of surveillance are increasingly comprehensive and extensive, drawing upon individual and cross-referenced data, providing far more information than traditional record keeping by hospitals, schools, or churches, for example (Moore, 2017, n.p.).

The quantified self (QS) movement (Wolf, 2010) was the first iteration of digital health tracking, and a key demonstration of neoliberal self-management health practices, which, like the earlier 1980s discourse advocated by neoliberal political rationalities (in particular, Margaret Thatcher's Conservative government), prioritises individual choice as a mechanism for the self-improvement of health. Self-quantification is the reliance upon science, and the technological extensions and affordances of scientific sensors in the monitoring of the self and individual health. Participants of the QS movement, through consumer devices, monitor everything that can be put into data to 'improve' and 'optimise' individual health. The 'quantified self' movement developed from a California-based laboratory in 2007, which now works as an international collaboration between users and producers of self-training tools (Wolf, 2010). Gary Wolf, co-founder (with Kevin Kelly) of the movement has referred to it as 'self-knowledge through numbers' (Wolf, 2010, n.p.). Swan (2013, p. 86) understands self-quantification as

> contemporary formalisations belonging to the general progression in human history of using measurement, science, and technology to bring order, understanding, manipulation, and control to the natural world, including the human body.

This movement, or rather its practices of capturing data, can now broadly be described as 'health tracking': the process of tracking aspects of our bodies and our minds, which promotes a way of looking at the world and learning through the process of data collection and interpretation. Much like the neoliberal public health promotion of the 1980s onwards, the QS movement, like health tracking, advocates that the best way to improve health is through individual responsibility for self-monitoring.

Another similarly techno-utopian perspective is that self-quantification can be considered as an alternative to Big Data practices, since self-management could be viewed as emancipatory when compared to the perspective of wider state surveillance (Nafus & Sherman, 2014). However, to contextualise this argument within the context of the surveillance capitalism society of 2021 and beyond, the techno-commercial infrastructures and data mining which many of these applications rely on as a foundation for their business model means very little health tracking data are private and are only visible to the eyes of their users (Zuboff, 2013). Though yes, we can argue that the variety of data capture enables users, citizens, and patients to track health practices and improvements over time, contributing to an ever-increasing archive of digital health information. Health tracking and quantifying the self is concerned with 'knowing thyself' through data acquisition (Wolf, 2007), as these technologies attempt to produce knowledge and understandings of the body. However, through individually quantifying behaviours and habits, capability to track and monitor expanding aspects of our bodies means: 'increasingly, the market sees you from within, measuring your body and emotional states, and watching you as you move around' (Fourcade & Healy, 2017, p. 23). Identifying with and understanding one's own body through such technologies can have positive aspects, but we must recognise the dangers of

> this growing trend of self-quantification and data-driven modes of health monitoring, particularly with regard to issues of privacy and data ownership as well as the marked shifts in healthcare responsibilities. (Ajana, 2012)

This may worryingly become embodied by the users themselves, for if 'health' becomes situated as best managed through these commercially developed and mined technologies, privacy is repackaged as in opposition to the 'collective' and 'public good', which is framed as making populations 'healthier' through data mining (Ajana, 2017). This philanthropic data discourse, which in recent years has attempted to legitimate data mining and privacy invasions, ensures

> privacy is dead, and profit is king (...), any reuse of data beyond the original purpose for which it was collected is a potential threat to privacy and civil liberties. (Kirkpatrick, 2017, p. 11)

Indeed, this is not always recognised by the users themselves, or even if it is, the lack of transparency and understanding of applications' 'terms and conditions' (T&C) means users have little to no knowledge or privacy power over their personal biometric or health-related data, or where it is sold on. As Kelvin (1973) argues, the role of privacy becomes a nullification mechanism for advocating surveillance. Therefore, self-trackers' voluntary self-surveillant practices problematically play directly into state discourses, as well as capitalist and corporate profit strategies.

Digital health practices and the affordances of health tracking devices, therefore, possess dimensions of both self-surveillance and wider surveillance. Health self-tracking, therefore, ensures that the body and health are subjected to regimes of neoliberal judgement dictate what are and are not healthy, productive and self-bettering behaviours, subsumed through discourses of competition and comparison (Ajana, 2017; Cederstrom & Spicer, 2015; Davies, 2016). In individualised, privatised terms, the responsibility for maintaining 'health' has now become internalised, and self-regulatory. Modes of monitoring consumption are advocated and encouraged through these devices: 'Care of the self is not an indulgence, or a distraction from the affairs of the polis, but rather a necessary condition of effective citizenship and relationships' (Heyes, 2006, p. 139). As a part of this individual management of self-care, reflexivity is paramount to ensure successful monitoring of individual health regulation. An abundance of health information and health data, even without access and literacy obstacles, does not necessarily mean that patients, citizens and users will act in the best interest of their health. As Husain and Spence (2015, p. 2) expand:

> we shouldn't confuse more healthcare with better healthcare. One of our roles as doctors is not just about treating the sick but also about protecting the well and protecting peoples' sense of wellbeing'. Furthermore, many health and fitness applications lack 'rigorous clinical evidence to demonstrate they can actually improve health outcomes.

We, in turn, should not confuse or conflate more data with healthier bodies. We can identify two opposing lines of argument in relation to digital health applications promoted within public health promotion strategies. On the one hand, it could be considered that they help or enable people to correlate personal decisions with the impact upon their health. On the other hand, it must be recognised that some of these apps are sometimes untested, unscientific, and inaccurate and do present questions of uncertainty; 'Make no mistake: diagnostic uncertainty ignites extreme anxiety in people' (Husain & Spence, 2015, p. 2). It is important to recognise the influences of a consumer tracking apps to actually provide better health outcomes to already healthy individuals, or whether they just provoke anxiety in the worried well.

Medical Versus Consumer Health Tracking

Digital health tracking and wellness apps renegotiate the boundaries between medical and lifestyle products. The identification and labelling of lifestyle products have been further developed by scientists who have called for a hybrid category that stands between medical and consumer applications (Saukko, 2010). Lifestyle and wellness apps, then can be defined as 'apps intended to directly or indirectly maintain or improve healthy behaviours, quality of life, and wellbeing of individuals' (EC Green Paper, 2014, p. 3). As part of digitised health promotion, health tracking technologies are increasingly promoted as having revolutionary capabilities to continually monitor bodily behaviours, reach certain social groups and tailor health messages. Broadly, digitisation and the internet's key role within healthcare practices

> has ceased to be that of information provision: contemporary web-based platforms and services integrate information provision and data collection by encouraging patients and citizens to contribute data and information about themselves. (Prainsack, 2013, pp. 111–112)

Health 'norms' of populations and groups are 'created' by using these health tracking devices to identify health differences and variations (Swan, 2013). These 'personal health climates' focus on collecting as much data as possible on individuals' health states, everyday habits, social and geographic locations. This goes further than public health policy, and arguably informs, 'constructs' and 'shapes' individual health decisions by 'nudging' people to make decisions, which are presented as better for their health (Swan, 2013).

Purpura et al. (2011, p. 6) have argued that increasing reliance on data, and quantified measuring of the body has left individuals increasingly unsure of how to manage their health. The sheer abundance of data and nutritional information available just further complicates 'health (mis)information', as everyone becomes an 'expert' on optimising good health. As Kristensen and Ruckenstein (2018, p. 12) assert: 'sensors and devices [have] become part of the processes in which the self is defined, extended, reduced, or restricted'. In the sense that the QS and health tracking movement is concerned with self-awareness by numbers or data (Moore, 2017; Wolf, 2010), a representation of data is similarly created either through a new medium or reproduction. Although medics use diagnostic technologies, which produce data, the difference here is that non-medical or 'lay people' attempt to understand their bodies through sensationalised visual representations from digital health tracking devices. It is through these social media self-representations that comparisons between 'healthy' bodies or lifestyles can be made. In turn, competition can also act as a motivator for self-trackers:

> The great appeal of competition, from the neoliberal perspective, is that it enables activity to be rationalised and quantified, but in ways that purport to maintain uncertainty of outcome. The promise of competition is to provide a form of socio-economic objectivity that is empirically and mathematically knowable, but still possessed of its own internal dynamism and vitality. (Davies, 2015, pp. 41–42)

Their perceptions of the digitised reproduction of bodily monitoring and biometrics may influence how this information is internalised and then acted upon by the health tracker. Citizens and patients using these platforms to manage their health engage with health improvement and medicine in a cyclical process of diagnosis, treatment, and increasing research. Although we could all be affected by illness or disease, which we could not have protected ourselves from, the neoliberal individualisation discourse places responsibility in the hands of the sufferer:

> If (…) people suffer from illnesses as a result of allegedly deliberate actions or actions against better knowledge, then they are to be taken to be accountable and indeed responsible for their condition. (Buyx & Prainsack, 2012, p. 81)

These arguments advocate individual health responsibilisation as the rhetoric to support the public health promotion of health tracking applications sees data as objective evidence-based health optimism and optimisation. Discussions around who is responsible for poor health often distract the focus and attentions of policy makers, from attending to the important underlying and socio-economic influences upon public health (Buyx & Prainsack, 2012). The same argument is often adopted by policy makers, governments and clinicians, as they make it the responsibility of patients and consumers to outsource and manage their health-care via tracking and wearables, without attending to the symptoms of ill health or poor mental health, in particular. The final section of this chapter will examine this in the context of the digital society of 2021.

Digital Society and the Covid-19 Pandemic

Today's digital society is underpinned by structures of platform capitalism, which refers to the market monopolisation of giant businesses (e.g. Google, Amazon, Facebook) carving up the capitalist economy into platform-based services (Srnicek, 2017) with related practices of surveillance capitalism integral to these business' economic models (Zuboff, 2013, 2019). This has led to the increasing datafication of health in our everyday lives. Datafication refers to the conversion of qualitative aspects of life into quantifiable data (Mayor-Schonberger & Cukier, 2013), specifically those data made analysable in relation to our health and bodies. The commercial digital health market alone is projected to grow to a global market value of $504.4 billion by 2025 (Statistica, 2020), this is set to aggressively grow in response to Covid-19 through investment in and advocation from industry, government, public health, and civil society. This occurs in a social landscape where contact tracing and diagnostic digital health tools flood the market and healthcare systems around the globe (Global Market Insights, 2020). Digital contact tracing and immunity certification have dominated public discourse and data-driven technological responses, such as centralised public health datastores (e.g. the NHS Track and Trace, NHS Covid-19 App). Indeed, these approaches have been central to many nations' responses to the virus. Furthermore, Covid-19 has hugely expanded what we can consider 'health data' to the extent where we can see that under surveillance capitalism in 2021, 'all data is health data' (Warzel, 2019). Aside from Covid-19 contact tracing applications (e.g. NHS Covid-19 App) and health tracking applications, we can now identify social media use and digital behaviours online, with the aim of offering insights into mental health. In response to Covid-19, my research conducted into the impact of national lockdowns on digital practices and health-related behaviours (ref: MRA-19/20-18193) illustrated how, with so many unknowns for citizens navigating a global pandemic, increasingly the public became lay experts of Covid-19 health and lifestyle related content on via digital platforms. In particular, the UK public turned towards the World Health Organization, BBC News, NHS website and social media platforms for health-related guidance. In the context of social media seeking and scrolling, in turn this led to 'algorithmic recommendations continually (…) [driving] them back to seek more "guidance", whilst having to simultaneously navigate a tsunami of misinformation, fake news, and conspiracy theories' (Kent, 2020a, n.p.). This raises, in turn, many questions which have been posed for years, such as 'can we trust social media to help with one's health management?'. This is a particularly important question during Covid-19 isolation's detrimental impact on mental health, induced by government lockdowns. During these health-anxiety inspiring times, the public wade through a wealth of health, wellness and Covid-19 guidance and tips on social media 'turning most of us into medical lay-experts continually attempting to decipher between what is legitimate information and what is nonsense' (Kent, 2020a, n.p.). This leads to shifting understandings of what are and what are not data related to our health and fitness practices, this is no longer clear to users, consumers, citizens, or patients. Covid-19 has exacerbated the tracking of health and bodies via contact tracing and has increased our interpersonal surveillance of others' health and lifestyle behaviours on social media.

This became particularly evident from the national lockdown 1.0 in the UK (March–July 2020) in which toxic productivity was 'performed' on social media (Kent, 2020b). A key example of this was the globally and widely used 'Instagram #stayhome logo, combined with an #instaworthy photo of artisan baking, home workout selfies, and nutritious #foodporn, which enabled the construction and performance of the "healthy and moral citizen"' (Kent, 2020a, n.p.). All these fragmented data representations of the self-help construct not only an online identity for users but also a 'health self', which is a construction of a health identity that users may desire others within the community to perceive (Kent, 2018, p. 62). Surveillance, therefore, becomes a continual system of health performativity and registration in adherence to government regulation and Covid-19 public health promotion. This illustrates the datafied power (Kristensen & Ruckenstein, 2018), and embodiment of platform and surveillance capitalism. This is particularly exemplified in social media performativity related to health and lifestyle during Covid-19 lockdowns and government restrictions in the UK. For those that dared showcase their life outside of their house, they presented it as a:

> prescription, for example in the UK in line with the parameter of the once #dailyexercise. Without this justification, a moral backlash can ensue, with comments, retweets, and DMs (direct messages), brandishing the individual an unruly, undisciplined citizen (…) behind the closed doors and screens of isolation, social media surveillance is certainly exacerbating moral judgement of others' health and lifestyle behaviours. (Kent, 2020b, n.p.)

Prior to 2020, if someone was outside of their home, this was not considered a health risk or a datapoint needed to assess someone's overall health risk level. Therefore, if we consider these practices through the concept of the risk society (Beck, 1992), risk is contextual to what we can examine and look at: 'it can be seen as a concept created to allow the quantification of circumstances and situations that do not really lend themselves to quantification' (Beck, 1992, p. 83). And yet, under platform capitalist structures and in the context of Covid-19, these increasingly unquantifiable practices are transformed into and reduced to quantifiable data for health purposes. Furthermore, advertising and retail companies, are too gathering personal data (what consumers eat and what fitness they do etc.), to make predictions about their health and well-being, and in turn market products to them accordingly (Ada Lovelace Institute, 2020). Under these data mining practices of platform and surveillance capitalism governments, private and public healthcare systems, employers, and insurers all now have increasing visibility into people's health and bodies (Ada Lovelace Institute, 2020). Data are therefore not only related to health via datasets, but also seek to make inferences about consumers' health. However, the reverse is also true. Data collected not for health or fitness related purposes can now be used for non-health purposes or insights (Ada Lovelace Institute, 2020). This not only shapes and influences decision-making about how citizens, patients and consumers conceive of their health, from the multitude of data collected about them, and marketed to them in 'health management' terms, generating evolving parameters for what human bodies, data and 'health' look like today. But, this health data, and its' quantification and tracking of human bodies becomes ever more valuable to these multitude of public and private stakeholders in the global Covid-19 pandemic, and beyond. Those who do have access to this data then, are the ones afforded with control over or access to data, as well as the extensive possibilities to influence people's health and lifestyles today.

Conclusion

This chapter has provided a historical contextualisation of health tracking and public health communication from the establishment of the NHS in 1948, to today's individualising practices of digital self-care and quantification of bodies within the context of our current digital society. The socio-economic, cultural and political shifts since 1948, combined with the development and widespread adoption of digital health and self-quantifying technologies have had dramatic implications for those who are responsible for healthcare. This chapter has traced the shifts from the first phase of the UK welfare state as inclusive guarantor of the health of the nation, to the second phase, the 'birth of neoliberalism', which promoted state-distancing individualised health management via the mechanism of choice, and the third and most recent phase of public health practices since the global 2008 financial crash and related austerity, which has led to the techno-commercial infrastructures of platform capitalism and now the digital surveillance society of the Covid-19 pandemic.

This chapter has illustrated how neoliberal governance has involved a reorganisation of the UK welfare state, and a devolution of responsibility for public health from the state onto individuals, increasingly advocated through the use of digital health tracking practices, and the quantification of bodies through platform and surveillance capitalism. As a practice, digital health tracking can be considered techno-deterministic and techno-utopian in their promotion of the idea that data capture is the best method to improve health and that these tools are the best available. These perspectives provide certain ways of knowing what data are, why they are important, who gets to interpret them and to what ends. As Ajana (2013, p. 10) asserts: 'citizenship is seen as becoming a hollowed out

concept whose carcass is increasingly shaped around techniques of identity management'. Like the 'wellness movement' (Cederstrom & Spicer, 2015; Leichter,
1997, p. 359) of the 1970s and 1980s, which encouraged lifestyle correction and
infused health behaviours within a moral discourse, to encourage certain health
and lifestyle behaviours through hegemonic socio-political discourses, with digital health design-based regulation as the normalised modality of citizenship
enactment (Yeung & Dixon-Woods, 2013). Indeed, when adopted in everyday
life, the integration of health tracking the body can become representative of
individual and public health identities. These practices are about managing and
being responsible for individual healthcare now, through technologies of governance, with a close eye on the future, the identification or (ideally) prevention
of potential pathologies (Rose, 2007). In the current digital neoliberal society,
citizens and patients must become active and responsible consumers of health,
medical services and products. This is a complex relationship of marketisation,
autonomisation, and responsibilisation (Rose, 2007).

Practices of quantifying and tracking the self, therefore, are paradoxical.
These devices and practices are not tracking the self, but the body, constructing a
dualism between the self and the body (Moore & Robinson, 2016). This dualism
stresses that: 'the body is not the self, the mechanism is just monitoring the shell
within which the ghost, that is you, can be better' (Duffy, 2014, n.p.). With Covid-
19 being the first pandemic of the algorithmic age (Ada Lovelace Institute, 2020),
it has further accelerated and normalised platform and surveillance capitalism
of human bodies, and the datafication of health in everyday life. The bounds
of what we once conceived as health data will continue to change and evolve.
Health and wellness in the digital economy changes our experiences of health,
healthcare, and where to turn to for health guidance and information. Most problematically, when the government advocates individual health tracking solutions
to public health problems, this continues to contribute to blurring the roles of the
NHS as a healthcare provider for its citizens, and citizens as self-managing consumers of healthcare. This ensures that the individualised neoliberal subject, who
self-manages healthcare is firmly here to stay, and will continue to be capitalised
upon in the increasingly digital society of the future.

References

Aguirre, A., Jr, Eick, V., & Reese, R. (2006). Introduction: Neoliberal globalization, urban
    privatization, and resistance. *Social Justice, 33*(3), 1–5.
Ajana, B. (2013). *Governing through biometrics: The biopolitics of identity.* Basingstoke:
    Palgrave MacMillan.
Ajana, B. (2017). Digital health and the biopolitics of the quantified self. *Digital Health.*
    doi:10.1177/2055207616689509
Anderson, W., & Gilllam, S. (2001). The elusive NHS consumer: 1948 to the NHS Plan.
    Economic Affairs, 12(4), 14–18.
Ayo, N. (2011). Understanding health promotion in a neoliberal climate and the making of
    health conscious citizens. *Critical Public Health, 22*(1), 1–7.

Beato, G. (2012). The quantified self. *Reason, 43*(8), 18–20.

Beck, U. (1992). *Risk society: Towards a new modernity.* London: Sage.

Brandt, M., & Rozin, P. (Eds.). (1997). *Morality and health.* London: Routledge.

Brenner, N., & Theodore, N. (2002). Cities and geographies of "actually existing neoliberalism." *Antipode, 34*, 349–379.

Brown, W. (2005). Neoliberalism and the end of liberal democracy. In W. Brown (Ed.), *Edgework: Critical essays on knowledge and politics* (pp. 37–59). Woodstock, NJ: Princeton University Press.

Buyx, A., & Prainsack, B. (2012). Lifestyle related diseases and individual responsibility through the prism of Solidarity. *Clinical Ethics, 7*(2), 79–85.

Cederström, C., & Spicer, A. (2015). *The Wellness syndrome.* London: John Wiley & Sons.

Crawford, R. (1977). You are dangerous to your health: The ideology and politics of victim blaming. *International Journal of Health Services, 7*(4), 663–680.

Crawford, R. (1980). Healthism and the medicalisation of everyday life. *International Journal of Health Care Services, 10*(3), 365–388.

Crawford, R. (2006). Health as meaningful practice. *Health: An Interdisciplinary Journal for the Social Study of Health, Illness and Medicine, 10*(4), 401–420.

Crouch, C. (2011). *The strange non-death of neoliberalism.* Cambridge: Polity Press.

Davies, W. (2015). *The limits of neoliberalism: Authority, sovereignty and the logic of competition.* London: Sage.

Davies, W. (2016). *The happiness industry.* London: Verso.

De Maria, A. (2012). Self quantification of health and fitness. *Journal of the American College of Cardiology, 60*(16), 1574–1575.

De Vogli, R. (2011). Neoliberal globalisation and health in a time of economic crisis. *Social Theory & Health, 9*(4), 311–332.

Dentzer, S. (2013). Rx for the 'blockbuster drug' of patient engagement. *Health Affairs (Millwood), 32*(2), 202. doi:10.1377/hlthaff.2013.0037

Duffy, D. (2014). Digital human. 'Quantisize'. *BBC Radio 4*, April 28. Retrieved from https://www.bbc.co.uk/programmes/b041vvw2. Accessed on June 1, 2018.

Fajans, J. (2013). *Self-experimentation & the quantified self: New avenues for positive psychology research and application.* Master thesis, Claremont Graduate University, Claremont, CA. Retrieved from https://www.slideshare.net/mrboodaddy/self-experimentation-the-quantified-self-new-avenues-for-positive-psychology-research-and-applicaiton. Accessed on May 4, 2017.

Foucault, M. (1975/1979). *Discipline and punish: The birth of the prison.* Harmondsworth: Penguin.

Foucault, M. (1997). *Essential works of Foucault, Vol. 1: Ethics, subjectivity and truth* (P. Rabinow, Ed.). New York, NY: The New Press.

Fourcade, M., & Healy, K. (2017). Seeing like a market. *Socio-economic Review, 15*(1), 9–29.

Gray, M. A. (1982). Inequalities in health. The Black report: A summary and comment. *International Journal of Health Services, 12*(3), 349–380.

Greene, J., & Hubbard, J. H. (2012). Why does patient activation matter? An examination of the relationships between patient activation and health-related outcomes. *Journal of General Internal Medicine, 27*(5), 520–526.

Harvey, D. (2005). *A brief history of neoliberalism.* New York, NY: Oxford University Press.

Hey, V. (2005). The contrasting social logics of sociality and survival: Cultures of classed be/longing in late modernity. *Sociology, 39*(5), 855–872.

Heyes, C. J. (2006). Foucault goes to weight watchers. *Hypatia, 21*, 126–149.

Husain, I., & Spence, D. (2015). Can healthy people benefit from health apps? *British Medical Journal.* doi:10.1136/bmj.h1887

Kelvin, P. (1973). A social–psychological examination of privacy. *British Journal of Clinical Psychology, 12*(3), 248–261.

Kent, R. (2018). 'Social media and self-tracking: Representing the 'health self'. In B. Ajana (Ed.), *Self-tracking* (pp. 61–76). London: Palgrave Macmillan.

Kent, R. (2020a). Forbes Magazine 'Should we all social media detox after the pandemic'. *Commentary*, May 7.

Kent, R. (2020b). Self-tracking health over time: From the use of Instagram to perform optimal health to the protective shield of the digital detox. *Social Media +Society Special Issue: Studying Instagram Beyond Selfies, 6*(3), 1–14.

Kent, R. (2020c). COVID-19, toxic productivity & technology overload: Our new visceral digital life. *Metric Life*, November. Retrieved from https://metriclife.net/publications/covid-19-toxic-productivity-technology-overload-our-new-visceral-digital-life/. Accessed on April 29, 2021.

Kirkpatrick, R. (2013). A new type of philanthropy: Donating data. *Harvard Business Review*. Retrieved from https://hbr.org/2013/03/a-new-type-of-philanthropy-don. Accessed on April 29, 2021.

Krieger, N. (2001). A glossary for social epidemiology. *Journal of Epidemiology and Community Health, 55*(10), 693–700.

Krieger, N. (2007). Why epidemiologists cannot afford to ignore poverty. *Epidemiology, 18*(6), 658–663.

Kristensen, B. D., & Ruckenstein, M. (2018). Co-evolving with self-tracking technologies. *New Media and Society, 5*(3), 219–238.

Lang, T., Barling, D., & Caraher, M. (2004). *Food policy: Integrating health environment, and society.* Oxford: Oxford Scholarship Online. Retrieved from https://oxford.universitypressscholarship.com/view/10.1093/acprof:oso/9780198567882.001.0001/acprof-9780198567882-indexList-1. Accessed on April 29, 2020.

Leichter, H. (1997). Lifestyle correctness and the new secular morality. In A. M. Brandt & P. Rozin (Ed.), *Morality and health* (pp. 359–378). London: Routledge.

Lorig, R., & Holman, M. (2003). Self-management education: History, definition, outcomes, and mechanisms. *Annals of Behavioural Medicine, 26*(1), 1–7.

Lucivero, F., & Prainsack, B. (2015). The lifestylisation of healthcare? 'Consumer Genomics' and mobile health as technologies for healthy lifestyle. *Applied and Translational Genomics, 4*, 44–49.

Lucivero, F., & Tamburrini, G. (2007). Ethical monitoring of brain–machine interfaces. *AI & Society, 22*(3), 449–460.

Lupton, D. (2013a). The commodification of patient opinion: The digital patient experience economy in the age of big data. *Sydney Health & Society Group Working Papers*, (3). Retrieved from http://hdl.handle.net/2123/9063. Accessed on October 6, 2014.

Lupton, D. (2013b). The digitally engaged patient: Self-monitoring and self-care in the digital health era. *Social Theory and Health, 11*, 256–270.

Lyon, D. (2003). *Surveillance as social sorting: Privacy, risk and digital discrimination.* Routledge: London.

Mayor-Schönberger, V., & Cukier, K. (2013). Big data: A revolution that will transform how we live, work and think. Retrieved from https://psycnet.apa.org/record/2013-17650-000. Accessed on April 29, 2021.

Mennel, S., Murcott, A., & van Otterloo, A. (1992). *The sociology of food: Eating, diet and culture.* London: Sage.

Moore, P. (2017). *The quantified self in precarity: Work, technology and what counts.* Abingdon: Routledge.

Moore, P., Piwek, L., & Roper, I. (2018). The quantified workplace: A study in self-tracking, agility and change management. In B. Ajana (Ed.), *Self-tracking* (pp. 93–110). London: Palgrave MacMillan.

Moore, P., & Robinson, A. (2016). The quantified self: What counts in the neoliberal workplace. *New Media & Society, 18*(11), 2774–2792.

Mozaffarian, D., Rosenberg, I., & Uauy, R. (2018). History of modern nutrition science—Implications for current research, dietary guidelines, and food policy. *BMJ, 361,* k2392. doi:10.1136/bmj.k2392

Nafus, D., & Sherman, J. (2014). This one does not go up to 11: The quantified self movement as an alternative big data practice. *International Journal of Communication, 8,* 1784–1794.

NHS COVID-19 App. (2021). Retrieved from https://www.nhs.uk/apps-library/nhs-covid-19/. Accessed on August 2, 2021.

NHS Digital. (2021). Retrieved from https://www.england.nhs.uk/tecs/. Accessed on August 2, 2021.

NHS Track and Trace. (2021). Retrieved from https://www.nhs.uk/apps-library/nhs-covid-19/. Accessed on August 2, 2021.

Oudshoorn, N. (2011). *Telecare technologies and the transformation of healthcare.* Houndmills: Palgrave.

Pantzar, M., & Ruckenstein, M. (2017). Living the metrics: Self-tracking and situated objectivity. *Digital Health, 3,* 1–10.

Poovey, M. (1998). *A history of the modern fact: Problems of knowledge in the sciences of wealth and society.* Chicago, IL: The University of Chicago Press.

Prainsack, B. (2014). Personhood and solidarity: What kind of personalised medicine do we want? *Personalised Medicine, 11*(7), 651–657.

Prainsack, B. (2015). Is personalised medicine different? *British Journal of Sociology, 66*(1), 28–35.

Prainsack, B., & Buyx, A. (2013). A solidarity-based approach to the governance of research biobanks. *Medical Law Review, 21*(1), 71–91.

Purpura, S., Schwanda, V., Williams, K., Stubler, W., & Sengers, P. (2011, May 7–12). Fit4Life: The design of a persuasive technology promoting healthy behavior and ideal weight. Paper presented at the ACM CHI conference on human factors in computing systems, Vancouver, BC.

Quigley, M. (2013). Nudging for health: On public policy and designing choice architecture. *Medical Law Review, 21,* 588–621.

Raphael, D. (2008). Grasping at straws: A recent history of health promotion in Canada. *Critical Public Health, 18*(4), 483–495.

Raphael, D. (2011). A discourse analysis of the social determinants of health. *Critical Public Health, 21*(2), 221–236.

Raphael, D. (2013). The political economy of health promotion: Part 1, national commitments to provision of the prerequisites of health. *Health Promotion International, 28*(1), 95–111.

Rivett, G. (2021). History of the NHS. *The Nuffield Trust.* Retrieved from https://www.nuffieldtrust.org.uk/health-and-social-care-explained/the-history-of-the-nhs/. Accessed on August 2, 2021.

Robins, K., & Webster, F. (1999). *Times of the technoculture: From the information society to the virtual life.* London: Routledge.

Ronquillo, Y., Meyers, A., & Korvek, S. J. (2020). *Digital health.* Treasure Island, FL: Statpearls Publishing. Retrieved from https://pubmed.ncbi.nlm.nih.gov/29262125/. Accessed on April 29, 2021.

Rose, N. (1999). *Powers of freedom: Reframing political thought.* Cambridge: Cambridge University Press.

Rose, N. (2007). *The politics of life itself: Biomedicine, power and subjectivity in the twenty-first century.* Oxford: Princeton University Press.

Ruckenstein, M., & Pantzar, M. (2017). Beyond the quantified self: Thematic exploration of a dataistic paradigm. *New Media & Society, 19*(3), 401–418.

Ruckenstein, M., & Schüll, N. D. (2017). The datafication of health. *Annual Review of Anthropology, 46,* 261–278.

Saukko, P. M., Reed, M., Britten, N., & Hogarth, S. (2010). Negotiating the boundary between medicine and consumer culture: Online marketing of nutrigenetic tests. *Social Science and Medicine, 70*(5), 744–753.

Scott, J. (1998). *Seeing like a state: How certain schemes to improve the human condition have failed.* New Haven, CT: Yale University Press.

Statistica. (2021). Global digital health market size in 2019 and a forecast for 2026. Retrieved from https://www.statista.com/statistics/1092869/global-digital-health-market-size-forecast/. Accessed on April 29, 2021.

Swan, M. (2012a). Health 2050: The realization of personalized medicine through crowd-sourcing, the quantified self, and the participatory biocitizen. *Journal of Personalized Medicine, 2*(3), 93–118.

Swan, M. (2012b). Sensor mania! The internet of things, wearable computing, objective metrics, and the Quantified Self 2.0. *Journal of Sensor and Actuator Networks, 1*(3), 217–253.

Swan, M. (2013). The quantified self: Fundamental disruption in big data science and biological discovery. *Big Data, 1*(2), 85–99.

Topol, E. (2012). *The creative destruction of medicine: How the digital revolution will create better health care.* New York, NY: Basic Books.

Townsend, A. (2013). Smart citizens. *FutureEverything Publications.* Retrieved from http://futureeverything.org/wp-content/uploads/2014/03/smartcitizens.pdf

Tritter, J. Q. (2009). Revolution or evolution: The challenges of conceptualizing patient and public involvement in a consumerist world. *Health Expectations, 12*(3), 275–287.

UK Government. (2021). NHS Test and Trace: What to do if you are contacted. Retrieved from https://www.gov.uk/guidance/nhs-test-and-trace-how-it-works. Accessed on April 29, 2021.

Warzel, C. (2019). All your data is health data: And Big Tech has it all. *New York Times,* August 13. Retrieved from https://www.nytimes.com/2019/08/13/opinion/health-data.html. Accessed on April 29, 2021.

Williams, R., & Miller, D. (1998). Producing AIDS News. In D. Miller, J. Kitzinger, K. Williams, & P. Beharrell (Eds.), *The circuits of mass communication* (pp. 147–166). London: Sage.

Wolf, G. (2010). The data-driven life. *New York Times,* April 28. Retrieved from http://www.nytimes.com/2010/05/02/magazine/02self-measurement-t.html?_r=3&ref=magazine&pagewanted=all. Accessed on June 13, 2018.

World Health Organisation. (2021). World Health Organisation main page. Retrieved from https://www.who.int/. Accessed on April 29, 2021.

Yeung, K. (2009). Towards an understanding of regulation by design. In R. Brownsword & K. Yeung (Eds.), *Regulating technologies* (pp. 79–80). Oxford: Hart Publishing.

Yeung, K., & Dixon-Woods, M. (2010). Design-based regulation and patient safety: A regulatory studies perspective. *Social Science Medicine, 71*(3), 502–509.

Zuboff, S. (2015). Big other: Surveillance capitalism and the prospects of an information civilization. *Journal of Information Technology, 30,* 75–89.

Chapter 5

Metrics of the Self: A Users' Perspective

Btihaj Ajana

Abstract

Self-tracking is becoming a prominent and ubiquitous feature in contemporary practices of health and wellness management. Over the last few years, we have witnessed a rapid development in digital tracking devices, apps and platforms, together with the emergence of health movements such as the Quantified Self. As the world is becoming increasingly ruled by metrics and data, we are becoming ever more reliant on technologies of tracking and measurement to manage and evaluate various spheres of our lives including work, leisure, performance, and health. This chapter begins with a brief outline of some of the key theoretical approaches that have been informing the scholarly debates on the rise of self-tracking. The chapter then moves on to discuss at length the findings of an international survey study conducted by the author with users of self-tracking technologies to discuss the ways in which they perceive and experience these practices, and the various rationales behind their adoption of self-tracking in the first place. The chapter also addresses participants' attitudes towards issues of privacy and data sharing and protection which seem to be dominated by a lack of concern regarding the use and sharing of self-tracking data with third parties. Some of the overarching sentiments vis-à-vis these issues can be roughly categorised according to feelings of 'trust' towards companies and how they handle data, a sense of 'resignation' in the face of what is perceived as an all-encompassing and ubiquitous data use, feelings of 'self-insignificance' which translates into the belief that one's data is of no value to others, and the familiar expression of 'the innocent have nothing to hide'. Overall, this chapter highlights the benefits and risks of self-tracking practices as experienced and articulated by the participants, while providing a critical reflection on the rise of personal metrics and the culture of measurement and quantification.

Keywords: Data; health; personal metrics; privacy; quantification; self-tracking

The Quantification of Bodies in Health: Multidisciplinary Perspectives, 93–118

Copyright © 2022 by Btihaj Ajana

Published under an exclusive license by Emerald Publishing Limited

doi:10.1108/978-1-80071-883-820211010

Introduction

We live in an age of intense measurement where metrics, data and quantification have become routine aspects of everyday life. As the world is becoming increasingly ruled by metrics and data, we are becoming ever more reliant on metric technologies and tracking practices to manage and evaluate various spheres of our lives including work, leisure, performance, and health. Over the last few years, we have witnessed a rapid development in digital tracking devices, apps and platforms, together with the emergence of health movements, such as the Quantified Self, and the promotion of data-driven forms of self-monitoring and analysis. Every day, millions of people around the world are routinely recording their activity levels, calorie intake, sleep patterns and a myriad of other physical and emotional variables, all with the aim to gain insights into their habits and behaviours, and improve their fitness, health, and life as a whole.

At the heart of this 'metric culture' (Ajana, 2018) of self-tracking is the philosophy of 'self-knowledge through numbers'; a form of 'wisdom' espoused by the Quantified Self community and one that encourages the gathering and analysis of data about the body and its vital aspects, and extracting meaningful insights for the purpose of self-improvement. Founded in 2007 by *Wired* magazine editors, Kevin Kelly and Gary Wolf, the Quantified Self initially started as a small gathering of 28 people in Kelly's home in San Francisco to discuss self-experimentation and analysis using sensor technology. Since then, it has become a global phenomenon with currently over 200 meetup groups in different countries around the world, and the term itself is now used to describe almost any form of self-tracking. However, not everyone who self-tracks necessarily self-identifies as a member of the Quantified Self. The growing metric culture of self-tracking goes beyond and above the confines of the Quantified Self community.

Moreover, the idea of monitoring the body and its activities is not completely new, nor is the use of metrics to chart progress and goal attainment. As Alexandra Carmichael (2010) reminds us '[p]eople have been recording their lives in analog format ever since they started drawing on cave walls'. For instance, back in the seventeenth century, Santorio Santorio, a Venice-based physician, famously devised a weighing chair to monitor his weight changes through food ingestion and discharges (Sysling, 2019, p. 6). A century later and on the other side of the Atlantic, Benjamin Franklin, who was influenced by Santorio, developed a system where his sins were tabulated and quantified in order to monitor his moral behaviour. In China, a similar system was in place in the sixteenth and seventeenth centuries where individuals recorded their daily good and bad deeds on *The Ledgers of Merit and Demerit* (Brokow, 1991) and counted their individual worth, accordingly. Also, the idea of the first pedometer goes all the way back to Leonardo da Vinci and a wheeled device he designed to count the daily steps made by marching Roman soldiers.

As such, people have long reflected on the state of their bodies and selves for centuries using analogues devices and diaries. Nevertheless, developments in digital technologies and sensors have certainly made it easier than ever to automate the process of self-tracking and quantification, embedding this practice into everyday products such as mobile phones and watches. Techniques and technologies that were traditionally confined to the expert professional sphere are increasingly made accessible to the everyday general user. There are now over 318,000 health apps on the markets (Mobius, 2019) and a wide range of wearable devices such as Fitbit Charge, Garmin Vivosport, Amazfit Bip and Apple Watch, all of which are designed to record various biometric data and fitness indicators, and provide feedback on activity and health in the form of illustrations and graphs.

It is often reported that the use of wearable tracking devices or apps has a positive impact on users' health and wellbeing, especially in terms of providing motivation and promoting behavioural change. The belief is that metric modes of self-analysis offer a much more reliable and efficient path towards self-knowledge and improvement, compared to traditional methods of self-reflection and introspection. 'Unless something can be measured, it cannot be improved' (Kelly in Takahashi, 2012) is seemingly the founding principle of the Quantified Self and a statement that symbolises the underlying ideology of self-tracking culture, its positivistic tendency, and its zealous dependence on numbers and quantification.

Unsurprisingly, the techno-social phenomenon of self-tracking has been receiving much attention recently, as evidenced in the mass media coverage of this trend and in the rapidly developing body of literature from medical researchers, cognitive and behavioural psychologists, as well as social scientists and humanities scholars. As of the literature from the latter, there has been a series of studies and critiques informed by the Foucauldian twin concepts of *anatomopolitics* and *biopolitics*. On the one hand, anatomopolitics refers to modes of (self-) discipline directed at the body of the individual with the intention to maximise its usefulness, capacities, and efficiency (Foucault, 1979, p. 139). Biopolitics, on the other hand, refers to the management of life and the living *en masse* by targeting the body of the population through aggregated processes of governance and statistical norms (Foucault, 1979). The literature informed by these concepts looks at the ways in which self-tracking practices can be seen as a form of biopower designed to subject the body and the self to normalising regimes of health and socially established beauty standards (anatomopolitics) (see, for instance, Sanders, 2017; Ajana, 2017; Elias & Gill, 2017; Charitsis, Yngfalk, & Skålén, 2019; Kent, 2018). At the same time, this body of literature is also interested in the ways in which the big data emerging from the use of mobile apps and wearable devices contribute to producing knowledge about the population for governance and health management purposes at the macro level (biopolitics) (Ajana, 2018; Neff, 2017; Neff & Nafus, 2016).

Other studies have drawn on the *post-phenomenological* approach, focussing on individual experience and perception, and on the relationship between the human subject and technology (see Kristensen & Prigge, 2018; Kristensen & Ruckenstein, 2018; Van Den Eede, 2015). This approach derives its main concepts from the work of philosophers such as Peter-Paul Verbeek (2005, 2008, 2011, 2015) and Don Ihde (1993, 2001) who developed useful typologies of human/technology constellations. These include 'embodiment relations' to analyse how self-tracking technologies affect bodily experiences and remediate users' relation to their health; 'hermeneutic relations' to analyse how users make sense of and interpret the data they generate; 'alterity relations' to analyse Quantified Self meetings and the communal aspect of self-tracking; and 'background relations' to analyse how self-tracking technologies are increasingly forming the backdrop of health experience and automating data generation and processing.

A related approach that has been recently adopted within the literature on self-tracking is that of *new materialism* which also resonates with the *Actor-Network Theory*. The focus here is on the 'material dimensions of human-data assemblages' (Lupton, 2017, p. 1). In this approach, the data deriving from self-tracking practices is seen as radically embodied and material, as opposed to the discourses found in some data science literature. The emphasis is placed on both human and non-human actors in a way that seeks to highlight the hybrid agency and co-constitutive, co-creative nature of human-technology relations (Esmonde, 2019; Esmonde & Jette, 2018; Fox, 2017; Lupton, 2019). As such, a new materialist approach to self-tracking seeks to understand various aspects of user-technology interactions including the meanings ascribed to self-tracking data by users and other entities, how self-tracking practices shape understandings of health and fitness, and the forms of power and agency emerging out of the enactment of these practices.

Some theorists have explored the phenomenon of self-tracking from a Marxist standpoint (e.g., Pitts, Jean, & Clarke, 2019) looking, for instance, at the ways in which the calculative rationale of self-tracking plays out at the workplace (Charitsis, 2019; Moore, Piwek, & Roper, 2018; Till, 2016; 2019) and feeds into the increasing precarity of the working conditions worldwide. Moore and Robinson (2016) invoke the example of Amazon and Tesco warehouses which, they argue, 'monitor every minute zero-hour contracted workers spend on the performance console using arm-mounted terminals'. They link this to Gilles Deleuze's notion of 'society of control', which is marked by modulations of power that are dispersed rather than centralised and where individuals are reduced to data and numbers, and subordinated to the capitalist logic of the neoliberal market.

The field of surveillance studies has also contributed to the theorisation of self-tracking practices, particularly with regard to their capacity to intensify forms of dataveillance (Charitsis, 2019; Lupton, 2016; Ruckenstein & Granroth, 2020; Sanders, 2017; Timan & Albrechtslund, 2018; Whitson, 2013) and the emerging strategies of resistance to datafication (Esmonde, 2020; Goodyear, Kerner, & Quennerstedt, 2019). These studies have drawn attention to the privacy issues raised by such developments as well as the extractionist and, at times, exploitative aspects of self-tracking data use by companies and the intersection of data-driven surveillance and socio-economic inequalities.

These are but some of the many approaches that have been animating the academic discussions on self-tracking in recent years. This chapter seeks to contribute to existing debates by drawing on the findings of an empirical study I conducted on users' experiences of self-tracking and their perception of the broader political and ethical issues pertaining to this practice. Some of the findings illustrate some of the theoretical approaches outlined above while others bring out new insights and further concerns. The study centres on an international online survey with 24 questions (both multiple-choice and fill-in-text based) regarding the use of self-tracking devices and apps. This online methodology was chosen due to a number of reasons, including the ability to:

- Reach a wide sample of participants in different countries;
- Cross-post the survey link to different platforms while gathering results in one source location;
- Motivate participation from users who would not otherwise be willing to spend much time being interviewed face-to-face or via email;
- Secure participants' privacy by default, by not collecting names or email addresses throughout the process.

The survey was shared across different platforms, forums and relevant communities including Fitbit Forum, MyFitnessPal online platform, Quantified Self meetup groups, Twitter, and relevant Facebook pages. Participants consented to taking part in the survey and having their anonymized answers included in subsequent publications. In addition to general demographic questions, the survey asked various questions around the relationship between the use of self-tracking techniques and self-knowledge, participation in corporate wellness schemes, data sharing practices, and the level of participants' awareness of the regulations relating to data use and sharing, privacy and surveillance. In what follows I will be analysing and discussing the answers to these questions and reflecting on the overall findings.

General Profile of the Survey Participants

A total of 505 participants have completed the survey and the greatest interest was received from participants in the United States (US) and the United Kingdom (UK). 68.5% of participants identified as female, 30.9% identified as male and 0.8% identified as 'other'. In terms of participants' age, 33.9% fell within the 26–35 age category, 26.7% within 36–45 category, 10.2% within 18–25 category, and 29.5% of participants were over 45.

Self-tracking Devices and Frequency of Use

Participants were asked which self-tracking devices or apps they use. Fitbit devices were the most used which concurs with previous reports about the popularity of Fitbit products within the general fitness-tracking market. For instance, in 2016, the International Data Corporation (IDC) stated that 'Fitbit's dominance remains unchallenged for now as the company's name is synonymous with fitness bands' (in Williams, 2016). More recently, a report by TechRadar ranked Fitbit Charge 3 as the best all-round fitness tracker one can buy at the moment (Peckham, 2020). Other popular brands used by the survey participants include Garmin, Apple Watch, and Nike +. Fitness apps such as Strava, RunKeeper, Apple Health and Endomondo were also popular among the participants, with MyFitnessPal being the most used app.

Participants were asked how long they have been using their self-tracking device/app. The categories (of length of use) were largely similar in size, as shown in the graph below (Fig. 5.1). In terms of frequency of use, 59.7% of users reported that they use their tracking devices/apps on a daily basis, both during

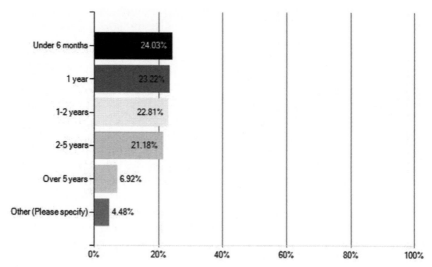

Fig. 5.1.   Length of Use.

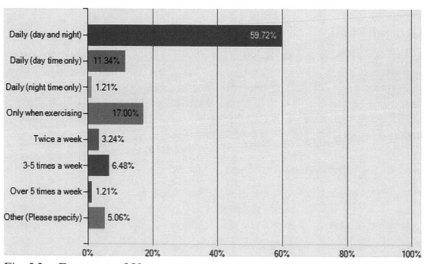

Fig. 5.2.   Frequency of Use.

daytime and at night, while 17% of participants reported that they only use them when exercising (Fig. 5.2). This suggests that the survey was completed by the most active users of the devices/apps, which indicates the high representativeness of this group within the survey sample.

What Do Users Track and Why?

Various biometric features and activity-related metrics can be captured and monitored through self-tracking devices and apps. Counting steps and the distance

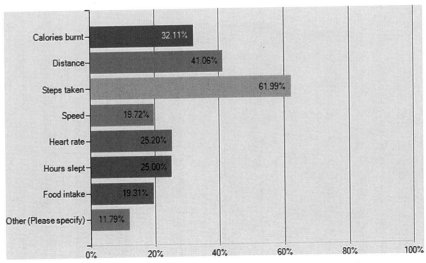

Fig. 5.3.   What Do You Monitor?

walked or run were the most tracked aspects among the survey participants (Fig. 5.3). These results confirm earlier reports suggesting that, despite the advanced developments in wearable sensors and biometric devices which enable the tracking of a wide array of bodily movements and biological signs (heart rate, blood sugar levels, blood pressure, and so on), step counting remains the most common aspect of self-tracking activity and the majority of fitness trackers are designed to act as pedometers primarily (Brown, 2016).

Reasons vary as to why people tend to track their activity and behaviour. The findings of this survey study suggest that the desire to increase motivation, monitor progress and collect data is the major driver behind the adoption of self-tracking practices (Fig. 5.4).

Other studies (GfK, 2016; Shin & Jarrahi, 2014) have also shown that much of the allure of self-tracking technologies and practices comes from the way they enable users to set daily goals, monitor habits and identify actions that can improve their fitness and overall health. The underlying belief is that when users are motivated by the rewarding feeling of achieving certain goals and making regular progress, they are likely to engage in more exercise or keep a healthy diet. Self-tracking devices and apps do act as, what Foucault (1997, pp. 224–225) terms, 'technologies of the self', that is to say, the instruments which

> permit individuals to effect by their own means or with the help of others a certain number of operations on their own bodies and souls, thoughts, conduct, and way of being, so as to transform themselves in order to attain a certain state of happiness, purity, wisdom, [and] perfection.

In this sense, self-examination through activity tracking and the monitoring of body, habits, moods, and behaviour becomes a means of improving these aspects

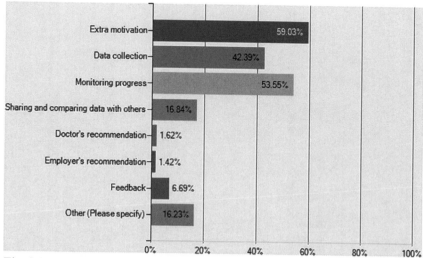

Fig. 5.4.   Why Track?

and enabling the attainment of an 'ideal' version of the self. This is facilitated all the more through the 'gamified' aspect of self-tracking technologies. Gamification refers to the process of applying game-based techniques and elements like digital points, badges, and leaderboards in non-game contexts. It is becoming a popular means of increasing motivation, instituting competition and rewarding performance. Technologies of self-tracking carry within them the promise of making physical activity more enjoyable and manageable through the gamification of health and the instrumentalization of exercise. Maturo and Setiffi (2016) argue that while quantification provides the 'rational' basis for exercise and dietary regimes, gamification provides the 'emotional support' needed to maintain motivation. As such, self-tracking technologies are increasingly designed to combine both quantification and gamification so as to promote 'numerical living' that can be 'fun and engaging' (Ruckenstein, 2014). For instance, Strava, an activity-tracking website and app popular among cyclists and runners, uses quantification and gamification to motivate users by awarding titles, like 'King of the Mountain', for the shortest time spent cycling up a particular hill. Many of the survey participants have indeed reported that using self-tracking devices or apps turns fitness and exercise into '*a fun game and adds joy to the experience*' (female participant, age range: 36–45). The self-tracking device itself is treated as '*a new toy that is fun to play with*' (male participant, age range: over 45), reaffirming the gamified and gamifying aspects of such technologies.

In her article, 'Gaming the quantified self', Jennifer Whitson (2013) argues that gamification encourages playful subjectivities and drives behavioural change to acquire new conducts. This is evident in the 'nudging' aspect of self-tracking devices which also function as triggers, reminding users to exercise regularly. For example, Fitbit's indicator lights up as an alarm when the device senses that the user has been sitting for too long. Apps like Aqualert and Plant Nanny act as a 'hydration reminder' encouraging the user to increase her water consumption. As one participant puts it,

> *[my device] reminds me to go out for walks, go to the gym, to be fitter. I'm always trying to raise my heart rate into the different zones and my FitBit challenges me to do that.* (female participant, age range: 18–25)

These are examples of what Natasha Singer (2015) calls 'the nurselike application of technology', whereby devices 'prod' the user to take action rather than just collect data. By playing the role of a 'friend' who knows the user well or the role of an authority such as a nurse or a doctor, self-tracking devices and apps aim to enhance the persuasive effect on one's behaviour. As Brian Jeffrey Fogg (2002) argues, 'computing technology that assumes roles of authority will have enhanced powers of persuasion'. Such technology can influence users' attitudes and lead to changes in habits and daily activities. As the following quotes from the survey participants testify:

> *I consider it [self-tracking technology] life changing. I have changed from a couch potato, to a fit active person. I rarely use my car. I have become familiar with my locality and its beauty.* (Female participant, age range: over 45)

> *It's made me more aware of my lifestyle and helps me be more active everyday, I try to reach a step goal of 10k steps per day and can get higher when I'm in a challenge on Fitbit.* (Female participant, age range: 26–35)

> *I used to be a couch potato now I do a minimum 10,000 steps a day.* (Female participant, age range: 26–35)

> *It has made me aware of how sedentary life styles are. I know how much effort it takes to get 10k steps, and makes me see why others are not active and the impact it has on their health. It means I encourage those around me to get Fitbit (or similar), including my kids, who then influence their peer group and teaching staff. It's amazing how many people around us have them now. It also makes me walk every day, rain or shine, which must be having an effect on the depression I have had all my life.* (Female participant, age range: over 45)

> *It motivates me to get moving, to eat right, to get to bed on time. I like knowing how much I can eat based on how much I burn. I've been working on losing weight for almost 3 years and have lost about 75 lbs. I would probably have given up long ago without the Fitbit and MyFitnessPal.* (Female participant, age range: over 45)

It is ridiculously motivating! Since retiring, my life style was very sedentary. I now walk 10k plus steps daily, all weathers. Without Fitbit, I would have made multiple excuses not to walk. I consider it to be life changing. I am fitter, healthier and stronger. (Female participant, age range: over 45)

The persuasive, gamifying and nudging functions of self-tracking technologies are often seen as positive motivational aspects that incite users to adopt 'healthier' lifestyle. As articulated in the above quotes, participants internalised the norms of self-tracking culture (such as walking 10,000 steps a day and dieting), 'regulating' their physical activity, food intake and other habits, accordingly. Parenthetically, the norm of 10,000 steps a day originated in Japan in the early 1960s through research led by Yoshiro Hatano. The research estimated that walking 10,000 steps would be enough to burn around 20% of our calorie intake (Cooper, 2013). Currently, across all health platforms and self-tracking devices, the 10,000 steps norm is set as the baseline that needs to be met by users if they are to be deemed as healthy and active citizens. In internalising such norms, the self-tracker ends up conforming to a pre-given standard of health and fitness and being (self-) assessed according to an idealised 'numeric identity' (Rowse, 2015). For this reason, Whitson (2013) regards self-tracking and its gamifying dimension as deeply rooted in self-surveillance practices which often align with institutionalised understandings and standards of health and wellbeing. This argument resonates with Foucault's notion of anatomopolitics, mentioned earlier, whereby the human body is made amenable to normative practices of (self-) discipline and control. In the case of the present study, even when users were ill or injured, they still maintained a sense of self-discipline, tracking their recovery and progress:

I have been using my Fitbit to track my recovery from a broken ankle since the summer, I am now up to 7000 steps a day and allowed to train in the gym, my physiotherapist has been impressed at how quickly I have come on and I credit that at least partially to the motivation of my Fitbit and using it to earn bounty points [...] yes, I am much more aware of days where I do very little, my overall activity had more than doubled in the 5 months from buying the Fitbit to breaking my ankle. Tracking improvements in my rehab was great too. (Female participant, age range: 26–35)

While the persuasive function of self-tracking technologies and their regime of self-discipline have certainly contributed to increasing participants' motivation, bodily awareness and overall level of activity, they have also led, in some cases, to feelings of anxiety and obsession over one's performance and progress. One female participant described her experience in the following way:

Occasionally I become preoccupied with my GPS that I stop enjoying my run because I feel like a bad run is a failure instead of just another run, good or bad. I become so obsessed with data that I sometimes cry if my pace run isn't to target or if I can't make it to the end of my long run without walking. (Female participant, age range: 26–35)

This illustrates the kind of pressure that is, sometimes, inflicted on the self as a result of processes of self-tracking and quantification, which in turn risks taking the pleasure out of physical activity itself due to excessive self-monitoring and self-imposed targets. As another participant stated, '*it is easy to focus too much on making a certain pace or burning a certain amount of calories instead of enjoying the activities and your surroundings*' (female participant, age range: 26–35). Some participants also reported that without tracking they feel as though their activity or exercise does not 'count'. As these quotes from various participants indicate,

My Fitbit recently broke down and although I continued to walk, I did feel as if it wasn't worthwhile!! (Female participant, age range: over 45)

I think there is a risk that people start doing these activities not because they are inherently good or valuable, but because it gives them more points or a better 'score', which in turn translates to better self-esteem. (Male participant, age range: 18–25)

These trackers could make some users too fanatical and obsessive when achieving goals or when competing. Some users do get very very stressed when the device or servers fail. (Male participant, age range: over 45)

It has been a bit of a stumbling block in some ways, especially food intake tracking because I tend to get a little hung up when eating food prepared by someone else that doesn't do things 'my way' (eg. weigh ingredients and total servings, etc.). I have been known to refuse to eat a food for which I did not know the specific gram weight. I can get a bit obsessive; I try to catch it as soon as I notice it or it is pointed out to me, and 'forcefully relax' my standards. (Female participant, age range: 36–45)

Some people may be exercising not for themselves but for the app. (Male participant, age range: 26–35)

I've thought a lot about peoples' 'obsession' with quantifying their lives and sharing that information. I'm hoping I'll never reach the point when not tracking my run will make it less enjoyable for me. That would be just sad. (Male participant, age range: 26–35)

The anxiety around performance and the potentially obsessive streak of self-tracking becomes, indeed, more pronounced in the case of participants who share their self-tracking data with others. As one participant admits, '*sometimes, if I know I am going to share data on social media I feel I need to go harder which stops me enjoying the exercise*' (female participant, age range: 26–35). Balancing between the ability to enjoy exercise and the need to perform adequately in front of the watchful gaze of an audience (on social media and other platforms) remains a challenging task for most users, as activity and self-representation become constructed and moderated in consideration of the imagined judgments of others. Here, feelings of accountability towards and competition with other users emerge, leading to an internalisation of self-discipline and striving for self-improvement.

Sharing in the Self-tracking Culture

The results of the survey indicate that 59.8% of participants tend to share their self-tracking data on social media, such as Facebook and Instagram, and other relevant platforms like Fitbit's and Strava's online forums. The chief reason being the sense of competition and pride, and the feeling of motivation that come part and parcel of sharing self-tracking data, goals and achievements with others: '*[I share] to push myself. So my friends can see what I've done and go out and push it a little more. Which in turn pushes me… And to be honest, to show off some times.:)*' (male participant, age range: over 45); '*You suddenly realize how competitive you are, even against yourself*' (female participant, age range: over 45); '*I found inspiration by checking other people's food diaries. Sometimes challenges with people on my friends list motivate me to move more*' (female participant, age range: 26–35). Accountability to oneself and to others thus becomes an inherent part in the performative sharing ritual of self-tracking data and experience. The belief is that social responses in the form of encouragement and acknowledgment as well as the fear of losing or visibly not meeting the set targets can be effective motivators for users to consistently engage in physical activity, pursue a healthy lifestyle and achieve their set goals: '*I take part in challenges with others in teams. Team accountability motivates me*' (female participant, age range: over 45).

Another key rationale found in the participants' responses relates to the sense of belonging that is instilled through acts of sharing. Many stated that the sharing of self-tracking data and experience reinforces the feeling of belonging to a community with shared objectives and interests. This resonates with Deborah Lupton's (2015, p. 12) claim that data sharing in the self-tracking culture tends to appeal to a deeply felt desire to be part of a community and a need to create social bonds and a sense of belonging. It is, indeed, this desire that the Quantified Self movement seeks to fulfil by offering a 'community of practice' that brings together individuals and groups who self-identify as Quantified Selfers or self-trackers. As Wenger-Trayner and Wenger-Trayner (2015, p. 2) argue, a community of practice is not only a community of those who share common interests but also groups who have a shared practice and a shared repertoire of resources including tools, stories, experiences and ways of tackling issues and problems. This definition chimes with the way the Quantified Self community encourages and facilitates the sharing of self-tracking experiments, data and stories for the purpose of learning, receiving feedback and exchanging relevant tips and information. According to Gary Wolf (2010), the co-founder of the Quantified Self, '[p]ersonal data are ideally suited to a social life of sharing. You might not always have something to say, but you always have a number to report'. The process of sharing within Quantified Self groups is performed through both online and face-to-face channels; through a dedicated website and forums, conferences and public symposiums and, most importantly, through the 'Show and tell' presentations which tend to be very candid exposition of personal experiences and difficulties encountered throughout the tracking journey. This social trend of participating in Quantified Self communities, established for the purpose of sharing health related information and experience, echoes Paul Rabinow's (1996) concept of 'biosociality'. This is a type of connection between individuals, which is centred on biologically based forms of socialisation. It gestures towards the interface between developments in biotechnologies, life sciences, social practices and individual and collective subjectivities (Valle & Gibbon, 2015). Olivia Banner (2014, p. 199) points out the intrinsic link between biosociality and the Foucauldian notion of anatomopolitics where the individual learns to discipline and control her body according to the terms delimited by her biosocial community. She goes on to argue that, by fostering the belief that the individual user can learn from other members, biosociality joins 'the individual practices associated with anatomopolitics to a biopolitics of the biosocial community' (Banner, 2014), as is the case with the Quantified Self.

Interestingly, though, few participants in the survey recognised the Quantified Self. The majority of respondents never heard of the term before coming across it in the survey question, which indicates that this is still a niche movement, after all, despite the fact that self-tracking itself, as a practice, has become a widely spread and mainstream activity. So, the process of sharing self-tracking data and experiences is not bound by the confines of particular biosocial communities or groups but takes place through the multitude of networks, online platforms and offline interactions.

Some participants indicated that they share their data for monetary incentives. This is the case of some of the 10.50% of participants who took part in corporate wellness schemes organised by their employers. In such cases, *'bonuses were offered to staff who walked 10,000 steps/day using company-issued pedometers'* (female participant, age range: 36–45). Some employers tracked the weekly exercise of their employees and entered those with top scores into a raffle (female participant, age range: 18–25). Other employers provided prizes such as Apple devices and other electronics to those who walked the greatest number of steps over a period of time. In addition to step tracking, weight monitoring was also part of some the corporate wellness programs. As this quote indicates:

> *It was an 8 week 'wellness' challenge. There was a weigh-in week prior and a weigh-out week after the 8 weeks. You get 2 points for 30 min of cardio, 3 points for 30 min of resistance throughout the challenge. At weight-outs, relative to weigh-ins: 5 points per pound lost, 10 pts for inch lost (bust, waist, hip, thigh), 25 pts for 1% body fat lost. #1 team of 6 people wins $800 each, #2 team of 6 people wins $650 each.* (Female participant, age range: 26–35)

Over the last few years, there has been indeed a growing interest in instituting wellness schemes at the workplace through the use of fitness-tracking devices and apps. For instance, companies such as Target, BP, Bloomberg, Barclays, and Google have been running wellness programs for their employees with the aim to encourage healthier and more active lifestyles. Some self-tracking devices are even designed specifically and exclusively for corporate wellness schemes. For example, Fitbit recently introduced a new activity and sleep tracker called, Fitbit Inspire, which is only available through corporate wellness schemes and health plans (Farr, 2019). Workplace wellness is now an $8 billion industry (Wadyka, 2020) and health itself has become 'a corporate concern', as Chris Till (2016) puts it. This is a development that is embedded in the double imperative of 'better health outcomes' and 'lower health costs' (Lupton, 2013, p. 3).

As such, the key rationale behind these schemes is to reduce healthcare and insurance costs while improving the productive capacity of employees. Based on a study of 36 corporate wellness schemes, a report from Harvard Business School found that for every dollar spent on wellness programs, medical expenses fell by $3.27 and employee absenteeism expenses fell by $2.73 (in Oppenheim, 2019). Another report from the Rand Corporation (2013) showed that corporate wellness schemes contribute to reducing stress, boosting productivity, and increasing employees' engagement. In a sense, corporate wellness schemes can be regarded as an example of what Boltanski and Chiapello (2005) term the 'new spirit' of capitalism whereby labour and organisational culture start to take on new qualities and ethos rooted in concepts of engagement, meaningfulness of work, and opportunities for self-development at and through work. As Dominique Genelot (in Boltanski & Chiapello, 2005, p. 63) argues, organisations must now be 'a site for creating meaning, for shared goals, where everyone can simultaneously develop their personal autonomy and contribute to the collective project'. So, in addition to their utilitarian aspect of cost reduction and increased productivity, corporate wellness schemes also appeal to the new spirit of capitalism in organisational culture which seek to give work a 'more human orientation' (Moore, 2018, p. 57) by providing employees with opportunities for self-improvement and instilling certain norms of health and team values. In doing so, these schemes also adhere to an 'economy of convention' (Boltanski & Thévenot, 2006; Diaz-Bone, 2018) in which the actors involved (employees, managers, team members, etc.) have to achieve a common goal by undertaking activities based on established beliefs (e.g. exercise is good; teamwork is good) and frames of action that are mediated through established metrics and tracking technologies.

Despite the putative benefits of wellness programs, there is a sense in which they can be seen as a 'colonization' of employees' private lives as leisure activities, including exercise, are becoming integrated more and more into the sphere of labour as well. One does not leave work when leaving the workplace but carries the demands of the employer into other personal spheres that are not necessarily work related (Holten, 2017). A female participant in the survey expressed a similar point in the following way: '*I have strongly rejected to participate, since I will not let my employer be a part of my life that for me is very private*' (age range: 26–35). And as another respondent (age range: 26–35) puts it: '*I would not like my employer to know how I exercise (why should they? and one more noisy observation to be judged by)*'. In his theory of communicative action, Jürgen Habermas (1987) raises this issue of colonisation by suggesting that the extreme 'mediatization of the lifeworld turns into its colonization' (Habermas, 1987, p. 318). That is to say, when media forms become the lens through which the world is 'enframed', in the Heideggerian sense, and life itself is experienced and lived, the protective boundaries surrounding the private sphere diminish and become absorbed into the media's capitalist logic, leading to system colonisation of lifeworld. Self-tracking technologies and the corporate wellness programs within which they became embedded take on this colonising aspect by defining what constitutes health and wellbeing in the first place and infiltrating almost every sphere of everyday life (from tracking sleep, weight and work performance to measuring sexual activity, fertility and other intimate aspects).

Moreover, linking the sharing of self-tracking data to financial incentives such as bonuses and discounts on insurance blurs the boundaries between what is voluntary and what is not. As attorney Dara Smith (in Wadyka, 2020) argues,

> [i]f the penalty for not participating is that your health insurance premiums will be higher, employees may feel like they have to share their health information in order to save money.

This can lead to coercive forms of self-tracking dressed up as voluntary participation in wellness schemes. Lupton (2014, pp. 5–10) developed a useful typology to differentiate between the various types of self-tracking, one of which she calls 'pushed self-tracking', an incentive-based form of self-monitoring that may be taken up voluntarily, but in response to external encouragement from other actors, as in health promotion initiatives. Another type of self-tracking is 'imposed self-tracking' which involves the use of tracking devices to monitor employees' productivity and health. The line between these two forms of tracking is very fine, according to Lupton, and one can argue that the above-mentioned examples from participants oscillate between these two types of tracking. Added to that the potential repurposing of the shared data for commercial benefits and for building customer profiles to use in targeted marketing and advertising. This is what Lupton refers to as 'exploited self-tracking' in which the commodification of personal data is a major feature.

Increasingly, various actors other than users themselves are interested in harvesting the self-tracking data. These range from public health institutions and private insurance companies to researchers and product developers. In the healthcare sector, self-tracking practices are looked up to as a means of realising the aspirations of participatory, preventative and personalised healthcare models. This is insofar as these practices can enable the capturing of quantifiable health data that can feed into decision-making vis-à-vis one's lifestyle, diet options, exercise activities, performance and habits. Both the public and the private health sectors are interested in how self-tracking data generated by individuals can feed into a larger big data ecosystem. The belief is that when ensembles of individuals' data are combined, a collective social picture will emerge, that of the population, its health, finances and productivity (Ajana, 2017).

To this end, self-trackers are encouraged to embrace data sharing and dona-tion as a way of enacting good bio-citizenship (see the example of Patients Like Me and its *Data For Good* campaign[1]). There is, in fact, a certain moral economy at work, which underpins data sharing practices and prescribes these as a form of altruism and civic duty, often packaged under the rubric of 'data philanthropy' (Ajana, 2017). But there remains a great tension between the notion of data phi-lanthropy and issues of data commercialisation. While many users of self-track-ing technologies operate under the assumption that the data they generate belong to them, the reality is that companies providing the technology often own the data. Service providers often leave users with no choice as to whether to save the data on the company's server or on their own devices. As such, users have hardly any control over how their data is stored and processed (Mulder, 2019). The tech-nically savvy members of the Quantified Self community tend to circumvent such issues by building their own tracking tools so that their data remains their own property. But that is not the case with the majority of everyday self-trackers who rely on commercial devices and apps to track their activities. There is, indeed, a delicate dance between commercial goals and the aim of 'self-knowledge through numbers' (Fotopoulou, 2018, p. 3).

The monetisation of data sharing is an issue that has been taken up by vari-ous scholars, recently, leading to the questioning of the essence of the term 'sharing' itself. For instance and taking cue from the work of Georges Bataille and Jean-Luc Nancy, Wolfgang Sützl (2016) distinguishes between the notion of 'exchange' and the notion of 'sharing'. He argues that sharing, as practiced by the likes of Uber and Airbnb, is more about capitalist notions of 'exchange' as a systemised infrastructure. He explains that, unlike exchange, sharing is pri-marily about *being* and only secondarily about *having*. So, whereas exchange is a rational and functional operation that is based on an economy of 'having' and 'possessing', sharing is an intimate experience of being which subsumes the meaning and the inner relationship one has towards that which is being shared and with whom it is shared. As such, Sützl warns that 'as economic exchange expands, it eliminates sharing by turning the commons into a com-modity', which in turn leads to 'pseudo-sharing', a business relationship mas-querading as communal sharing (Belk, 2014). Pseudo-sharing benefits from the association of commonality and sociability that comes with the word itself, thereby masking the economic rationality at work. Russell Belk argues that the ubiquitous 'share' button on social networking sites and online platforms can be regarded as a nicely packaged invitation to provide content to sustain these sites, encourage more participants, and, in so doing, provide information that can be sold to advertisers, marketers, and research firms. This 'sharing' framing *mystifies* the profitable transactions that exploit information (Belk, 2014). It can therefore be argued that, by generating data and information, self-trackers end up unwittingly contributing to the expansion of capital and the intensification of exchange.

---

[1] Available at: https://www.patientslikeme.com/research/dataforgood.

Attitudes Towards Privacy and Data Protection

The generation, collection and 'sharing' of data have various implications vis-à-vis privacy issues, some of which might evade the awareness of self-trackers. The survey, as such, asked the participants whether they were familiar with the privacy statements and data regulations surrounding self-tracking, and whether they had any concerns about what happened to their data and who had access to it. 50% of participants reported that they were not familiar with the regulations concerning the data they generated through their use of self-tracking devices and apps. And strikingly, the majority of respondents noted that they were not concerned about the exposure or use of their data by others. Some did not even see why self-tracking data should be private ['*I've never given it a second thought. I can't easily come up with a reason for keeping such information private, either*' (female participant, age range: 26–35); '*I think those concerns are overrated and somewhat paranoid*' (female participant, age range: 26–35)], trusting that companies would not share their data: '*I have a decent amount of trust in tracking companies not to release information. More so, I don't feel there is any particularly damaging information that would be released anyway*' (male participant, age range: over 45); '*I trust the large corporations (Garmin, Google, etc.) 100% in keeping my data safe, and use it for good purpose. I worry about the public getting to this information, so that bad persons (e.g. thieves) can use the information to their advantage and my disadvantage (steal from me when they know I'm not home). But I trust that the large corporations keep my data safe, and won't share it with the wrong people*' (male participant, age range: 18–25). Others think that *their 'details are boring*' (female participant, age range: 36–45) or not significant enough to raise concern, as articulated in the following quotes:

> *I'm but one in seven billion people on the rock called earth, about half have access to the internet, and probably less than a handful have any interest in me or my whereabouts, I'm not planning to run for president or a similar occupation that would bring me to the lime-light, but sure, I would prefer my information stay private, but in today's society, it comes with the cost of convenience.* (Male participant, age range: 18–25)

> *I don't care – I'm not interesting enough to get monitored.* (Female participant, age range: over 45)

> *Nope. I've never really been bothered by who's watching me or 'spy-ing' on me. I consider myself quite boring and don't imagine anyone using my data for anything other than averages and understanding what to sell me online.* (Female participant, age range: 18–25)

> *If people find out my weight or what I eat it's not the end of the world.* (Female participant, age range: 36–45)

> *I don't think any of the information they have will be of any use.* (Female participant, age range: 26–35)

I've got nothing to hide. But would be annoyed if they added ads.
(Female participant, age range: 36–35)

Had not thought that my data would be of any interest to anyone.
(Female participant, age range: over 45)

*There's nothing worth worrying about in how many steps/calories/
floors etc – that data is of no benefit to anyone other than myself.*
(Female participant, age range: 26–35)

*No, I don't think I'm important enough that anyone would look for
my data specifically. If my data is being used for research purposes
without my knowledge, I would be annoyed, but I don't fear it because
it doesn't really impact me. I would probably volunteer my data for
research if asked.* (Female participant, age range: 18–25)

*No because really what can they learn from what I eat? I don't mind
if they share what I do as long as they don't hack my bank account.
If it helps research and knowledge then all the better.* (Female participant, age range: 26–35)

Some participants have resigned to the fact that their data are hardly secure
and inevitably shared all the time, believing that the benefits often outweigh privacy concerns and that using data for medical research and knowledge advancement is a legitimate reason for data repurposing:

*None of my data is safe and secure. Big companies lose data every
day, I am tracked everywhere I go, every website, every app, purchase
and so on. I just assume that any data I store with someone is possibly going to be stolen or used to sell me something.* (Male participant, age range: 26–35)

*There is an extent to which we can't escape such data collection these
days unless we completely go off the grid. I don't like this, but convenience often leads me to just accept it. If this data is being used to
help improve the health of future generations, then I am fine with it
being collected, but if it is being used to sell me or others something,
that really bothers me.* (Male participant, age range: 26–35)

*My concerns are small and speculative versus the tangible benefits I
receive each day.* (Male participant, age range: 26–35)

I think the more the data is shared the more we can learn. (Male
participant, age range: 18–25)

I always assume it's being used by somebody for something. (Female
participant, age range: 26–35)

I think that the more we know about what keeps people healthy the better, more data, more understanding is the hope. (Female participant, age range: over 45)

At this point, I am just going to assume any data I provide to anyone is going to be used to either advertise towards me or to put me on a government watch list, but living off the grid is too hard, so I might as well lean all the way in. (Female participant, age range: 26–35)

Google and Facebook have more data on me then I have on myself. (Male participant, age range: 26–35)

Nevertheless, some participants, especially from the United States, expressed their concern regarding the interest of insurance companies in the data and how data could be used against them in certain circumstances. As indicated in the following statements:

Yes, I wouldn't want anyone to have access to my data, this is personal and because we don't know how it will affect us in the future I would rather not have this recorded anywhere, just in case one day someone somewhere would make it count on health/life insurance policy. (Female participant, age range: 26–35)

Sometimes when tracking food and alcohol consumption as it could be used against insurance policies although in the up side the exercise and diet part is a good sign. (Female participant, age range: over 45)

Yes. That medical or health care insurance companies might see how much or how little I sleep, eat, and exercise. (Male participant, age range: 36–45)

I know this is valuable information for health insurances, potential employers, etc. I hope that the data will not be abused, but to be honest, I have been too lazy to check what the privacy regulations are. (Female participant, age range: 26–35)

Yes. I fear health insurance companies may get hold of this info and negatively use it in determining insurability or coverage. (Female participant, age range: 36–45)

Yes – considering insurance companies and the like and whether they would ever use them to predict premiums in an area, but also the GPS tracking side. If someone wanted too, it wouldn't be hard to spot my habits near work and home. (Female participant: 26–35)

> *I might be paranoid but I think that eventually there'll be huge soci-*
> *etal pressure to exercise regularly (if there isn't already) and that*
> *those who don't might eventually be ineligible for free healthcare etc.*
> *If/when the UK has privately owned healthcare, your digital fitness*
> *record could end up affecting your premiums.* (Male participant, age
> range: 26–35)

Since the survey was conducted prior to the implementation of The General
Data Protection Regulation (GDPR) in May 2018, it did not ask participants
about their understanding of the GDPR rules and the effects they have had on
data sharing and privacy issues. This, I believe, would be a topic worthy of further research. Some scholars have recently started examining the implications and
assessing the effectiveness of the GDPR with regard to the landscape of self-
tracking culture. For example, a very recent study conducted by the legal scholar
Trix Mulder (2019) examined the privacy policies of various heath apps, including apps designed specifically for the medical sector as well as general self-tracking apps, such as Fitbit, Strava and Nike Running, and she compared these to the
GDPR provisions. The findings of the study suggest that even where companies
provide privacy statements, it is impossible to get a complete picture of what
the app providers do with the personal data they collect, as the language these
companies use tends to be vague and leaves the reader with many questions. The
study even found that almost 50% of the analysed apps used privacy as a positive
marketing statement leading you to believe that 'your' privacy is important even
when this is not reflected in the companies' privacy policies.

Also, the GDPR foregrounds the issue of consent, that is, the requirement for
companies to obtain permission from data subjects before processing and sharing
their data. The regulation defines consent as

> any freely given, specific, informed and unambiguous indication
> of the data subject's wishes by which he or she, by a statement or
> by a clear affirmative action, signifies agreement to the processing
> of personal data relating to him or her. (Article 4 (11) GDPR)

Companies responded to the introduction of the GDPR by including privacy
pop-up windows on their platforms giving users the choice to accept or reject the
use of technologies such as 'cookies' to track their online activities and collect
data about them. As shown in Figs. 5.5 and 5.6, 'Accept' tend to be the default setting while 'Show purposes', which provides users with further information on the
types of data being collected and to what ends, tends to come in very small fonts
in comparison with 'Accept'. In fact, and as Frederike Kaltheuner (2018) from
Privacy International points out, Quantcast, a US-based advertising company
that also sells 'consent solutions' to websites and publishers as in Figs. 5.5 and
5.6, prides itself for its (deceptive) design which is able to achieve 90% consent
rate. In a way, users are also complicit in this as they tend to see the warning page
about privacy and data collection as an irritant and quickly click 'Accept all' to
make it disappear (Lynskey, 2019). As such, users tend to formally consent to

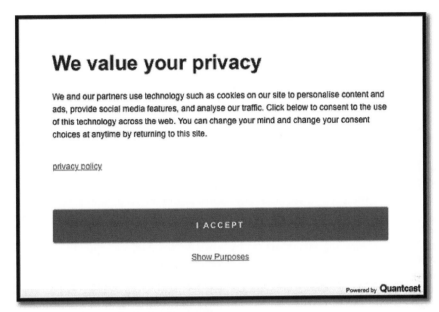

Fig. 5.5.   Privacy Notice by Quantcast.

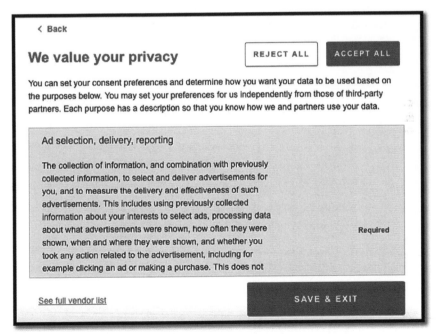

Fig. 5.6.   Privacy Options by Quantcast.

privacy policies without knowing what happens to their personal data and often without even reading the privacy statements (Kon, n.d.).

Conclusions

In this chapter, I drew on the results of an international survey involving users of self-tracking technologies to examine experiences and perceptions of self-tracking practices and attitudes towards privacy and data regulations. As the findings of the study demonstrate, self-tracking carries many benefits to the user, particularly with regard to increasing motivation and encouraging a healthier and more active lifestyle. Nevertheless, the data-driven and quantifying aspects of self-tracking can sometimes lead to excessive forms of self-monitoring which can increase the pressure on the user to perform according to certain standards of health, resulting in feelings of inadequacy, at times, and inability to enjoy the exercise activities themselves. Participants' attitudes towards privacy and data protection are seemingly dominated by a lack of concern regarding the use and sharing of self-tracking data with third parties. Some of the overarching sentiments vis-à-vis these issues can be roughly categorised according to feelings of 'trust' towards companies and how they handle data, a sense of 'resignation' in the face of what is perceived as an all-encompassing and ubiquitous data use, feelings of 'self-insignificance' which translates into the belief that one's data is of no value to others, and the familiar expression of 'the innocent have nothing to hide'. Whether the implementation of the GDPR has changed users' attitudes towards issues of privacy, consent and data protection is a question that warrants further research. Overall, more multidisciplinary studies are needed to explore the ways in which the proliferation of self-tracking technologies in everyday life is impacting people's understanding of their health and bodies, and shaping the wider socio-technical ecosystem within which we live.

References

Ajana, B. (2017). Digital health and the biopolitics of the quantified self. *Digital Health, 3*(1), 1–18.

Ajana, B. (Ed.) (2018). *Metric culture: Ontologies of self-tracking practices*. Bingley: Emerald Publishing.

Banner, O. (2014). 'Treat us right!' Digital publics, emerging biosocialities, and the female complaint. In A. Poletti & J. Rak (Eds.), *Identity technologies: Constructing the self online* (pp. 198–216). Madison: University of Wisconsin Press.

Belk, R. (2014). Sharing versus pseudo-sharing in Web 2.0. *Anthropologist, 18*(1), 7–23.

Boltanski, L., & Chiapello, E. (2005). *The new spirit of capitalism*. London: Verso.

Boltanski, L., & Thévenot, L. (2006). *On justification: Economies of worth*. Princeton, NJ: Princeton University Press.

Brokow, C. J. (1991). *Ledgers of merit and demerit*. Oxford: Princeton University Press.

Brown, A. (2016). What tracking metric do you care about? In *Wearable technologies*. Retrieved from http://www.wearable-technologies.com/2016/04/what-tracking-metric-do-you-care-about

Carmichael, A. (2010). Self tracking: The quantified life is worth living. *H+ Magazine*. Retrieved from http://hplusmagazine.com/2010/02/08/self-tracking-quantified-life-worth-living/

Charitsis, V. (2019). Survival of the (data) fit: Self-surveillance, corporate wellness, and the platformization of healthcare. *Surveillance & Society, 17*(1/2), 139–144.

Charitsis, V., Yngfalk, A. F., & Skålén, P. (2019). 'Made to run': Biopolitical marketing and the making of the self-quantified runner. *Marketing Theory, 19*(3), 347–366.

Cooper, B. B. (2013). Is 10,000 steps really the best measurement of our health? In *TNW*. Retrieved from http://thenextweb.com/apps/2013/11/29/10000-steps-really-best-measurement-health/#gref

Diaz-Bone, R. (2018). Economics of convention and its perspective on knowledge and institutions. In J. Glückler, R. Suddaby, & R. Lenz (Eds.), *Knowledge and institutions* (pp. 69–88). Cham: Springer.

Elias, A. S., & Gill, R. (2017). Beauty surveillance: The digital self-monitoring cultures of neoliberalism. *European Journal of Cultural Studies, 21*(1), 59–77. doi: 10.1177/1367549417705604

Esmonde, K. (2019). Training, tracking, and traversing: Digital materiality and the production of bodies and/in space in runners' fitness tracking practices. *Leisure Studies, 38*(6), 804–817.

Esmonde, K. (2020). 'There's only so much data you can handle in your life': Accommodating and resisting self-surveillance in women's running and fitness tracking practices. *Qualitative Research in Sport, Exercise and Health, 12*(1), 76–90.

Esmonde, K., & Jette, S. (2018). Assembling the 'Fitbit subject': A Foucauldian-sociomaterialist examination of social class, gender and self-surveillance on Fitbit community message boards. *Health*. doi: 10.1177/1363459318800166

Farr, C. (2019). Fitbit has a new health tracker, but you can only get it through your employer or insurer. In *CNBC*. Retrieved from https://www.cnbc.com/2019/02/08/fitbit-releases-insprire-for-employers.html

Fogg, B. J. (2002). Persuasive technology: Using computers to change what we think and do. *Ubiquity*. Retrieved from http://dl.acm.org/citation.cfm?id=763957

Fotopoulou, A. (2018). From networked to quantified self: Self tracking and the moral economy of data sharing. In Z. Papacharissi (Ed.), *A networked self: Platforms, stories, connections* (pp. 144–159). New York, NY: Routledge.

Foucault, M. (1979). *History of sexuality: The will to knowledge*. London: Allen Lane.

Foucault, M. (1997). Technologies of the self. In P. Rabinow (Ed.), *Ethics: Subjectivity and truth* (pp. 223–252). New York, NY: The New Press.

Fox, N. (2017). Personal health technologies, micropolitics and resistance: A new materialist analysis. *Health, 21*(2), 136–153.

GfK. (2016). A third of people track their health or fitness. Who are they and why are they doing it? Retrieved from https://www.prnewswire.com/news-releases/a-third-of-people-track-their-health-or-fitness-who-are-they-and-why-are-they-doing-it-595221791.html

Goodyear, V. A., Kerner, C., & Quennerstedt, M. (2019). Young people's uses of wearable healthy lifestyle technologies: Surveillance, self-surveillance and resistance. *Sport, Education and Society, 24*(3), 212–225.

Habermas, J. (1987). *The theory of communicative action, vol. 2. Lifeworld and system: A critique of functional reason*. Boston, MA: Beacon Press Books.

Holten, E. (2017). In: Ajana, B. (dir) *Quantified Life*, documentary film. Retrieved from https://www.youtube.com/watch?v=qI75kMqctik

Ihde, D. (1993). *Postphenomenology: Essays in the postmodern context*. Evanston: Northwestern University Press.

Ihde, D. (2001). *Bodies in technology*. Minneapolis: University of Minnesota Press.

Kaltheuner, F. (2018). I asked an online tracking company for all of my data and here's what I found. In *Privacy International*. Retrieved from https://privacyinternational. org/long-read/2433/i-asked-online-tracking-company-all-my-data-and-heres-what-i-found

Kent, R. (2018). Social media and self-tracking: Representing the 'health self'. In B. Ajana (Ed.). *Self-tracking* (pp. 61–76). Cham: Palgrave Macmillan.

Kon, G. (n.d.). Does anyone read privacy notices? The facts. In *Linklaters*. Retrieved from https://www.linklaters.com/en/insights/blogs/digilinks/does-anyone-read-privacy-notices-the-facts

Kristensen, D. B., & Prigge, C. (2018). Human/technology associations in self-tracking practices. In B. Ajana (Ed.), *Self-tracking: Empirical and philosophical investigations* (pp. 43–60). Cham: Palgrave Macmillan.

Kristensen, D. B., & Ruckenstein, M. (2018). Co-evolving with self-tracking technologies. *New Media and Society, 20*(10), 3624–3640. doi: 10.1177/1461444818755650

Lupton, D. (2013). *Digitized health promotion: Personal responsibility for health in the Web 2.0 era*. Sydney Health & Society Group Working Paper N°5. Retrieved from https://ses.library.usyd.edu.au/handle/2123/9190

Lupton, D. (2014). Self-tracking modes: Reflexive self-monitoring and data practices. Paper, 'Imminent citizenships: Personhood and identity politics in the informatics age' workshop, 27 August 2014, ANU, Canberra, Australia. Retrieved from https://papers.ssrn.com/sol3/papers.cfm?abstract_id=2483549

Lupton, D. (2015). Lively data, social fitness and biovalue: The intersections of health self-tracking and social media. In Preprint chapter, J. Burgess et al. (Eds.), *The Sage handbook on social media*. London: Sage. Retrieved from https://papers.ssrn.com/sol3/papers.cfm?abstract_id=2666324

Lupton, D. (2016). The diverse domains of quantified selves: Self-tracking modes and dataveillance. *Economy and Society, 45*(1), 101–122.

Lupton, D. (2017). Data thing-power: How do personal digital data come to matter? Retrieved from https://papers.ssrn.com/sol3/papers.cfm?abstract_id=2998571

Lupton, D. (2019). Toward a more-than-human analysis of digital health: Inspirations from feminist new materialism. *Qualitative Health Research, 29*(14), 1998–2009. doi: 10.1177/1049732319833368

Lynskey, D. (2019). The tech industry's disregard for privacy relies on the consent of its customers. *New Statesman*. Retrieved from https://www.newstatesman.com/science-tech/social-media/2019/06/tech-industry-s-disregard-privacy-relies-consent-its-customers

Maturo, A., & Setiffi, F. (2016). The gamification of risk: How health apps foster self-confidence and why this is not enough. *Digitised Health, Medicine and Risk, 17*(7/8), 477–494.

Mobius, M. D. (2019). 11 surprising mobile health statistics. Retrieved from https://www.mobius.md/blog/2019/03/11-mobile-health-statistics/

Moore, P. (2018). *The quantified self in precarity: Work, technology and what counts*. London: Routledge.

Moore, P., Piwek, L., & Roper, I. (2018). The quantified workplace: A study in self-tracking, agility and change management. In B. Ajana (Ed.), *Self-tracking* (pp. 93–110). Cham: Palgrave Macmillan.

Moore, P., & Robinson, A. (2016). The quantified self: What counts in the neoliberal workplace. *New Media & Society, 18*(11), 2774–2792.

Mulder, T. (2019). Health apps, their privacy policies and the GDPR. *European Journal of Law and Technology, 10*(1), 1–20.

Neff, G. (2017). Exploring the world of self-tracking: Who wants our data and why? In *The Oxford Internet Institute*. Retrieved from https://www.oii.ox.ac.uk/blog/exploring-the-world-of-self-tracking-who-wants-our-data-and-why/

Neff, G., & Nafus, D. (2016). *Self-tracking*. Cambridge, MA: MIT Press.

Oppenheim, S. (2019). How the corporate wellness market has exploded: Meet the latest innovators in the space. *Forbes*. Retrieved from https://www.forbes.com/sites/serenaoppenheim/2019/06/11/how-the-corporate-wellness-market-has-exploded-meet-the-latest-innovators-in-the-space/

Peckham, J. (2020). Best fitness tracker 2020: The top 10 activity bands on the planet. In *Techradar*. Retrieved from https://www.techradar.com/uk/news/wearables/10-best-fitness-trackers-1277905

Pitts, F. H., Jean, E., & Clarke, Y. (2019). Sonifying the quantified self: Rhythmanalysis and performance research in and against the reduction of life-time to labour-time. *Capital and Class, 44*(2), 219–240.

Rabinow, P. (1996). *Essays on the anthropology of reason*. Princeton, NJ: Princeton University Press.

Rand Corporation. (2013). Workplace wellness programs study: Final report. Retrieved from https://aspe.hhs.gov/system/files/pdf/76661/rpt_wellness.pdf

Rowse, L. M. (2015). *Statistics of the Self: Shaping the self through quantified self-tracking*. Scripps Senior Theses. Paper 695. Retrieved from http://scholarship.claremont.edu/cgi/viewcontent.cgi?article=1656&context=scripps_theses

Ruckenstein, M. (2014). Visualized and interacted life: Personal analytics and engagements with data doubles. *Societies, 4*(1), 68–84.

Ruckenstein, M., & Granroth, J. (2020). Algorithms, advertising and the intimacy of surveillance. *Journal of Cultural Economy, 13*(1), 12–24.

Sanders, R. (2017). Self-tracking in the digital era: Biopower, patriarchy, and the new biometric body projects. *Body & Society, 23*(1), 36–63.

Shin, G., & Jarrahi, M. (2014). Studying the role of wearable health-tracking devices in raising users' self-awareness and motivating physical activities. Retrieved from https://wish2014.files.wordpress.com/2014/10/sub-12-shin_jarrahi_wish_workshop_paper_2014.pdf

Singer, N. (2015). Technology that prods you to take action, not just collect data. *New York Times*. Retrieved from http://www.nytimes.com/2015/04/19/technology/technology-that-prods-you-to-take-action-not-just-collect-data.html?_r=0

Sützl, W. (2016). Being with one another: Towards a media phenomenology of sharing. *APRJA*. Retrieved from https://aprja.net//article/view/116036

Sysling, F. (2019). Measurement, self-tracking and the history of science: An introduction. *History of Science, 58*(2), 103–116. doi: 10.1177/0073275319865830

Takahashi, D. (2012). Quantifying our lives will be a top trend of 2012. In *VB*. Retrieved from http://venturebeat.com/2012/01/21/quantifying-our-lives-will-be-a-top-trend-of-2012/

Till, C. (2016). Why do companies want us to be healthy? Corporate wellness, self-tracking and philanthrocapitalism. In *This is not a Sociology Blog*. Retrieved from https://christopherharpertill.wordpress.com/2016/04/06/why-do-companies-want-us-to-be-healthy-corporate-wellness-self-tracking-and-philanthrocapitalism/

Till, C. (2019) Creating 'automatic subjects': Corporate wellness and self-tracking. *Health, 23*(4), 418–435.

Timan, T., & Albrechtslund, A. (2018). Surveillance, self and smartphones: Tracking practices in the nightlife. *Science and Engineering Ethics, 24*, 853–870.

Valle, C. G., & Gibbon, S. (2015). Introduction: Health/illness, biosocialities and culture. In *SciELO.org*. Retrieved from http://www.scielo.br/scielo.php?script=sci_arttext&p id=S1809-43412015000100067

Van Den Eede, Y. (2015). Tracing the tracker: A postphenomenological inquiry into self-tracking technologies. In R. Rosenberger & P. P. Verbeek (Eds.), *Postphenomenological investigations: Essays on human–technology relations* (pp. 143–158). Lanham: Lexington Books.

Verbeek, P. P. (2005). *What things do – Philosophical reflections on technology, agency, and design*. Pennsylvania: Penn State University Press.

Verbeek, P. P. (2008). Cyborg intentionality: Rethinking the phenomenology of human–technology relations. *Phenomenology and the Cognitive Sciences, 7*(3), 387–395.

Verbeek, P. P. (2011). *Moralising technology, understanding and designing the morality of things*. London: University of Chicago Press.

Verbeek, P. P. (2015). Beyond interaction: A short introduction to mediation theory. *Interactions, 22*(3), 26–31.

Wadyka, S. (2020). Are workplace wellness programs a privacy problem? In *Consumer Reports*. Retrieved from https://www.consumerreports.org/health-privacy/are-workplace-wellness-programs-a-privacy-problem/

Wenger-Trayner, E., & Wenger-Trayner, B. (2015). Communities of practice: A brief introduction. Retrieved from https://wenger-trayner.com/wp-content/uploads/2015/04/07-Brief-introduction-to-communities-of-practice.pdf

Whitson, J. R. (2013). Gaming the quantified self. *Surveillance and Society, 11*(1/2), 163–176. Retrieved from https://ojs.library.queensu.ca/index.php/surveillance-and-society/article/view/gaming/gaming

Williams, S. (2016). Fitbit's dominance in wearables market remains unchallenged, Apple suffers decline. In *Channel Life*. Retrieved from https://channellife.co.nz/story/fitbits-dominance-wearables-market-remains-unchallenged-apple-suffers-decline

Wolf, G. (2010). The data-driven life. *The New York Times*. Retrieved from http://www.nytimes.com/2010/05/02/magazine/02self-measurement-t.html?_r=0

Chapter 6

Whose Bodies? Approaching the Quantified Menstruating Body Through a Feminist Ethnography

Amanda Karlsson

Abstract

Studies on the socio-technical relations between bodies and self-tracking apps have become more relevant as the number of digital solutions for monitoring our bodies are increasing and becoming even more embedded in our everyday lives. While a strong body of literature within the fields of self-tracking and the quantified self has evolved during the recent years, the author suggests it is time we (once again) start paying attention to the specific bodies in question when we look into the quantification of bodies, particularly about the question as to whose bodies are we talking about when we say, 'quantified bodies'. The author also proposes that, when discussing the quantification of bodies, we take interest in the bodies designing, producing, and guiding the logic behind the algorithms embedded in the technological solutions in question. By suggesting this focus on bodies as knowledge producing, the author draws from a feminist perspective of situated knowledges (Haraway 1988; Harding, 1986, 2004) with a particular interest in knowledge production and the understanding of bodies as active, epistemological objects. Feminist theory of science replaces, so to speak, the idea of a universal human identity with a knowing subject who can occupy many different positions – in co-creative and transforming constellations. Following this line of thought, all kinds of knowledge production must be bodily anchored and situated. However, knowledge production always takes place in *relation* to or with something/someone else/other. As explained by philosopher Rosi Braidotti '[t]he post-human knowing subject has to be understood as a relational embodied and embedded, affective and accountable entity and not only as a transcendental

The Quantification of Bodies in Health: Multidisciplinary Perspectives, 119–134
Copyright © 2022 by Amanda Karlsson
Published under an exclusive license by Emerald Publishing Limited
doi:10.1108/978-1-80071-883-820211011

consciousness' (Braidotti, 2018, p. 1). Thus, the bodies in this chapter are the bodies who menstruate. The author wishes to discuss a particular socio-technical relation between smartphone applications (apps) to track and monitor the female cycle; period-apps, and the menstruating bodies engaging with these apps. Building on early feminist thoughts from the science and technology studies (STS), the author seeks to move beyond the algorithmic quantification of bodies to study the network of knowledge production formed by bodies, materialities, technology and history with all its reminiscence of stigma and taboo surrounding these leaking bodies (Shildrich, 1999). These inquiries are not only theoretical accounts but are also rooted in empirical soil. Based on a feminist ethnography of Danish women's everyday engagement with period-apps, the female developers from the Femtech-industry and the women-only groups within the quantified self-movement, the author aims to provide a broad perspective on what the author defines as the *gendered data body*. The author argues for a feminist approach to better understand the socio-technical relations and the socio-cultural discourses the menstruating body is situated in, as well as to better understand the unique relation between knowledge production and technology as being constitutional for the gendered data body.

Keywords: Feminist STS; self-tracking; period-tracker; knowledge production; menstruation; quantification

> Technology is not neutral. We're inside of what we make, and it's inside of us. We're living in a world of connections – and it matters which ones get made and unmade. (Donna Haraway cited in Kunzru, 1997)

In the development of self-tracking technologies, norms and values have seeped in between decisions and solutions. These norms and values are expressed in the intended use and in the marketing of technological devices. Thus, technology is political and can have an impact on societal change, or it can affirm an existing culture and view of humanity. The latter can be seen in a number of the available period-apps, which are full of flowers and butterflies, presenting a narrative about menstruation as a fairy tale for girls in kindergarten. But it can also be seen more subtly in the period-apps that have a strong focus on fertility and thus assume that all women who menstruate want to know when they are fertile. 'Technology is not neutral', says Donna Haraway, and she is right. Because behind the algorithms, the great designs, and the affordances we embed in our everyday lives are people with visions, ideas, and beliefs about concepts such as bodies, health, and gender. Thus, technologies are a good way of looking at normativities, and this is also the case with period-apps. It matters which connections are made, and it matters which stories are told. I suggest we re-imagine the idea of self-tracking as an individual practice and instead look at the communal aspects and potentials that self-tracking holds. However, we can only do so by paying attention to the specific bodies in question when we say *quantified bodies*. This chapter is about bodies who menstruate and who are using and producing technologies to navigate the menstrual cycle. In other words – or in Haraway's words – this chapter is based on connections made between women engaging with self-tracking technologies.

The Quantified Menstruating Bodies

In recent years, a growing amount of feminist research on women's health has begun confronting both political status quo in the design process (Brewer, Kaye, Williams, & Wyche, 2006; Light, 2011) and taboo and stigma surrounding women's bodies (Balaam et al., 2017; Bardzell, 2010; Bardzell & Bardzell, 2011a, 2011b; Eaglin & Bardzell, 2011; Søndergaard & Koefoed, 2016). The old stigma of menstruation, reproduction and sexuality is challenged by these scholars, and the story about women's sexuality and women's embodiment is told differently. By critiquing epistemologies and core assumptions within technological solutions (Wajcman, 1991) and design (Goodall, 1983), feminism can give voice to a different story by challenging the great narratives. By using the speculum as an example of a completely stagnated development within reproduction and contraceptives, one study emphasises how research on women's reproductive health lacks development and vision (Almeida, Comber, & Balaam, 2016). However, things have slowly started to change with the rise of the Femtech,[1] providing the market with many solutions targeted at women's health. Research points out that it is primarily women who download self-tracking health apps (Fox & Duggan, 2013), and a recent qualitative study about women's engagement with digital health technologies concludes that women are both digitally engaged patients and digitally engaged care takers (Lupton & Maslen, 2018). Research examining engagement with digital health technologies from a gender perspective and looking at the use of gender-specific apps is evolving, asking questions such as: How are women beginning to think about their bodies in the process of quantification? And do they trust data over embodied knowledge? Critical reviews of fertility and sexual performance apps question the normative stereotypes and assumptions about women and men as reproductive and sexual subjects that these apps suggest as well as the constantly disrupting app notifications of future bleeding days reminding women to control their bodies (Lupton, 2014; Lupton & Pedersen, 2015). Not all women track their menstrual cycle to become pregnant and would therefore prefer to be able to switch off notifications about ovulation (Epstein et al., 2017). Another study found similar issues with apps leaving no room for non-normative gender identities, women experiencing irregular periods or women struggling with infertility (Figueiredo, Caldeira, Eikey, Mazmanian, & Chen, 2018; Gambier-Ross, McLernon, & Morgan, 2018).

Other studies suggest that women track their cycle for various other reasons associated with menstrual stigma (Karlsson, 2019). Some track their sexual activity to have a 'written proof' of a healthy relationship (Epstein et al., 2017). Based

---

[1]Femtech is a term, coined by period tracker Clue's CEO, Ida Tin in 2013, describing an industry of software solutions to monitor and navigate women's health digitally.

on a systematic evaluation of the functionality accuracy and features of more than 100 free menstrual cycle tracking apps, one study concludes that most of the free smartphone apps for tracking menstruation appear to be inaccurate (Moglia, Nguyen, Chyjek, Chen, & Castano, 2016). From a speculative design perspective, another study investigates the mediating ability of self-tracking technologies to track and support the flux and changing body that most women experience, which are factors that have been historically used as a tool for subjugation (Homewood, 2018). All the issues listed above touch upon ancient theoretical accounts of the female body and emphasise how studying self-tracking of the body calls for a concept that can admit of the interplay between a human being's embodied experience and the ideological and practical systems that seek to define that body.

Theorising Bodies

A man has a body, a woman *is* her body. Still, even though the woman is historically viewed as bodily anchored, as *being* her body and thus more *natural* than the man, the woman's body is also feared because it is perceived as boundless and uncontrollable. Therefore, this marginalised, different and slightly dangerous body has, to a greater extent, been subjected to the investigative gaze which has also given rise to oppression of the female body and the need to try to control it (Shildrick & Price, 1999, p. 3). The female body has become 'the other body' – the other sex, as famously described by Simone de Beauvoir in her work *Le deux-ième sexe* (1949). This body-rooted 'otherness' has made feminist theorists and thinkers throughout history anxious to define the female body simply out of fear of succumbing to essentialism and to a pure biological reading of the body. To achieve equality between the sexes, feminist thinkers have tried to go *beyond* the body, erase the differences and escape biological influence. And instead, the potential of the woman as an intellectual organ has been investigated and pursued to achieve the same status as man (Shildrick & Price, 1999). Nevertheless, the body is an obvious starting point for a feminist ontology, since body and corporeality have historically been a strong counterpoint to the Cartesian dualism mindset in which body and spirit have been separated. Thus, feminist theory of the body is a confrontation with the traditional Western philosophical notions of reason and nature, which postulates that everything that has to do with rationality and reason is distinctly masculine, and everything that has to do with nature, body and matter is distinctly feminine. Feminist thinkers throughout the late eighties and nineties, the so-called third wave, wanted to remove the divide between nature and culture, between the artificial and the organic, and reinstall bodily, materiality and lived bodies in feminist theory without submitting to biological reductionism. Donna Haraway (1991), Judith Butler (1993) and Elizabeth Grosz (1994) all take the body as the starting point for their analysis. From different perspectives, they try to rise above essentialist interpretations of the body. Butler reduces the body to be culturally constituted, as performative actions are constantly repeated. According to Butler, the boundaries of the body, its surface, are constructed and constantly interpreted through cultural meanings and understandings. Gender is something we 'do', not something we 'are'. In doing so, Butler also challenges the concept of 'woman'. Haraway cannot determine the social position of the body in a power relationship because she does not prioritise the human subject over other species. However, Haraway sees the body as an active, epistemological object, and she insists that all objectivity is bodily anchored – situated – in the eye that sees (Haraway, 1991). Unlike Butler, Grosz insists on the biological difference between the sexes. Grosz rejects a constructionist gender theory and professes the post-constructionist gender-theoretical direction. Like the other two, Grosz also focusses on materiality, corporeality, which she regards as central to her study, because 'the body must be seen as capable of doing much more than culture allows' (Grosz, 1994, p. 84). By insisting on seeing the subject as bodily, we can, according to Grosz, never succumb to dualism. If, on the other hand, we try to write off the significance of the body for the creation of the subject, in this case the gendered differences, then we have lost. Other scholars of feminist studies have addressed the issues of 'matter' that call for a different ontological approach, where matter, biology and bodies are not merely constituted as products of discursive practices or social constructs (Butler, 1993) but are in fact worldly phenomena (Barad, 2003; Fausto-Sterling, 2000; Frost, 2011). (New) materialism is not just about acknowledging and accounting for non-human actors when studying, for instance, digital assemblages (Fox & Alldred, 2017; Lupton, 2018). It is also about the network created between and with both humans and non-humans. It is about knowledge translation, and it is about uniting and about becoming. Thus, new materialism becomes a new way of thinking qualitative research. Posing questions such as: What counts as knowledge? Who/what can render herself/ it knowledgeable? And who will benefit from that knowledge? In the following, I will look into how knowledge, technology and gender intersect and what it means for women's engagement with self-tracking technologies.

Perspectives on Gender and Technology

Research on the relationship between gender and technology has been focussing on how different gender perceptions and gender stereotypes are inscribed in technology, but also how technology disrupts, reinforces, or changes perceptions and systems around gender. Common to much of the literature that emerged through the 1980s was a desire to change and create a more balanced and equal world. Mostly, it was expressed as better conditions for women, but also a desire for a much higher degree of involvement in the sciences (Adam, 1998; Harding, 1986; Johnson, D. 2010; Wajcman, 2010). Wajcman puts it this way:

> Rather than asking how women can be more equitably treated within and by science, the question became how a science apparently so deeply involved in distinctively masculine projects can possibly be used for emancipatory ends. (Wajcman, 2010, p. 146)

Throughout history, technology has been associated with the masculine, and in the definition of technological solutions, knowledge and artefacts associated with women have been overlooked. The question of whether a technology, in casu a period app, is a tool for emancipation, or whether it is (yet) another patriarchal tool for reproductive control, resonates with the debates around the development and introduction of new reproductive technologies (Adrian, 2015). In 1970, radical feminist Shulamith Firestone introduced the idea of the artificial uterus as the only way to eliminate the difference between the sexes. This created a stir among other radical feminists, who criticised Firestone's perspective for being just another way for patriarchy to control the female reproductive body. What these technophile and technophobic positions had in common is that they were preoccupied with breaking down the patriarchal system of power (Adrian, 2015, p. 55) and creating a more balanced world. So, technologies are indeed a good way of looking at normativities. When we look at technologies, at how they are used, and how and where they are situated – also historically – it becomes clear which norms are dominating in society, and which connections are made and unmade. The introduction of new technologies, like self-tracking apps, can say something about our current time. The relationship between gender and technology, as well as the relationship between technology and society, is constituted as '… an ongoing process of mutual shaping over time and across multiple sites' (Wajcman, 2010, p. 150). Feminist research in the intersection between body and technology suggests alternative perspectives and ways of conceptualising the female body, other than medical and aesthetic perspectives. One of the most influential contributions in this matter is Haraway's cyborg figure (2004) that not only dismantles bodily biological origins, but also illustrates the enormous influence tech-culture has on us now and even back then in the budding, postmodern times when the manifesto was written. Both then and today, the cyborg provides an excellent vision of how we co-create with technology, and how it helps to expand and change how we define and conceptualise bodies. The boundaries between nature and culture as well as human and non-human are blurred, and the cyborg '… opened up new possibilities for feminist analyses to explore the ways in which women's lives are intimately entwined with technologies' (Wajcman, 2010, p. 148).

Precisely a certain scepticism in relation to conceptual categories and dichotomies – and a preoccupation with practices, things and places – characterises science and technology studies (STS). Feminist contributions to STS research are also preoccupied with science and technology and their interaction with society. Both STS and feminist STS are focussed on 'core interests and problems rather than disciplinary canons, and comprise an open-ended and heterodox body of work' (Suchman, 2008, p. 140). Research within STS is interested in the fragmentation of the 'couples' of culture and nature, discursivity and materiality, human and non-human. What becomes particularly significant in feminist STS is the attention to the hegemonic conditions that lurk in these 'couples.' One quickly observes that it is the first term that is considered the privileged one. Bearing in mind that the woman is reduced to body (nature) and man to thought (culture), and that the body is consistently under-prioritised, or completely absent in traditional Western philosophical thinking, this observation becomes central to the argument for a feminist contribution to the study of technology – the design and development of it, the use of it and also the critique of it. As Wajcman puts it:

While it is not always possible to specify in advance the characteristics of artefacts and information systems that would guaran-
tee more inclusiveness, it is imperative that women are involved
throughout the processes and practices of technological innovation. (Wajcman, 2010, p. 150)

Whose bodies are technologies designed for? Feminist activist and journal-
ist Caroline Criado-Perez outlines several valid examples of why the absence of
(female) bodies in product development, artificial intelligence and design processes is problematic. The concept of the universal body can have fatal consequences for those bodies who do not fit into the physical measures of a male body.
Bulletproof vests designed for a body without breasts, women with incipient cardiac arrest who are not discovered and rescued in time because we only know the
symptoms of cardiac arrest from a male body to name a few (Criado-Perez, 2019).
Two decades earlier, Alison Adam examined the epistemological basics of artificial intelligence. Adam demonstrates how these epistemological starting points
are deeply rooted in an old Western philosophical position on human intelligence.
Adam questions Allen Newell's Human Problem Solving (SOAR) project, where
the empirical material behind the project was 'unspecified subjects,' who later
turned out to be male, white college students (see Adam, 1998, p. 94 and Hackett,
Amsterdamska, Lynch, & Wajcman, 2008, p. 143). Adam starts an important critique of the epistemological starting point for knowledge production and thus the
necessity of a feminist theoretical contribution to AI and robot research (Hackett
et al., 2008). These accounts of recent and prior origin emphasise the importance
of situated knowledges (Haraway, 1988), meaning that all knowledge must be
bodily grounded. In continuation of the women's movement and the liberation
process in the early seventies, where women insisted on the right to knowledge
about their own bodies, the need for a new knowledge paradigm arises – a rene-
gotiation of *who can know* and who has the right to knowledge. With the establishment of a new understanding of knowledge as anchored in the subject – the
body – the idea of the universal point from which all knowledge springs disappears. As a direct critique of and response to the idea of pure objectivity, feminist
standpoint theory puts the subjective practice of all knowledge production in
the foreground (Haraway, 1988; Harding, 1986, 2004). Feminist theory of science replaces, so to speak, the idea of a universal human identity with a knowing
subject that can occupy many different positions in co-creative and transforming
constellations (Adam, 1998; Haraway, 1988). The knowledge in this chapter is
not detached but has clear subjective anchors in the bodies that have produced it.
Knowledge takes its starting point in the female body as a knowledge-producing
materiality. In the following, I will outline the empirical material – the specific
bodies in question.

Methods and Material

In addition to the theoretical accounts outlined above, this chapter also draws
from empirical sources including interviews and observations I conducted

Table 6.1.   Overview of Collection of Empirical Material.

Interviews with 15 Danish App Users (Aged 18–49)	Interviews with Three Female App Developers	Observation Study and Interviews with Women
Conducted in Denmark 2017–2019	Conducted via Skype, Jitsi 2018–2019	Conducted at the QS Conference in Amsterdam in 2017
To acquire knowledge on motives behind digital self-tracking of the menstrual cycle	To acquire knowledge on considerations regarding the development of apps for tracking women's bodies	To acquire knowledge on how the QS and QSXX meetings function

between 2017 and 2019. Table 6.1 serves as an overview of how, when and why the empirical material was collected.

The 15 Danish women were recruited between 2017 and 2019 via Facebook and Twitter. I was sampling for what I define as 'experienced menstruators'; women who have had some years of experience with a menstruating body (Karlsson, 2019). Sexual orientation and ethnicity were not selection criteria in this study. I did not ask my interviewees about them either; however, throughout the individual interviews, eight of my interviewees referred to their male partners, one refereed to her female partner, and the rest did not refer to a partner or to their sexual orientation. Who is a woman? This continues to be an important question discussed in post-colonial and queer-feminist literature in particular.[2] A future study could definitely benefit from a higher degree of diversity in the sampling process and from considering the question of 'who is a woman'. I am thus aware that my knowledge is also situated – being a white, cis-gendered, heterosexual, well-educated and menstruating 42-year-old woman. My perspective does not pretend to be conclusive, as it is my perspective based on my choices in interaction with my empirical material.

Knowledge-producing Bodies

Knowledge production always takes place in *relation* to or with someone/something else. As explained by Braidotti:

---

[2]For feminist theory to have impact, it has been of great importance to have the common concept 'woman' as a starting point for transforming the private into political actions. However, the second wave of feminists' idea of a 'global sisterhood' was critiqued for being an extremely white, middle-class sisterhood. These essentialist notions of 'woman' were challenged mainly by feminists of colour not feeling included in the sisterhood of second-wave feminists, simply because they felt various factors of suppression other than being a woman; the women shared a gender perspective but were separated by racial privilege (Hooks, 1981; Hill-Collins, 2000).

[t]he post-human knowing subject has to be understood as a
relational embodied and embedded, affective and accountable
entity and not only as a transcendental consciousness. (Braidotti,
2018, p. 1)

My study has shown that embodied knowledge from self-tracking practices
does not stay bound to the individual. Knowledge is shared, distributed, discussed and debated. It travels across countries from body to body; from developer
to end-user; from interviewee to me as a researcher. In one interview, I wanted to
show my interviewee how the tracking of premenstrual symptoms (PMS) works
in Clue, and while we were both looking, my cycle appeared in Clue's interface on
my smartphone, and my interviewee suddenly burst out: Oh, you are experiencing PMS right now, I couldn't even tell, are you feeling okay? Another woman
shared with me how I could customise the notifications in my app, so instead
of 'your PMS is on its way', it would notify me with 'hey sexy – you look awe-
some'. This communal feeling and the sharing of knowledge about how to use
technology to navigate the female cycle have emancipatory potential to challenge
the cultural and historical stigma around the menstruating body. Still, the device
has a central function in the sharing of stories; the app is the mediator and thus
it matters where it comes from and what kind of stories it is shaped by. When it
comes to digital solutions for tracking various bodily matters, we know they are
designed and shaped based on certain cultural beliefs and within specific social
and cultural contexts and often with a specific group of users in mind (Light,
Burgess, & Duguay, 2018; MacKenzie & Wajcman, 1985; Wajcman, 1991). For
the app developers I have interviewed, it is obvious that it is about giving women
a voice, or 'to create a more balanced world' (Tin, Clue). It is about making room
for *other bodies* and making it possible to be in the world with the full story about
those bodies. Something we have witnessed before during the women's movement
in the late sixties.

Our Bodies, Ourselves has served as a way for women, across eth-
nic, racial, religious and geographical boundaries, to start examining their health from a perspective that will bring about change.
The change begins within the individual, who then brings about
effective community change. The struggle continues. La lucha
continua. (Boston Women's Health Book Collective (BWHBC),
1998, p. 15)

In 1969, the BWHBC met for the first time, and since then the book, and
the knowledge it holds, has travelled across countries informing women about
women's health. The women from the collective wanted to shift the power balance regarding knowledge about their health, their bodies – from being in the
hands of mainly male doctors to being in their own hands– and to take back
their embodied selves. What we see now in the Femtech-industry are examples of
women taking back knowledge and entering a male-dominated area to be part of
designing and developing digital solutions for women's health. I have conducted

interviews with three women from the industry who each started their business because they were looking for a (digital) solution they could not find, and then they decided to develop it:

> It makes a difference if your experiences with breast pumps have been so horrible that you feel motivated to start a company that develops better breast pumps. Or if you have already built 20 apps and can see an opportunity to build another one just for the profit. Those are two very different starting points. (Ida Tin, Clue)

It matters where we are situated, who we are, what motivations and stories we are shaped by, which connections are made and unmade. 'It matters what stories make worlds, what worlds make stories' (Haraway, 2016, p. 2). In the QSXX, women discuss and debate various matters related to their bodies (e.g. hormones, diets, menstrual cycle, fertility), sharing knowledge and trying to learn from each other's experiences in a women-only forum. One of the founders of the QSXX in New York describes that the motivation for starting the women-only meetings was to create a space where one could speak openly about specific bodily matters without the interference of men. She describes how the QSXX started as 'a free and safe space for conversation' whereas regular QS is a space for 'showing and presenting your results' (QSXX organiser in New York). And that emphasises the fundamental difference between the two settings. One of the women I met at the conference in Amsterdam told me about her first experience presenting in the QS scene:

> I thought about what it would be like to talk about my tracking in a 'show and tell'.[3] Obviously, I have a visible body and that is how I get to places, right, but I couldn't imagine getting up in front of a bunch of people and talking about that body. In a context where I have to be professional and wanting people to take me seriously you know? I couldn't find a way around my female, readily objective, viable body. (Woman, QS)

Referring to her body as something she 'could not find a way around' in a setting where she had to 'be professional' stresses the historical notions of her *being* her body to an extent where she cannot distance herself from that body and look at it as an object of study. That supports the reasons why the QSXX was formed – to create a place for specific bodies. It also, quite sadly, supports the idea of women's bodies still being surrounded by a resilient, cultural taboo (Chrisler, 2011; Chrisler, Marván, Gorman, & Rossini, 2015; Delaney, Lupton, & Toth, 1976; Phipps, 1980). And it most certainly reveals a market for apps that serve as places for women to privately engage with their menstruating bodies

---

[3] A show and tell is a seven-minute format around which each presentation in the quantified-self meetings is built up. You get seven minutes to tell what you did, how you did it, and what you have found out through your self-tracking.

(Karlsson, 2019). The question remains as to whether these apps can be used for emancipatory ends or whether they are simply capitalising on existing taboos and reproducing menstrual stigma.

The Gendered Data-body

> In terms of quantifying oneself, I think it somehow takes us out of our bodies and into the app. In that sense, I feel that it is a relief to just check the app, so I do not have to pay bodily attention – to notice my period. (Eve, aged 31)

Eve describes how the boundary between app and body is exceeded and how it is a relief that she can move her bodily attention from the body itself and into the app. Several women I interviewed described a similar dynamic in terms of 'keeping up with themselves', and that the app has opened up a new world – a deeper inner world. It is interesting how the app becomes a way to sense the body, and how it is experienced as an artefact that makes it easier to keep up with the body, the flux, the pain, and the changes throughout the cycle: 'It is as if the app brings me closer to my biological body', says Judith, aged 36. The algorithm can learn about a body and show bleeding and pain patterns based on the data it is fed. It can notify and nudge the app user to make specific choices based on these patterns. A notification on upcoming PMS (premenstrual syndrome) can potentially make the user anxious and hyperaware of her surroundings as well as her inner emotions such as mood and pain. This awareness can then make her feed the algorithm with data about her experience of PMS that she just became aware of – and then the feedback loop begins! App notifications and bodily experiences reinforce and reassure each other and potentially create new emotions founded in this socio-technical relationship between app and bleeding body (Karlsson & Olesen, Forthcoming). This extra dimension of body that the algorithm co-creates, and what I define as the *gendered data-body*, is not really the body, but it is not *not* the body either. The algorithm functions as a validation of what is already bodily experienced; it reassures embodied experiences. Knowledge about the menstruating body is co-produced in the assemblage of algorithm (and the company behind the app) and body. Still, the algorithm does not know menstruation in its material form – the shedding of the uterine lining and the pain involved in that process. It may foresee the time of the process, but it cannot know the process itself. To fully understand menstruation, we need to understand it on a much deeper level than an algorithm is capable of, since the concept of menstrual blood is not just shaped by the biological matter but also by culture.

The Configuration of Menstruation

Historically, the blood carries with it references to both life and death. The blood is purity, life and beginning, but the blood is also dirty, death and ending. Menstrual blood is not life-giving or pure, but rather the proof of a life that did not become. Semen that went to waste. Something abject:

Not me. Not that. But not nothing, either. A 'something' that I do
not recognize as a thing. (Kristeva, 1982, p. 2)

According to the French philosopher Julia Kristeva, menstrual blood is part
of what we understand as the abject. Menstrual blood – the abject – is neither
a subject nor recognisable as an object. The abject is the fluid, boundless, the
balance between the subject and the object; it has been a part of me, but as it
leaves my body it becomes something else, which is in the void between 'inside'
and 'out' of the body (Kristeva, 1982). I find Kristeva's understanding of and
use of the term 'the abject' relevant in a study of what the menstrual blood itself
means for menstruation; which potential agency has the blood in our relation to
the menstruating body and not least to the app, where the amount of bleeding
can be tracked? Kristeva describes abjection as the process by which the subject
distances itself from that which can potentially harm it. Following Kristeva, the
interesting thing about seeing menstrual blood as the abject is also that it is what
fundamentally separates the woman from the man and thus constitutes the most
fundamental biological difference between the two sexes. Anthropologist Marilyn
Strathern describes in her famous ethnographic text about the Mount Hagen people of New Guinea (1972) how children from an early age are told that when their
mothers menstruate, it is as if her whole body is smeared with faeces or poison.
Children thus associate menstruation with something dangerous and disgusting –
long before they know what it really means (Strathern, 1972, p. 173). Twenty years
later, Sophie Laws writes about men's attitude towards menstruation. Laws builds
her study on interviews with Western men and sheds light on how stories and
especially jokes about menstruation are adopted from an early age and often used
by boys without them really knowing what they are referring to (Laws, 1990). In
my interviews it also emerged, both explicitly and more subtly, that avoiding stu-
pid, derogatory remarks is a good reason to navigate one's period in an app and
not in a shared online calendar or another 'publicly' accessible medium (Karlsson, 2019). Quantifying the menstrual abject blood also becomes a Cartesian
cleansing of the dirty and tabooed, which in its computerised and datafied form
is transformed to be pure and free of stigma (Søndergaard, 2016). Although the
blood was remarkably absent in my interviews – with both the users and the producers of apps, it could be read between the lines how the menstrual blood brings
with it grief, shame and hope throughout a woman's life. The menarche, which
marks the transition from girl to woman, is both a day of joy and a reminder to be
careful not to become pregnant. Later in life, the absence of blood may manifest
itself as fear of being pregnant, or the opposite, when the blood suddenly appears
and announces that a pregnancy is lost or never was. Then the menopause, which
marks the transition from fertile to non-fertile – the aging female body, which in
a youth-fixated culture is neither welcome nor appreciated (Chrisler, 2011). When
we begin to understand menstruation as a configuration of both matter and culture, we also begin to understand why there is a market for period-apps in the first
place. However, to dismiss these technologies as being nothing but subjugating
tools reproducing stigma, before looking into their unifying potentials to disman-
tle that exact same stigma, would be a mistake.

If the 'good ones' don't want to enter this industry then we have lost twice. Then we have lost the opportunity we had to do something great and we have lost it to those who don't care about ethics and only want to exploit. (Ida Tin, CEO, Clue)

Conclusion

Whose bodies are we talking about when we say quantified bodies? If we acknowledge that all knowledge is situated, bodily anchored, located in a specific body, then we must include the bodies guiding the logic behind the algorithms. We must show an interest in what stories, beliefs and values shape these bodies and how this can be seen in the technologies at hand. In this chapter, I have tried to look at various positions from which knowledge is produced and shared in gendered technology. How using period apps can be a way of reclaiming bodily knowledge – making the private political (again) by raising awareness of women's health through the Femtech-industry and collectively initiating cultural change by destigmatising menstruation and women's bodies. Knowledge is situated and shared in many ways. Women designing for women, women meeting and sharing in QSXX groups, the period app initiating the sharing of knowledge between individual women. The gendered data-body, then, is not just the representation of the fleshly body. Not simply numbers representing and notifying women of future bleeding days and upcoming PMS. The gendered data-body is constituted by many entities; the app user herself, the algorithm, the designers behind the algorithm and the app, the blood, the stigma surrounding menstruation and the culture that maintains that stigma. It is the connections made and the stories told. Through various sources of empirical material, I have explored how these tools for sharing knowledge and re-producing knowledge on women's bodies initiate communal activities and aspects. Are the women engaging with these self-tracking technologies initiating a new (techno-feminist) movement? Maybe. Does this sharing of embodied knowledge have the potential to create cultural change? Definitely.

References

Adam, A. (1998). *Artificial knowing: Gender and the thinking machine.* London: Routledge.

Adrian, S. (2015). Assisteret befrugtning, en feministisk teoretisk udfordring? *Kvinder, Køn & Forskning, 3*, 51–65.

Almeida, T., Comber, R., & Balaam, M. (2016). "HCI and Intimate Care as an Agenda for Change in Women's Health", *CHI* San Jose CA, USA.

Balaam, M., Hansen, I. K., D'Ignazio, C. Simpson, E., Almeida, T., Kuznetsov, S., Catt, M., Søndergaard, M. L. (2017). "Hacking Women's Health", *CHI 2017*, May 6–11, 2017, Denver, CO, USA.

Barad, (2003). Posthumanist Performativity: Toward an Understanding of How Matter Comes to Matter. *Signs: Journal of Women in Culture and Society, 28*(3).

Bardzell, S. (2010). Feminist HCI. In *Proceedings of the 28th international conference on Human factors in computing systems – CHI '10*, Atlanta, Georgia, USA.

Bardzell, J., & Bardzell, S. (2011a). Pleasure is your birthright: Digitally enabled designer sex toys as a case of third-wave HCI. In *Proceedings of the SIGCHI conference on human factors in computing systems (CHI 2011)*, Vancouver, BC, Canada (pp. 257–266).

Bardzell, S., & Bardzell, F. (2011b). Towards a Feminist HCI Methodology: Social science, feminism, and HCI. In *SIGCHI conference on human factors in computing systems (CHI'11)* (pp. 675–684).

Beauvoir, S. (1949). *Le deuxième sexe*. Paris: Editions Gallimard.

Boston Women's Health Book Collective (BWHBC). (1998). *Our bodies, ourselves for the new century: A book by and for women*. New York, NY: Simon & Schuster.

Braidotti, R. (2018). A theoretical framework for the critical posthumanities. *Theory, Culture & Society*, *0*(0), 1–31.

Brewer, J. Kaye, J., Williams, A., & Wyche, S. (2006). Sexual interactions: Why we should talk about sex in HCI. *Ext. Abstracts CHI 2006*, ACM Press.

Butler, J. (1993). *Bodies that matter – On the discursive limits of "sex"*. London: Routledge.

Chrisler, J. (2011). Leaks, lumps and lines: Stigma and women's bodies. *Psychology of Women Quarterly*, *35*(2), 202–214.

Chrisler, J., Marván, M., Gorman, J., & Rossini, M. (2015). Body appreciation and attitudes toward menstruation. *Body Image*, *12*, 78–81.

Criado-Perez, C. (2019). *Invisible women: Exposing data bias in a world designed for men*. London: Chatto & Windus.

Delaney, J., Lupton, M., & Toth, E. (1976). *The curse: A cultural history of menstruation* (1st ed.). New York, NY: Dutton, cop.

Eaglin, A., & Bardzell, S. (2011). Sex toys and designing for sexual wellness. In *Proceedings of the 2011 annual conference on human factors in computing systems*, Vancouver, BC, Canada (pp. 1837–1842).

Epstein, D., Lee, N., Kang, J., Agapie, E., Schroeder, J., Pina, L., ... Munson, S. (2017). Examining menstrual tracking to inform the design of personal informatics tools. *chi2017*.

Fausto-Sterling, A. (2000). *Sexing the body: Gender, politics and the construction of sexuality*. New York, NY: Basic books.

Figueiredo, M., Caldeira, C., Eikey, E., Mazmanian, M., & Chen, Y. (2018). Engaging with health data: The interplay between self-tracking and emotions in fertility struggles. In *Proceedings of the ACM on human-computer interaction*, Vol. 2, CSCW, Article 40, New York, United States.

Firestone, S. (1970). *The dialectic of sex: The case for feminist revolution*. New York, NY: William Morrow and Company.

Fox, N., & Alldred, P. (2017). *Sociology and the new materialism – Theory research action*. London: SAGE.

Fox, S., & Duggan, M. (2013). "Tracking for Health", *Pew Research Center, California Health Care Foundation*.

Frost, S. (2011). *The implications of the new materialisms for feminist epistemology. Power in Knowledge*. New York, NY: Dordrecht.

Gambier-Ross, K., McLernon, D., & Morgan, H. (2018). A mixed methods exploratory study of women's relationships with and uses of fertility tracking apps. *Digital Health*, *4*, 1–15.

Goodall, P. (1996). Design and gender. In J. Bird, B. Curtis, M. Mash, T. Putnam, G. Robertson, S. Stafford, L. Tickner (Eds.), *The block reader in visual culture*. Routledge.

Grosz, E. (1994). *Volatile bodies – Towards a corporeal feminism*. Bloomington, IN: Indiana University Press.

Hackett, E., Amsterdamska, O., Lynch, M., & Wajcman, J. (2008). *The handbook of science and technology studies* (3rd ed.). London: The MIT Press.

Haraway, D. (1988). Situated knowledges: The science question in feminism and the privilege of partial perspectives. In *Feminist studies* (pp. 575–599), Feminist Studies, Inc.

Haraway, D. (1991). *Simians, cyborgs and women – The reinvention of nature.* London: Free association Books Ltd.

Haraway, D. (2004). A manifesto for cyborgs: Science, technology, and socialist feminism in the 1980s. In *The Haraway reader.* New York, NY: Routledge.

Haraway, D. (2016). *Staying with the trouble: Making kin in the chthulucene.* Durham, NC: Duke University Press.

Harding, S. (1986). *The science question in feminism.* Milton Keynes: Open University Press.

Harding, S. (2004). *Rethinking standpoint epistemology: What is strong objectivity? The Feminist Standpoint Theory Reader: Intellectual and Political Controversies.* London: Routledge.

Hill-Collins, P. (2000). *Black feminist thought: Knowledge, consciousness, and the politics of empowerment.* New York, NY: Routledge.

Homewood, S. (2018). Designing for the changing body: A feminist exploration of self-tracking technologies. *CHI'18 Extended Abstracts, April 21–26, 2018, Montreal, QC, Canada.*

Hooks, B. (1981). *Ain't I a woman: Black women and feminism.* Boston, MA: South End Press.

Johnson, D. (2010). Sorting out the question of feminist technology. In L. Linda, S. Vostral, & K. Boyer (Eds.), *Feminist technology.* University of Illinois Press.

Karlsson, A. (2019). A room of one's own? Using period-trackers to escape menstrual stigma. *Nordicom Review, 40*(s1), 111–123.

Karlsson, A., & Olesen, F. (forthcoming). Emotional engagement with technology – How women (use technology to) navigate emotions throughout their menstrual cycle.

Kristeva, J. (1982). *Powers of horror – An essay on abjection.* New York, NY: Columbia University Press.

Kunzru, H. (1997). "You are cyborg", *Wired Issue* 5.02 Feb.

Laws, S. (1990). *Issues of blood: The politics of menstruation.* London: The Macmillan Press LTD.

Light, A. (2011). HCI as heterodoxy: Technologies of identity and the queering of interaction with computers. *Interacting with Computers, 23*(5), 430–438.

Light, B., Burgess, J., & Duguay, S. (2018). The walkthrough method: An approach to the study of apps. *New Media and Society, 20*(3), 881–900.

Lupton, D. (2014). Quantified sex: A critical analysis of sexual and reproductive self-tracking using apps. *Culture, Health & Sexuality: An International Journal for Research, Intervention and Care, 17*(4), 440–453.

Lupton, D. (2018). 'I just want it to be done, done, done!' Food tracking apps, affects and agential capacities. *Multimodal Technologies and Interaction, 2*(2), 1–15.

Lupton, D. (2018). A much better person: The agential capacities of self-tracking practicies. In B. Ajana (Ed.), *Metric culture: Ontologies of self-tracking practices* (pp. 57–75). London: Emerald Publishing.

Lupton, D., & Maslen, S. (2018). The more-than-human sensorium: Sensory engagements with digital self-tracking technologies. *The Senses and Society, 13*(2), 190–202.

Lupton, D., & Pedersen, S. (2015). *What is happening to your body and your baby: Findings from an Australian survey of women's use of pregnancy and parenting apps.* News & Media Research Centre, University of Canberra, Canberra, Australia.

MacKenzie, D., & Wajcman, J. (1985). Introductory essay: The social shaping of technology. In D. MacKenzie & J. Wajcman (Eds.), *The social shaping of technology: How the refrigerator got its hum* (pp. 2–25). Milton Keynes: Open University Press.

Moglia, M., Nguyen, H., Chyjek, K., Chen, K., & Castano, P. (2016). Evaluation of smartphone menstrual cycle tracking applications using an adapted application scoring system. *Obstetrics & Gynecology, 127*(6), 1153–1160.

Phipps, W. (1980). The menstrual taboo in Judeo-Christian tradition. *Journal of Religion and Health, 19*(4), 298–303.

Shildrick, M., & Price, J. (1999). *Feminist theory and the body: A reader*. Edingburgh: Edinburgh University Press.

Søndergaard, M. L. (2016). Sharing the abject in digital culture. *Excessive Research, 5*(1).

Søndergaard, M. L., & Koefoed, L. (2016). PeriodShare: A bloody design fiction. *Proceedings NordiCHI 2016*. Extended Abstract.

Strathern, M. (1972). *Women in between: Female roles in a Male world, Mount Hagen, New Guinea*. London: Seminar Press.

Suchman, L. (2008). Feminist STS and the science of the artificial. In *The handbook of science and technology studies* (3rd ed.). London: The MIT Press.

Wajcman, J. (1991). *Feminism confronts technology*. University Park, PA: Penn State University Press.

Wajcman, J. (2010). Feminist theories of technology. *Cambridge Journal of Economics, 34*, 143–152.

Part III

Body Quantification and Mental Health

Chapter 7

#Wellness or #Hellness: The Politics of Anxiety and the Riddle of Affect in Contemporary Psy-care

Ana Carolina Minozzo

Abstract

The classification of psychological suffering stumbles on the challenge of quantifying the 'un-quantifiable' upon the systematic categorising and description of affective and mental states and their transformation into illnesses and disorders. In this chapter, the author will explore the affect of anxiety through a critical recent history of its diagnosis and treatment in the context of psychological care. By unpacking the strategies employed by mainstream psychiatry in the Diagnostic and Statistical Manual of Mental Disorders (DSM), published by the American Psychiatric Association since the mid-twentieth century, it is possible to unveil the dynamics of a reduction of the subject to a productive-biological body in the last decades. This chapter thinks through what happens to the equation 'body-world' through the critical genealogy of affect and its relation to diagnoses and treatments of anxiety and depression. It grapples with the ethics of techno-scientific global financial capitalism – heralded by pharmacological corporations and governmentality – which replicates a modern scientific view of the body, affect and suffering in a world of renewed paradigmatic demands. The author argues that by consistently pathologizing and working towards the elimination of anxiety, the hegemonic clinic erases the possibility of such 'subjective truth', reducing the subject to the status of 'dividual'.

Keywords: Anxiety; diagnosis; affect; body; the real; governmentality

The Quantification of Bodies in Health: Multidisciplinary Perspectives, 137–156
Copyright © 2022 by Ana Carolina Minozzo
Published under an exclusive license by Emerald Publishing Limited
doi:10.1108/978-1-80071-883-820211012

> *Until we can understand the assumptions in*
> *which we are drenched we cannot know ourselves.*
>
> Adrienne Rich (1968)

During the recent Covid-19 pandemic, prescriptions for antidepressant, anti-anxiety and anti-insomnia drugs were reported to have risen in 21% in the United States.[1] In the United Kingdom, early reports also suggested an increased demand between 10% and 15% for antidepressant drugs in pharmacies in the first months of the crisis.[2] The Office of National Statistics (ONS) reported that half of the British population experienced 'high anxiety' during the weeks of lockdown.[3] Anxiety, interestingly, is the sole category for measuring negativity in wellbeing in the UK since the ONS implemented such tracking in 2010, cancelling out 'happiness', 'worthwhileness' and 'life satisfaction'.[4] Whilst uncertainty, vulnerability, and stress, coupled with precarity, lace the impoverishment of overall wellbeing in critical times, what would be the line dividing a pathological disorder and a healthy, if anything, reaction to torment in light of troubling circumstances? To gauge the status and politics of the contemporary pathologising of distress and the possibilities of our relation to it, we must begin by asking other elementary questions: If anxiety is negative, then how much anxiety is too much? And how could we measure it? The classification of psychological suffering stumbles upon the challenge of quantifying the 'un-quantifiable' through the systematic categorising and description of affective and mental states and their transformation into illnesses and disorders.

In this chapter, I will explore the of anxiety through a critical recent history of its diagnosis and treatment in the context of psychological care. By unpacking the strategies employed by mainstream psychiatry in the Diagnostic and Statistical Manual of Mental Disorders (DSM), published by the American Psychiatric

---

[1]According to the Report 'America's State of Mind', published in April 2020 by the private healthcare provider Express Scripts, anti-anxiety benzodiazepines prescription rose 34% during the first month of Covid-19 crisis, whilst antidepressant SSRI/SNRI pills saw an increase in 18% of prescription filed by health care provides across the USA. Retrieved from: <https://www.express-scripts.com/corporate/americas-state-of-mind-report?mod=article_inline> [Accessed 13/05/2020].

[2]Ruchira Sharma, 'Coronavirus and Mental Health: Pharmacists are struggling to source antidepressants, after a rise in demand during lockdown'. Retrieved from: *iNews.* 4 May 2020 <https://inews.co.uk/news/health/mental-health-coronavirus-antidepressants-medication-supplies-uk-lockdown-rise-demand-2842273> [Accessed 13/05/2020].

[3]The British ONS has published Covid-19 specific research. Retrieved from: <https://www.ons.gov.uk/peoplepopulationandcommunity/wellbeing/bulletins/personalandeconomicwellbeingintheuk/may2020#elevated-levels-of-anxiety> [Accessed 13/05/2020].

[4]All of the 'wellbeing' data generated by the British ONS can be found online. Retrieved from: <https://www.ons.gov.uk/peoplepopulationandcommunity/wellbeing> [Accessed 13/05/2020].

Association (APA) since the mid-twentieth century, it is possible to unveil the dynamics of a reduction of the subject to a productive-biomedicalised body in the last five decades. Such process, as this chapter will demonstrate, echoes a mode of governance that finds its realisation not only in the clinic but also in contemporary modes of consumption and discourses and policies of wellbeing. What becomes apparent is a process of quantification, qualification, and management of affects – or, as I propose here, an affective-politics that assembles body and psyche in a particular mode of alienation.

Affects and their bodily inscription, however, seem to resist, if we follow a psychoanalytic logic, such efforts of division and, ultimately, administration of the body and psychic life towards a pharmacological productive utopia. In the specific case of anxiety, we will see its transformation from a core category of stress diagnosis to an abrupt fading in favour of a biological rise of depression as the 'illness of the century'. Such diagnostic-culture, inaugurated in the late-1970s, is framed by a logic of categorisation and control of the body, which becomes a particularly complex locus of 'dividualisation' (Deleuze, 1992) – a concept Deleuze utilised to address the mode of subjective production of the contemporary society of control – and entails a loss of the possibility of experience of subjective truth in symptoms that anchor the psychoanalytic conception of anxiety.

This chapter thinks through what happens to subjectivity, affect and its relation to diagnoses and treatments of anxiety and depression. It grapples with the ethics of techno-scientific global financial capitalism – heralded by pharmacological corporations and governmentality – which replicates a modern scientific view of the body, affect and suffering in a world of renewed paradigmatic demands. I argue that by consistently pathologising and working towards the elimination of anxiety, the hegemonic clinic erases the possibility of a 'subjective truth', reducing the subject to the status of 'dividual'. The problem I engage with addresses the question 'can the dividual speak' and, if so, is the clinic ready to listen?

Anxiety: An Affect Beyond the Mirage of the Subject

For Georges Canguilhem, what characterises a form of suffering that is 'enough of a problem' to be considered a 'pathology' comes always in contrast with an idea – or ideal – of normativity that frames the subject ideologically through ranking possibilities of recognition of such suffering (Canguilhem, 1991). Thus, there is not a 'normal' neither a 'pathological' in itself, rather, there are only these qualifications within the relation between an organism and the environment. Therefore, context and the context produced by the qualifications generated by the psychologies (and in an ample manner, the *psy-* field) are crucial elements of any interpretation over 'suffering'. In short, what Canguilhem defends is that the characterisation of what it is to suffer 'normally' or not is a producer of this very suffering too.

In another text, 'What is Psychology?,' from the late 1950s, Canguilhem adds one more layer to his critique of the 'sciences' of *psyche* by asserting that 'it is inevitable that in presenting itself as the general theory of behaviour, psychology will incorporate some idea of Man' (Canguilhem, 2016, p. 202). For this reason, he completes, 'it is necessary that we allow philosophy to question psychology about where this idea comes from, and whether it may not be, ultimately, some philosophy' (Canguilhem, 2016, p. 202). Given his proposition, we can map our field of enquiry as follows. Primarily: the context producing and qualifying suffering as well as the ideological normativity implicated when assessing this suffering – in this case, the contextualisation of anxiety as a negativity. These initial points are fundamental in the attempt of inquiring about this affect in a non-normative manner and asking what is the role of both diagnosis –in particular in its hegemonic psychiatric approach – and cultural discourses over the contemporary understanding of anxiety. That is, how diagnosis and culture produce our relation to this affect at an individual level. Secondly, there is an idea – and again, an ideal – of subjectivity predicted in the very object of psychology, and by being so, questions brought by philosophy cannot be dismissed, once it is an objectivity of the subject that is being proposed. Thus, if ever speaking of an 'anxious self' or 'anxious subject', it is necessary to make it clear what this notion of self in question is and how it is produced.

In both aspects, there is something that sets psychoanalysis apart from other psychological practices. As Foucault (2008a) questions in *Mental Illness and Psychology* (1954; revised in 1962), the limits between what is considered a 'pathology' of the organic or physical domain and the 'mental', or more subjective realm, are worked through a complementary psyche-soma that extends beyond a simple or linear 'cause and effect' relation in psychoanalysis. As an example, we could look at the early texts on hysteria written by Freud and Breuer in the seminal *Studies on Hysteria*, wherein psychological phenomena implicate the body and are implicated by the body (Breuer & Freud, 1893). More clearly, in accepting the Freudian notion of the drive (*pulsion, Trieb*, first mistranslated as 'instinct' into English), a complex interrelation of mind/body, without necessarily privileging any part over the other as such is required. This conceptual 'privileging' meaning, thus, what is still present in the organicist psychiatric discourse that locates, or better, makes attempts at locating, suffering on the brain, or treating a mental 'malaise' through a rebalancing of chemical substances, natural or not to the human organism. Psychoanalysis therefore sits in between the organic-medical discourse and a philosophical understanding of the self/subject that amplifies the understanding of a self beyond the physical body yet not transcending it completely – in the sense of a soul versus flesh narrative, that nineteenth century psychology set as the line between religion and science (Guéry & Deleule, 2014). Exploring affects under a psychoanalytic theoretical umbrella allow us to trace a cartography in which the subject is not only produced and situated in relation to certain discourses, but also functions as a reproducer and locus of embodiment of a diagnostic-culture or principles of governmentality.

In psychoanalysis, anxiety is defined as an affect, mobilising therefore 'body' and 'mind' equally. Anxiety

> includes in the first place particular motor innervations or discharges and secondly certain feelings; the latter are of two kinds – perceptions of the motor actions that have occurred and the direct

feelings of pleasure and unpleasure which, as we say, give the affect its keynote. (Freud, 1917, p. 395)

In other words, the affect of anxiety situates the subject in relation to what is beyond oneself, stretching both perception and feelings. This move or encounter with an abyss or a beyond oneself is at the centre of the unsettling, overwhelming but also creative potential of this 'exceptional affect' (Soler, 2014) that marks an appearance of what Lacan named the register of the Real. What makes anxiety really compelling also theoretically is how both Freud and Lacan have cast it as an affect of 'excess'. For Freud, as per his 1917 *Introductory Lecture* on Anxiety, anxiety is an excessive affect that escapes the ego's attempts of repressing or representing a libidinal vicissitude – castration anxiety points thus to the threat an overwhelming libido poses to the ego, which, in its turn acts as a psychic gatekeeper of stability in Freudian topology.

Lacan was rather sceptical of life under a strong and stable ego, as, to him, the ego pertained to the register of the Imaginary. The Imaginary in Lacan can be summarised as the function that offers coherence to the world 'outside' through the 'image', or the mirage of the subject. Its limits, so the limits of this anchoring 'mirage' and 'subjective coherence', are particularly relevant to the understanding of anxiety, as in anxiety the fictional character of this subjective mirage becomes evident – or better, the mirage is under threat, the abyss comes near (Lacan, 1960). For Lacan, it is in anxiety that the Real makes an 'apparition', since

anxiety highlights how much of the subject is not captured by language, or how much is left over after the most exhaustive attempts to encapsulate or represent the subject in words. (Gallagher, 1996, p. 5)

Because of its relation to the Real, anxiety points at a failure of fantasy, and this theoretical relation is developed in detail throughout Lacan's *Seminar X* on Anxiety, delivered between 1962 and 1963. Fantasy functions as a cover up for a fundamental 'structural fault' of the subject, and it fails to provide this efficient covering up in the moment of anxiety. This fact alone alludes to something beyond symbolisation, something that fails and in failing is unique to each subject that is evident in anxiety. In other words, the mirage of the subject is destabilised in anxiety. The curtain is lifted, a veil evaporates.

The psychoanalytic view of anxiety reiterates the same particular psychoanalytic understanding of the symptom and diagnosis. This means that it goes against the logic of contemporary hegemonic discourses in psychology and psychiatry, in which anxiety is treated as a generator of 'disorders' in its own right or as an isolated symptom to be 'cured' or 'managed away'. For Lacan, as much as for Freud, anxiety is not 'the problem', let alone 'a problem to be eliminated' in the search of some 'cure'. What the trail of anxiety reveals to us in the following psychosocial analysis of its journey in and out of the clinic from the mid to late twentieth century until the current moment is an affective-politics, or an affective domination, that steers the subject away from any possibility of living with their anxiety, their affects or conceiving life beyond the curtain or the veil of fantasy.

Unwanted Anxiety: The Historical Framework of Pathologising Anxiety

Twentieth century psychiatry is characterised as and effort of 'descriptive psychopathology' (Berrios, 1996) and of an aetiological mapping of discontent, suffering and illness within a system of biological and individualised causality, culminating in the DSM-III, IV and V (Rose, 2018). This debate involves complex philosophical and ideological assumptions that permeate wider discourses in psychiatry, psychologies and psychoanalysis that meet precisely at the complicated, yet often oversimplified, definition of what is normal and what is pathological in affective life. In other words, the riddle of quantifying and qualifying 'how much anxiety is too much?'

Eighteenth and early-nineteenth century medical literature discussed what were considered both 'subjective' (fear, phobia, etc.) and 'objective' (digestive, respiratory, etc.) aspects of what was later combined into the understanding of 'anxiety' disorders or symptoms as unrelated phenomena that were formative or other illnesses and of madness. In other words,

> it seems clear that, by the mid-nineteenth century, the term anxiety was used in medical writings to describe a mental state that fell within the range of normal human experiences but was able to cause or lead to disease, including insanity. (Berrios, 1996, p. 266)

It was only in the later decades of the nineteenth century that the prominence of a 'nervous' system, or a ganglionar system, gave rise to an understanding of anxiety as having something to do with an excessive production of some sort from within the body and a link with perception – or what was being sensed from outside. This focus on the nerves and neurology in the works of physicians such as Xavier Bichat, Bénédict Morel, and chiefly George Miller Beard (Shorter, 2005) both in the United States and in Europe would see the diagnosis of 'neurasthenia' grow in popularity, containing symptoms of what we would now understand as anxiety or even an anxiety or panic attack (Berrios, 1996). In the context of such diagnoses of a 'weakness of the nerves' and of the enigma of hysteria, psychoanalysis emerges as an approach that accounted for the unconscious traces and logics at the heart of symptoms. The psychoanalytic emphasis on anxiety can be found in a very early theoretical proposition written by Freud, 'On the Grounds for Detaching a Particular Syndrome from Neurasthenia Under the Description "Anxiety Neurosis"' (1894). Anxiety neurosis was here being called as such 'because all its components can be grouped round the chief symptom of anxiety, because each one of them has a definite relationship to anxiety' (Freud, 1894, p. 91). Freud, in this paper, recognises the potential similarities in diagnosis both cases of neurasthenia and anxiety neurosis, but he moves on to clarifying the difference between the two as lying precisely on the specific sexual origins of anxiety neurosis – the sexual can be interpreted with a more contemporary inflection as libidinal or concerning what Lacan names *jouissance*, an enjoyment beyond the scope of the subject.

Freud also defends the psychoanalytic method as – it seems, at least in contrast with neuropathological methods – the only one capable of providing in depth enough interpretations that would not only prove his theory of anxiety neurosis right as really unveil symptoms since

> it is impossible to pursue an aetiological investigation based on anamneses if we accept those anamneses as the patients present them, or are content with what they are willing to volunteer. (Freud, 1895, p. 129)

In other words, we cannot take presented symptoms or narratives of complaints at face value, once they are not the 'full picture'. The unconscious marks a division among methods, interpretations, and treatments, in this instance, particular to anxiety neurosis, and in more general terms on the psychoanalytic approach to symptoms.

The psychoanalytic influence in psychiatry will have consequences to our relationship with the affect of anxiety thereafter, so much so that in the early twentieth century, the widespread nonspecific naming of the modern sense of discontent, or *Unbehagen*, was 'neurotic anxiety'. In this period 'anxiety and its sibling condition, "neuroses", became the central themes of what came to be called the stress tradition' (Horwitz, 2010, p. 113), thus revealing a certain trend of 'pathologising' of anxiety, despite anxiety being considered a common affliction of the post-World War II world. However ubiquitous or familiar to the post-war subject, anxiety was also the main category of discriminating in the clinic what was 'normal' and what was 'pathological' in that same period. Depression, at that point, as Horwitz (2010, 2013) defends, was 'in practice' – and by that he means, in the practice of psychiatrists in the United States – more commonly associated with the psychotic sphere and was a characteristic diagnosis reserved for severe melancholic cases of hospitalised patients. This trend will come to a halt towards the later decades of twentieth century precisely, as we will see in what follows, due to a disappearance of the influence of psychoanalytic theory in the field of mainstream psychiatry. Before the 1980s, psychiatric diagnoses 'reflected the centrality of the 'psychoneuroses', which were grounded in anxiety' (Horwitz, 2010, p. 115) and the first two editions of the DSM, from 1952 to 1968, respectively, are considered to be the most flavoured by psychodynamics – the type of psychotherapeutic knowledge that considers the dynamic unconscious of psychoanalysis. From the third edition onwards, however, the is an increased trend in further categorising mental illness in search of a 'reliable' efficiency in diagnosis that culminates in the fifth and most recent edition of the manual, the DSM-V, from 2013, with its bulk of over 900 pages of 'disorders' and their respective diagnostic checklists (Dunker, 2015; Ehrenberg, 2015; Herzberg, 2009). This change in approach will reshape the status of anxiety and, consequently of a biological narrative of depression in the turn of the twenty-first century. It also presents us with a paradigmatic shift regarding the quantification of the body, psyche, and affect.

The process of mapping and categorising mental states and affects and transforming them into recognisable symptoms is at the heart of the birth of the DSM, making it into a quantifying *dispositif par excellence*. The DSM emerges as a 'promise', at least, of a more 'pragmatic' and 'detailed' approach to substitute the then existing diagnostic forms, which were mostly based on prototypical descriptions and hypothetical case-studies rather than 'checklists'. The prototypical approach was already seen in earlier key texts of psychiatry such as Philippe Pinel's *A Treatise on Insanity*, from 1806, wherein distinctions of 'treatable' and 'untreatable' patients and principles of moral and medical treatments of what he called insanity were laid out systematically. This was even though Pinel had 'a single view of madness, characterised by many symptoms' (Ehrenberg, 2009, p. 36), rather than 'different types of madness', as we can see in a psychoanalytic and psychodynamic approach that divided, at a basic level, psychoses and neuroses as different structures. In the early twentieth century, Pinel's approach was still dominant in psychiatry, making use of clinical vignettes of patient's cases that guided doctors by some type of comparison. Psychoanalysis relied on clinical analysis and conjectural 'judgement', rather than on a clear-cut dividing line between what caused or classified a symptom as pathological or even as a symptom in the first place. A similar reliance on the doctor in question was present in the traditions that favoured a prototypical approach, and it was in part promising to facilitate these individual judgements on the side of the doctor that the first major manual of mental illness was published in the United States by the APA at the beginning of the twentieth century, in 1918. The 'Statistical Manual for the Use of Institutions for the Insane' was published ten different times (Dunker, 2015; Horwitz & Wakefield, 2012) before being substituted by the first edition of the DSM, in 1952.

At the time, however, different authors would already have diverging views on mental illness and founding heavy names of the discipline such as Emil Kraepelin and Eugen Bleuler, for example, presented contrasting views over the focus either on biological components or, rather, more 'holistic' aetiological approaches. Psychiatry was a mixed field, yet 'in the 1950s and 1960s, while psychoanalysis occupied the commanding heights of American psychiatry' (Scull, 2019, p. 133), the first edition of the DSM is published. This first edition 'reflected the movement of psychiatric practice from state mental hospitals to outpatient treatment and thus paid more attention to the psychoneuroses' (Horwitz & Wakefield, 2012, p. 93) instead of psychosis – the latter more frequently 'reserved' to hospital wards. The paradigm of the asylum and of a medicalised culture that excluded the insane from society, as explores in depth in his work on psychiatric power and biopolitics (Foucault, 2008b) starts cracking from this point onwards. Anxiety, therefore, was a common handle in clinical practice in the mid-twentieth century due to the influence of psychoanalysis and what we may call 'everyday' madness and suffering (Crocq, 2015, 2017). Anxiety was, therefore, not a disorder in itself, but a signal to something else that had to be treated in a contextual and individual basis.

The influence of North American psychiatry is politically relevant once such paradigmatic frameworks have reflected systems of classification and of quantification across the globe. In the 1950s and 1960s, the then dominant group at the APA, under the auspices of Adolf Meyer, conferred their psychodynamic preference on the manual, and such psychoanalytic 'flavour' was not lost even with the changes imposed by the following second version of the DSM, published in the late 1960s (Scull, 2019). The second edition was published after the release of the 6th edition of the International Classification of Diseases (ICD), published by the World Health Organization that had been formed in 1948; this sixth edition has inaugurated the ICD model existent to date. Envisaging a pairing of the DSM with the ICD-6, as this was the first of its kind to list mental health disorders, the APA launched the DSM-II. The 1968 edition

> did not make any major changes in the account of the anxiety disorders or in the pivotal role of anxiety in psychopathology. It maintained anxiety as the key aspect of the psychoneuroses. (Horwitz & Wakefield, 2012, p. 95)

Anxiety was still a central component of the frame that conferred a diagnostic platform to the then dominant diagnoses at the period, but that was about to change in the next decade.

The third edition of the DSM, published in 1980, inaugurates a decisive distancing from the psychoanalytic approach and, with that, manages to re-signify the status of anxiety. This will be critical in inaugurating a novel kind of quantification of affect, favouring biologist explanations of psychic distress, and giving birth to depression as the illness of the century. To comprehend the motor of this change from the ubiquity of anxiety towards mass-depression diagnoses, there are some elements to consider of the politics of psychiatry at the time and also the influence of products being marketed by the pharmaceutical industry (Scull, 2019). Such factors will have an important role in producing the 'grammar' of anxiety in the last half of the twentieth century. What we see as a drastic change implemented in the DSM-III is a moving away from the prototype-based model and an introduction of the checklist-logic of diagnosis. A group of biologist psychiatrists based at Washington University in St Louis led by Robert Spitzer and known as neo-Kraepelinian – for their biologist inclination – was tasked with the formulation of the third edition of the manual, their core interest was to define psychiatry as a medical discipline (Shorter, 2005). This alignment with the medical discourse was achieved by the introduction of a new system based on a list of criteria, 'Spitzer's task force was a political animal, and its aim was to simplify the diagnostic process by reducing it to a tick-the-boxes approach' (Scull, 2019, p. 172). This system inaugurated in the third edition of the manual is still guiding its current version, the fifth, since such an approach of a checklist that classifies, qualifies, and quantifies is seen as more 'scientific' than narrative models of treatment that preceded it.

In this new model, anxiety no longer features as an aspect of psychic experience and neurotic distress, rather, each 'type' of suffering is allocated into an individual category. Anxiety now is divided into subcategories of phobias, separation anxiety, panic disorder and so on (Shorter, 2005) leaving the category of General Anxiety Disorder, or GAD, as the only nonspecific category of diagnosis. GAD could only be 'ticked' however, when no other type of anxiety was present. This move alone demarcates a significant effort in qualifying the affect of anxiety.

Conversely, the broad category of Major Depressive Disorder, or MDD, appears as the go-to general diagnosis of distress (Mojtabai & Olfson, 2008). The results of this 'grammatical' shift are critical. Whilst the numbers of diagnoses of depression in the United States during the 1960s accounted for roughly one third of the diagnoses related to anxiety, in the 1980s depression will take over anxiety. This trend will only intensify in the following years and according to the US National Centre for Health Statistics, by the early 2000s the proportion of anxiety versus depression diagnoses shifts completely – from about 50 million overall yearly diagnosis of mental health a year, over 20 million were of depression whilst only 6 million were diagnosed as anxiety (Herzberg, 2009).

Depression travels, then, as we are able to trace historically, from belonging mostly to the melancholic and hospitalised world all the way into ordinary experience. It moves from being a peripheral category into being a dominant diagnosis of the 'stress tradition' (Crocq, 2015, 2017). Alongside the moving away from the anxiety-paradigm of the psychoneuroses that marked so heavily the psychodynamic approach of the earlier versions of the DSM, by the late 1970s 'depression' as an overarching category itself also appears to 'fit the professionally desirable conception of a severe and specific disease that could be associated with biological causes' (Horwitz, 2010, p. 123). Therefore, it served well the then dominant group within the hegemonic forces of the psy-field, whilst it also brought the roots of the 'discontent' close to the body, to the organism. The new 'malaise' favoured biologism, in contrast with a hard to measure psychoanalytic neurotic anxiety, and it also served, by consequence, the thriving pharmaceutical industry (Herzberg, 2009).

Quantifying Affect: From Discontent to Medication

The 'fall' of anxiety thus hardly represents the diminishing of anxious states in the experience of individuals, rather, it is a 'fall' reliant not solely on diluted socio-political changes and their production of subjectivity, but also on the politics of the systems of diagnosis and treatments and their representation of contemporary capitalist interests. The publication of the DSM-III and the shift towards a biological cause of distress facilitates a 'chemical imbalance' narrative that was accompanied by mass marketing campaigns aimed at both the general public and clinicians as well as profitable drug patents (Shorter, 2009; Whitaker, 2010). The most famous case study of the sort is the 1987 pill launched by Eli Lilly: Prozac. Within 10 years of its launch, 10% of the North American population was already taking it (Segal, 2017). In the United States, in 1988, the National Institute of Mental Health (NIMH) launched the 'Depression Awareness, Recognition, and Treatment Program' (DART), and Prozac (fluoxetine) featured in 8 million brochures and 200,000 posters sponsored by its manufacturer (Segal, 2017). The serotogenic rebalance becomes the pharmacological promise of the following decades, giving Prozac many successful companion drugs known as Selective Serotonin Reuptake Inhibitors (SSRIs), such as citalopram, escitalopram, sertraline, or paroxetine.

What is curious is that anxiety returns 'blurred' within depression through psycho-pharmaceutical treatments named 'antidepressant' (Herzberg, 2009). Such is the terminology factor in the fall and rise of certain diagnosis that in an article in *The Guardian*, from June 2017, the dean of The Royal College of Psychiatrists, Dr Kate Lovett, is quoted affirming that:

> Antidepressants are used in the treatment of both depression and anxiety disorders. They are an evidence-based treatment for moderate to severe depression and their prescription should be reviewed regularly in line with clear national guidance. (Campbell, 2017)

Under such discourse, as stressed in the 'scientific' tone of an adjective such as 'evidence-based', contemporary antidepressants work in a 'versatile' fashion, both when you are 'up' or 'down', anxious or depressed. The first patented drug to benefit from this shift back to a 'new age of anxiety diagnosis', in which anxiety returns in a biologised form was Paxil (paroxetine) approved in the United States in 1999 for the treatment of Social Anxiety Disorder, known as SAD, and in 2001 for GAD (Rose, 2007). The product now generates three billion dollars in sales a year (Horwitz, 2010) and a good part of such 'success', especially in the United States, is due to the heavy television advertising of the drug promoted by GlaxoSmithKline

> suggesting to individuals that their worry and anxiety at home and at work might not be because they are just worriers but because they are suffering from a treatable condition. 'Paxil … Your life is waiting', (Rose, 2007)

read the adverts. Other drugs have been approved for the treatment of anxiety in its many categories as stated in the most recent editions of the DSM since the late 1990s. Zoloft (sertraline) and Effexor (venlafaxine, officially a serotonin and norepinephrine reuptake inhibitor, or SSNRI) have also been marketed for Post-traumatic stress disorder (PTSD) and GAD, respectively.

The profitability behind the shift towards a checklist-approach of diagnosis also reveals a tragic unethical mingling of Big Pharma and governing bodies. For the latest edition of the DSM, for example, the DSM-III,

> it was reported that the pharmaceutical industry was responsible for half of the APA's $50 million budget, and that eight of the eleven-strong committee which advised on diagnostic criteria had links to pharmaceutical firms. (Davies, 2015, p. 124)

The ethically problematic conflict of interests present in the structure that creates diagnostic criteria, funds research and, in general terms, produces the 'grammar of suffering,' reveals 'the entanglement of psychic maximization and profit maximization' (Davies, 2015, p. 124), crossing through the vocabulary available for identifying and recognising mental suffering.

There are other links between this model of diagnosis and the operative global financial capitalist system once a manual such as the DSM comes to operate as a neo-colonising discourse through the imposition of its frameworks of categorisation of psychic experience. This relation is clearer if we look into the DSM's presence around the world. Despite being a North American psychiatric manual, the DSM has its scope and influence more 'globally'. If at the start of the DSM project and with the DSM-II in particular, there was a preoccupation in matching the 'international' standards of the ICD, after the third edition of the DSM, the 'power' shifts hands. With the publication of the DSM-III, in 1980 things move to the opposite direction and the ICD goes on to follow the trends in diagnosis already present in the DSM. Until the ICD-9, from 1975, the umbrella-terms of 'psychosis' and 'neurosis' were present. In the following version of the international manual, the first post-DSM-III, the ICD-10, from 1992, a longer list of very specific and detailed types of 'disorders' appears, reflecting the 'categories' checklist system (Shorter, 2009). Despite the gaps in publishing time, both manuals present a similar development of the trends in diagnosis, especially in terms of moving away from a psychodynamic-influenced language and a shift towards further divisions and categories. Ingrid Palmary and Brendon Barnes (2015) comment on the 'hegemonic' power of the North American psychiatric manual in their study of critical psychology and diagnoses in African countries. Reproducing colonial dynamics, as seen in Nigeria for example, the DSM,

> was consistently used in such a way that the clinician could devalue the meanings given by the client and focus only on those parts of the narrative that were congruent with the way mental health was understood in the DSM. (Palmary & Barnes, 2015, p. 398)

They add: 'In this way, Western psychological knowledge is reproduced as the true focus whilst local knowledge is rendered irrelevant or at most a cultural variation' (Palmary & Barnes, 2015, p. 398).

This 'imported' and 'exported' grammar of suffering that is at the core of the project of the ICD for public health, whilst crossed by the logic of the DSM also represents a colonising 'globalization of the manners of suffering' (Dunker, 2015, p. 23) that accompanied the globalisation of financial capital within the neoliberal ideology. The subject 'of' neoliberal capitalism becomes, through such diagnostic systems and multinational pharmaceutical corporations, a 'global' paradigm, and the potentiality of affects such as anxiety or the possibilities involved in experiencing psychic distress are erased systematically by the hegemonic practices in the field of psy, serving the 'powers' of 'globalised' financialisation of human capital. In such quantifying culture, the subject is locked out of from the possibility of seeing what is beyond the lifting of curtains of fantasy, as Freud and Lacan proposed. Affect is divided and conquered in a neo-colonising effort.

The connection of this diagnostic-culture to neoliberalism goes further and deeper. If we echo Canguilhem's concern with ideological inscriptions of the grammar of what is 'normal' and what is 'pathological', we are taken to an affective-politics that produces a biologised negativity in anxiety and profits from it. In this manner, when we accept that the DSM provides categories for recognition of distress, it must be recognised that this language is not neutral and value-free but rather reflects a dominant ideological rhetoric of the specific epoch, in this case the crisis in welfarism and the emergence of neoliberalism. (Cohen, 2016, p. 79)

Neoliberalism and a broader 'culture organised by the criteria of performance/ production' (Dunker, 2015, p. 23) sees a reverberation in the field of psy through the relationship established with medication. To put it simply, where do we draw the line between the use of a substance to ease a painful difficulty/suffering and eliminate 'all' suffering and discomfort? Or even, when does medication become what doping is to an athlete, an aid to up one's performances and increase benefits? Therefore, a 'diagnostic grammar' – informed and formed by the 'alliances' between hegemonic powers in the field of psy and neoliberal productivity and consumption standards – provides not only a possible manner of experiencing a discontent-turned-disease, as well as it delineates the 'exclusion' of modes of suffering from its grammar. Anxiety, in the shift in diagnosis observed since the 1980s, turns into a 'stranger'. The initial mass-pathologising of anxiety, followed by its breaking down into specific categories and diagnostic 'submission' to depression, as well as its 'management' through medication, accompany a cultural arrangement that is also observable outside of the clinic.

Wellness or Hellness

An individualist concept of 'wellbeing' has permeated neoliberal times as our attitudes towards 'being not well' reflect the logic of quantification, categorisation and, ultimately, financialisation of late capitalist ideology. Such an arrangement of 'wellbeing', extrapolates Foucault's account of modern governmentality as developed since the late eighteenth century under the paradigm of interiority and self-reference that permitted biopolitical subjectivation (Foucault, 2004) – and towards which psychoanalysis is also allegedly a contributor. The effort to 'feel good' in one's body is, in the contemporary context, also framed by the disciplinary and controlling assumption of the totality of conscious speech as promoter of attitude and behavioural changes – an assumption heavily questioned by psychoanalysis, which relies, on the contrary, precisely on the potential of representational lacunae, or gaps in language, which consist of the unconscious (Leader, 2009). As mentioned, Freud taught us to take symbolisation and narrative with a 'pinch of salt', being more concerned with what lays underneath a complaint. In current wellbeing discourse, 'mind and body' are articulated in such a manner that digital apps, checklists, as well as medication and even some 'yoga pants' have become the vocabulary to address bodies that are not 'balanced enough' and in need of management. All the while Big Pharma and the trillions of dollars – worth 'wellness industry'[5] revel in profits (Cederström & Spicer, 2016).

---

[5]Patricia Reaney, 'Global spa, wellness industry estimated at $3.4trillion: report'. *Reuters*, 1st October 2014 <http://uk.reuters.com/article/us-life-wellness-idUKKC-N0HP2OK20140930> [Accessed 13/05/2020].

Among the solutions offered by Big Pharma, therapeutic practices based on self-monitoring, thinking 'positive' and setting clear 'goals' such as Cognitive Behavioural Therapy (CBT) and Positive Psychology have thrived under the logic of isolating symptoms and de-politicising suffering (Scull, 2019). Currently, in the United Kingdom, guidelines[6] for treating GAD promote the use of SSRI drugs as well as self-monitoring and individual or group self-help based on the principles of CBT. A more 'effective' or simply put, 'cheaper' and easy to measure approach to therapy than long term psychotherapy, CBT has been part of the NHS since the New Labour government of Tony Blair, promoted by his advisor from the London School of Economics, Richard Layard (Layard & Clark, 2014). The notions of 'efficiency' and 'productivity' unfold both in terms of governmental spending and of a mode of management of the self that delineates a problem based on the patient's complaint and works towards a clear goal that involves 'thinking and behaving' differently to rid oneself of an unwanted symptom. It is a 'win win' situation, only that it reinforces the isolation of symptoms and of the individual and one's competence in just 'acting' and 'changing' one's own patterns that are causing suffering. Such suffering which is often costly to the state and, under this logic, should be 'easily' and strategically dealt with.

As a paradox, yet reflecting the logic of such a therapeutic approach, governments, corporations, and independent institutions have been investing in measuring 'happiness' exponentially in recent years, despite data on soaring inequality, precarity and mental health issues under austerity that circulate on the press. Economic problems and economic solutions to increase 'happiness' naturalise the paradigm of human capital even further, departing from a privatisation of suffering towards self-productivity management. 'Happiness' or 'wellbeing' seem secondary in such measuring policies once questions such as 'what are these 'sufferings' telling us' are, if not ignored, bypassed by productivity metaphors. Cederström and Spicer comment on the rise of 'happiness officer' jobs and 'wellness contracts' in corporate institutions and universities, which are turning 'being happy' compulsory (Cederström & Spicer, 2016). 'Happiness pulses' and 'happy city' projects also echo such 'happiness is the new black' trend that leaves precisely the 'meaning' of what is considered as 'happy' out of the debate, as seen in a number of academic and theoretical critiques of the neoliberal 'culture of happiness' (Ahmed, 2010; Binkley, 2014; Cederström & Spicer, 2016; Davies, 2015; Segal, 2017).

In psychoanalytic terms, wellness culture presupposes an ideal-self, an Imaginary body, in the Lacanian sense of the term, towards which all such fantasies of an ideal state of plenitude and control are projected. In this sense, if we consider the promises of an ideal, purified, and efficient self present in such discourses of consumption, there is a type of 'collective' fantasy being composed, and fantasies can only but leave something hanging out of them, something that will not

---

[6]National Institute for Health Care Excellence, Principles of care for people with Generalised Anxiety Disorder, <https://www.nice.org.uk/guidance/cg113/chapter/1-Guidance#principles-of-care-for-people-with-generalised-anxiety-disorder-gad> [Accessed: 13/05/2020].

fit into the frame of this projected ideal of selfhood. In a Lacanian view of this relation to fantasy, the cyclical attempt at fulfilling a fantasy and embodying an ideal that is impossible to ever be attained will open space for a failure, and this very failure will make way for, interestingly, anxiety. This opens to a paradoxical cycle. In one hand, there is the ubiquitous invocations for an individual 'work' on one's wellbeing, which passes through for example, mass medicalisation, to Positive Psychology all the way into wellness trends. On the other hand, we can see these discourses promoting an 'easily-reachable' type of ideal wellbeing or ideal 'tuning' of the body and mind. However, by understanding this 'ideal' as a fantasy, thus, one that leaves the subject to face the impossibility of ever feeling so 'good', we can see this 'fantasy of control' opening the way to anxiety or even more anxiety, paradoxically. Therefore, it might be possible to trace a seemingly conflicting cycle in which the subject is caught: from discontent to wellness; from such recourse to failing to feel as good as promised; from there to more anxiety and then back over to another wellness too; maybe another medication or a different diet this time. Metaphorically, wellness can easily become hellness.

Psychoanalytically, the process of continuous and repeated frustration present in the case of the 'management' discourses of the field of psy and wellness culture promoting a logic of a possible and ideal 'feeling-well', operates as an object that takes the space of a lack and, as Salecl defends, based on Lacan, 'anxiety is not incited by the lack of the object but rather by the lack of the lack, that is, the emergence of an object in the place of lack' (Salecl, 2004, p. 32). When this object fails to fulfil its promise, the subject is confronted with the depth of their anxiety, unable to situate themselves facing the desire of the Other. In the case of such discourses around wellbeing, it is interesting to trace, as per Salecl's logic, the repetition of this cycle once the 'ideal' object appearing as an impossible ideal comes in precisely as a model of feeling 'better', feeling 'balanced', 'producing enough' – thus, an antidote to its own problem. As a promise, this state of 'feeling-well,' presupposed when all discontent is turned into disease, categorised, and offered a remedy, for example, as in the biologist and DSM-style psychiatric practice, turns out to produce further discontent.

The discourses of 'management of the self' present in all these spheres – from diagnosis to treatment and consumption – also reveal typical characteristic of neoliberal capitalism: a constant praise and calculation of the 'individual' that at the same time leaves no space for the 'singular'. That is, the very promotion of a 'fit-efficient-pure-controlled' model for consumption or as goal and standard in Mental Health care presupposes that this ideal operates as a model that would work for 'everyone', cancelling or at least limiting the possibilities of singular, unique to each subject, potentialities. The diagnostic-culture of our times, considering diagnosis and the promotion of wellbeing under such logic, reinforces, paradoxically, a state of constant anxiety that echoes a somewhat subjective precarity that anchors the mode of governance of contemporary capitalism.

Can the Dividual Speak?

What the assemblage of wellness, psychiatric diagnosis, medicalization of psychic experience and ultimately quantification of affect reveal is an affective-politics that accounts for body and psyche in a particular mode of alienation. Under the current affective-politics, we can identify pharmacological corporations and governmentality replicating a modern scientific view of the body: described, divided, quantified, and qualified. However, the demands for taming affective experiences are coupled with mechanisms of consumption and identification that result in post-modern technologies of subjectivity. This double-alienation that entails a colonisation of affect seen through the trail of anxiety are interestingly elucidated in Deleuze's mapping of the birth of the *dividual* (1992). Whilst Foucault delineates the modern individual as a locus of reproduction of a disciplinary society based in exclusions and division that took shape during the eighteenth and nineteenth centuries, Deleuze proposes that this modern individual has been further reduced into a *dividual*, the locus of reproduction of the society of control – one not based on exclusion, but based on identification, participation, and endless quantification (Dosse, 2016). The shift into what he calls a society of control encompasses a transformation of 'molds' into 'modulations' of subjective production (Deleuze, 1992). When thinking the trail of anxiety through this prism we can find concomitant 'mold' and 'modulation'-like qualities of the current psy-discourse. This particular encounter of *dispositifs* is precisely what qualifies the current affective-politics as I argue in conclusion.

Wellbeing and governance have not become connected only in the last decades. On the contrary, it is an old modern alliance as it was particularly elaborated by Foucault in '*The Birth of Biopolitics*' lecture series from 1978 to 1979. In these lectures, he points to the fact that, 'wellbeing' is a term that emerged in the 18th century as a 'symbol' of state power in its full effectiveness, thus, having been crucial in ideological control and the mechanisms of biopower since the dawn of modernity (Foucault, 2008b). Social regulation through the care of the body is, under this prism, bound to capitalism as the refinement of 'life-sciences' is historically linked to what Foucault calls the 'liberal art of governing.' Deleuze calls such *dispositifs* 'molds' (1992) and defines their logic as follows:

> The disciplinary societies have two poles: the signature that designates the individual, and the number or administrative numeration that indicates his or her position within a mass. This is because the disciplines never saw any incompatibility between these two, and because at the same time power individualises and masses together, that is, constitutes those over whom it exercises power into a body and molds the individuality of each member of that body. (Deleuze, 1992, p. 5)

In this sense, the project of the DSM as a whole could be compared to a 'mold' as it offers a homogenisation of whatever heterogeneity is present in the forms of discontent and suffering experienced in society. The DSM and the *raison d'être* of efforts in categorising and identifying aetiological frames for mental illness marked across the field of psy, as seen in this chapter, provide a 'name', a 'number', and a 'diagnosis' through which an individual can be 'positioned within a mass'. Such reduction of the multiplicity in manners of suffering to the same common 'grammar' – and as Dunker (2015) remarks, a particularly 'normative' grammar – generate an imposition of uniformity on symptoms based on a contemporary western paradigm of pathology, resulting in a 'neutralization of the critical potential that psychological symptoms bring to the understanding of a determined social context, as the role that symptoms have always played' (Dunker, 2015, p. 35). Furthermore, there is also a neutralisation of the potential to 'produce new modalities of the social bond' (Dunker, 2015, p. 35) carried by 'discontents' in their singularity and multiplicity. Another 'mold'-like characteristic of the diagnostic-culture inaugurated in the 1980s can be observed in its biologist, or organicist, traits that 'reduce discontent to sensorial pain and suffering' (Dunker, 2015, p.33). Therefore, reducing the subject to the 'fleshy' body.

In the 'modulation' of 'societies of control' that unfold in the twentieth century, the picture is slightly more complex yet not too dissimilar. Deleuze describes the shift as follows:

> In the societies of control, on the other hand, what is important is no longer either a signature or a number, but a code: the code is a password, while on the other hand the disciplinary societies are regulated by watchwords (as much from the point of view of integration as from that of resistance). The numerical language of control is made of codes that mark access to information, or reject it. We no longer find ourselves dealing with the mass/individual pair. Individuals have become 'dividuals,' and masses, samples, data, markets, or 'banks'. (Deleuze, 1992, p. 5)

One manner of illustrating what Deleuze means by 'modulated dividuals' is the 'quantified self' movement in relation to wellbeing. Noting that people usually refuse or at least do not collaborate with reporting on their mental health for research, Davies (2015) cites the digital platforms and devices operated by companies such as Google or Nike through which users are 'happily' willing to offer details, 'and report on various aspects of their private lives- from their diets, to their moods, to their sex lives' (Davies, 2015, p. 221). Such 'enthusiasm for self-surveillance' is welcomed by corporations that are now investing in novel health and fitness products (e.g. Fitbit, Strava or even the Apple Watch) that

> can be sold alongside quantified self apps, which will allow individuals to made constant reports of their behaviour (such as jogging), generating new data sets for the company in the process. (Davies, 2015, p. 221)

Data thus become a 'password' and offer recognition in the digitally informed social sphere. At the same time, each tap, each word, each interaction is translated into chunks of big data that, in its turn, bounces back in the form of targeted advertising operated through algorithms on the web.

In this sense, the alliance between the DSM-model and the pharmaceutical industry, which relies heavily in marketing, echoes the 'modulation' of experience. Consumption of medication becomes the 'password' and the body, the fleshy body, is modulated as 'medication adjustments' operate by isolating parts and functions of the body, creating 'artificial zones of contention, excitation, anaesthesia and separation that work as protective walls against discontent and zones of exception against suffering' (Dunker, 2015, p. 28). 'Dividuality' and the modus operandi of the society of control are evidenced in the new function of psychopathological diagnosis under the current diagnostic-culture explored in this chapter. Instead of representing a force of exclusion from social life, as the asylum did for example, the consumption of medication(s) justified by a systematic categorisation of affects, symptoms and manners of suffering and being provide, as a modulating mapping of the fleshy body, a type of 'fantasy' of recognition in the model of a 'password'. As Dunker summarises, yet without referring to Deleuze's ideas,

> if previously the psychopathological diagnosis could mean a terrifying and at times irreversible inclusion in the juridical-hospital frame or moral-educational exclusion, now it seems to have become a powerful and disseminated means of determination and recognition, if not even a means of destitution of the responsibility of a subject. (Dunker, 2015, p. 33)

A diagnosis can, under the paradigm of productivity, offer a form of relief from such a burden.

Deleuze, however, leaves an impression that in the present time, Foucault's 'disciplinary societies' were being substituted by this new order of control, as if one followed the other. This 'misunderstanding' is, as defended by Deleuzian-scholar Gerald Raunig, in part due to the nature of the text itself (Raunig, 2009). 'Postscript on Societies of Control', the text, is extremely short, barely reaching five pages of length, and written in a very poetic – and apocalyptic if one may add – style. What Raunig stresses is that 'modulation' 'is the name of this merging of discipline society and control society: as the aspects of discipline and control are always to be seen as intertwined' (Raunig, 2009). Thus, the seeming linearity of temporal sequence open for interpretation in the original text is one of its 'weaknesses'. Deleuze's text reads as follows:

> But everyone knows that these institutions are finished, whatever the length of their expiration periods. It's only a matter of administering their last rites and of keeping people employed until the last installation of the new forces knocking at the door. These are the societies of control, which are in the process of replacing the disciplinary societies. (Deleuze, 1992, p. 4)

Indeed, this passage evokes a temporal linearity that does not translate in the shifts from enclosed confinement of institutions towards an open and multiple form of ever-changing casts. Rather, as Raunig points, what we experience in the twenty-first century and what characterises modulation is 'an accumulation of both aspects' (Raunig, 2009), a simultaneous presence of both models, intertwined and intercalating. Social subjugation and 'forced adaptation' – the hetero into homogeneous, from mass to individual – accompanies the 'modes of self-government in a totally transparent, open milieu, and discipline through personal surveillance and punishment couples with the liberal visage of control as voluntary self-control' (Raunig, 2009) that 'modulates' a 'dividual'.

The encounter of modulating-molds and of *dispositifs* of subjective production and reproduction explicated in this chapter and found in tracing the trail of anxiety in mainstream psychiatric discourses allows us to elucidate, even if a little, the current arrangements of colonisation of psychic experience and affective life. Given this cartography of anxiety and the place of an anxious *dividual* in it, we can finally ask whether the *dividual* can speak. If anxiety is the compass that can lead us to a world beyond the veils of fantasies, if it can push novel arrangements of the social bond, it seems that an anxious *dividual* is left at the cliff-edge of an existential abyss that only grows deeper on the hands of hegemonic psy-discourses.

References

Ahmed, S. (2010). *The promise of happiness*. London: Duke University Press.

Berrios, G. E. (1996). *The history of mental symptoms: Descriptive psychopathology since the nineteenth century*. Cambridge: Cambridge University Press.

Binkley, S. (2014). *Happiness as enterprise: An essay on neoliberal life*. New York, NY: State University of New York Press.

Breuer, J., & Freud, S. (1893). On the psychical mechanism of hysterical phenomena. In *The standard edition of the complete psychological works of Sigmund Freud, Volume II (1893–1895): Studies on hysteria* (pp. 1–17). London: Hogarth Press.

Campbell, D. (2017). NHS prescribed record number of antidepressants last year. *The Guardian*, Thursday, 29 June. [Online] Retrieved from https://www.theguardian.com/society/2017/jun/29/nhs-prescribed-record-number-of-antidepressants-last-year. Accessed on May 13, 2020.

Canguilhem, G. (1991). *The normal and the pathological*. New York, NY: Zone Books.

Canguilhem, G. (2016). What is psychology? *Foucault Studies, 21*, 200–213.

Cederström, C., & Spicer, A. (2016). *The wellness syndrome*. London: Polity.

Cohen, B. (2016). *Psychiatric hegemony: A Marxist theory of mental illness*. London: Palgrave Macmillan.

Crocq, M. A. (2015). A history of anxiety: From Hippocrates to DSM. *Dialogues in Clinical Neuroscience, 17*(3), 319–325.

Crocq, M. A. (2017). The history of generalised anxiety disorder as a diagnostic category. *Dialogues in Clinical Neuroscience, 19*(2), 107–116.

Davies, W. (2015). *The happiness industry: How the government and big business sold us wellbeing*. London: Verso.

Deleuze, G. (1992). Postscript on societies of control. *October, 59*, 3–7.

Dosse, F. (2016). Deleuze and Foucault: A philosophical friendship. In N. Morar, T. Nail, & D. Smith (Eds.), *Between Deleuze and Foucault*. Edinburgh: Edinburgh University Press.

Dunker, C. (2015). *Mal-Estar, Sofrimento e Sintoma*. São Paulo: Boitempo Editorial.

Ehrenberg, A. (2015). *The weariness of the self: Diagnosing the history of depression in the contemporary age*. London: McGill-Queen University Press.

Foucault, M. (2004). *Abnormal: Lectures at the Collège de France, 1974–1975*. New York, NY: Palgrave Macmillan.

Foucault, M. (2008a). *Mental illness and psychology*. Oakland, CA: University of California Press.

Foucault, M. (2008b). *The birth of biopolitics: Lectures at The Collège de France 1978–79.* London: Palgrave Macmillan.

Freud, S. (1894). On the grounds for detaching a particular syndrome from neurasthenia under the description 'Anxiety Neurosis'. In *The standard edition of the complete psychological works of Sigmund Freud, Volume III (1893–1899): Early psycho-analytic publications* (pp. 85–115).

Freud, S. (1895). A reply to criticisms of my paper on anxiety neurosis. In *The standard edition of the complete psychological works of Sigmund Freud, Volume III (1893–1899): Early psycho-analytic publications* (pp. 119–139).

Freud, S. (1917). Introductory lectures on psycho-analysis. In *The Standard Edition of the Complete Psychological Works of Sigmund Freud, Volume XVI (1916–1917): Introductory Lectures on Psycho-Analysis (Part III)* (pp. 241–463). London: Hogarth Press.

Gallagher, C. (1996). High anxiety – A theoretical and clinical challenge to psychoanalysis. *The Letter*, 6(Spring), 1–23.

Guéry, F., & Deleule, D. (2014). *The productive body.* Winchester, UK: Zero Books.

Herzberg, D. (2009). *Happy Pills in America: From Miltown to Prozac.* Baltimore, MD: Johns Hopkins University Press.

Horwitz, A. (2010). How an age of anxiety became an age of depression. *The Milbank Quarterly*, 88(1), 112–138.

Horwitz, A. (2013). *Anxiety: A short history.* Baltimore, MD: The Johns Hopkins University Press.

Horwitz, A., & Wakefield, J. (2012). *All we have to fear. Psychiatry's transformation of natural anxieties into mental disorders.* New York, NY: Oxford.

Lacan, J. (1960). The subversion of the subject and the dialectic of desire in the Freudian Unconscious. In *Écrits: The first complete edition in English (2005)* [B. Fink, Trans.]. New York, NY: W.W. Norton and Company.

Lacan, J. (2016). *Anxiety. The seminar of Jacques Lacan Book X.* London: Polity Press.

Layard, R., & Clark, D. M. (2014). *Thrive: The power of evidence-based psychological therapies.* London: Penguin.

Leader, D. (2009). The New Black: Mourning, Melancholia and Depression. London: Penguin

Mojtabai, R., & Olfson, M. (2008). National patterns in antidepressant treatment by psychiatrists and general medical providers: Results from the National Comorbidity Survey Replication. *Journal of Clinical Psychiatry*, 69, 1064–1074.

Palmary, I., & Barnes, B. (2015). Critical psychology in Africa. The impossible task. In I. Parker (Ed.), *Handbook of critical psychology* (pp. 397–405). London: Routledge.

Raunig, G. (2009). In modulation mode: Factories of knowledge. *Transversal*, August. [Online] Retrieved from <http://eipcp.net/transversal/0809/raunig/en≥. Accessed on May 13, 2020.

Rose, N. (2007). *The politics of life itself – Biomedicine, power, and subjectivity in the twenty-first century.* Oxford: Princeton University Press.

Rose, N. (2018). *Our psychiatric future: The politics of mental health.* London: Polity Press.

Salecl, R. (2004). *On anxiety.* London: Routledge.

Scull, A. (2019). *Psychiatry and its discontents.* Oakland, CA: University of California Press.

Segal, L. (2017). *Radical happiness: Moments of collective joy.* London: Verso.

Shorter, E. (2005). *A historical dictionary of psychiatry.* Oxford: Oxford University Press.

Shorter, E. (2009). *Before Prozac: The troubled history of mood disorders in psychiatry.* Oxford: Oxford University Press.

Soler, C. (2014). *Lacanian affects: The function of affect in Lacan's Work.* London: Routledge.

Whitaker, R. (2010). *Anatomy of an epidemic: Magic bullets, psychiatric drugs, and the astonishing rise of mental illness in America.* Cambridge, MA: Crown Publisher-Random House.

Chapter 8

Me Apps: Mental Health and the Smartphone

Zeena Feldman

Abstract

This chapter considers how mental health care is done in and by digital culture in the UK. The author examines how treatments for anxiety and depression operate in today's technosocial age of smartphone hegemony. Smartphones, the author argues, offer valuable insight into contemporary health and wellbeing precisely because they are emblematic of the neoliberal production logics, knowledge claims and modes of address that structure this moment in digital culture history. The author also shows how this moment is the outcome of key shifts in computing hardware, software, and content. Empirically, this research focusses on mapping Britain's terrain of smartphone interventions for anxiety and depression. Working from a dataset of 635 apps, the author develops a four-part framework for understanding products and services in this crowded marketplace relative to an app's (1) intended audience; (2) communicative affordances; (3) business model; and (4) therapeutic approach. Through this framework, the author proposes the notion of *me apps* to codify the individualised, commercialised, and desocialised mode of address enacted by most of the apps in the dataset. The author shows that the ideology of me apps, and the modes of address they employ, frame mental illness as an individual problem and regard treatment as an individual endeavour. The end of the chapter considers the possibility of an alternative vision for designing technologies of mental wellbeing.

Keywords: Mental health; smartphones; apps; depression; anxiety; digital culture; wellbeing

The Quantification of Bodies in Health: Multidisciplinary Perspectives, 157–177
doi:10.1108/978-1-80071-883-820211013

Digital Technology and Wellness: An Introduction

This chapter considers how mental health care is done in and by contemporary digital culture. Specifically, I explore how treatments for anxiety and depression operate in the technosocial age of smartphones and hyperconnectivity. How do repertoires of care for these conditions map onto the pocket computers that now saturate everyday life? In what ways do these technological interventions position mental health and the ailing subject? And how do they connect to the ideological values and imperatives of our socioeconomic moment?

The internet-enabled smartphone is ubiquitous across Global North geographies. In the UK – where this research is situated – smartphone ownership now outstrips that of desktops, laptops, and tablets (Ofcom, 2015) and by 2020, '96% of households in Great Britain had internet access, up from... 57% in 2006 when comparable records began' (ONS, 2020a). This hyperconnectivity has wide-ranging implications for everyday life. It affects how the rhythms, routines and practices of everyday life are organised, from economic activity to learning, communicating, and 'doing' health (ONS, 2020a). It affects the full spectrum of human experience.

Today, smartphones act as a main interface by which we access that spectrum. They provide the interface through which we articulate ourselves and relate to world around us, so much so that these devices have become our appendages, quite literal 'extensions of (wo)man' (McLuhan, 1964). Through their ubiquity, smartphones have forged an unprecedented intimacy between body, mind, and screen, between corporeality, sociality, and knowledge. Indeed, Ofcom's (2016) communications market report found that in Scotland, nearly 70% of respondents had experienced someone walking into them because that person was looking down at their smartphone rather than paying attention to the materiality around them.

This technological hegemony is significant and approached here as a means of locating how mental illness – in particular, anxiety and depression – is currently being problematised and attended to by app developers, clinicians, and users. As I will argue, smartphones offer valuable insight into contemporary health and well-being precisely because they are emblematic of the production logics, knowledge claims and modes of address that structure this moment in digital culture history.

My focus on anxiety and depression is also significant. These two interrelated conditions (McManus, Bebbington, Jenkins, & Brugha, 2016) are among today's most prominent and mainstream mental health issues. Indeed, depression is the world's leading mental health diagnosis (Global Burden of Disease Study Collaborators, 2013) and a leading cause of disability, suicide, and cardiovascular disease (Chesney, Goodwin, & Fazel, 2014; Correll et al., 2017). In the UK, it is a key public health concern and one that has been exacerbated by Covid-19. Our Office for National Statistics (ONS), for example, found that 'Almost one in five adults (19.2%) were likely to be experiencing some form of depression during the coronavirus (COVID-19) pandemic' – nearly double the number of those affected before the pandemic (ONS, 2020b).

As depression rates rise in the UK, so too have referrals to talking therapies. NHS Digital's (2020) annual report on the Improving Access to Psychological

Therapies (IAPT) programme finds that in 2019–2020, there were '1.69 million referrals to talking therapies, up 5.7% from [the previous year]'. This emphasis on talking therapy as treatment suggests a link between depression and sociality (or lack thereof). As David Taylor notes, 'Humans are social animals whose mental health depends upon frequent interaction with others and with the outside world' (Robinson, 2020). Covid-19 has clearly upset sociality, with many of us working from home and physically isolated from our social networks. Taylor warns that 'Being asked to stay inside with little or no contact with other people can be expected to cause increased rates of anxiety and depression' (Robinson, 2020). Thus, in their capacity to forge and sustain social connections, smartphones may offer hope to those struggling with mental illness.

In their relative affordability and accessibility, smartphones may also be well-placed to respond to the considerable economic costs and resource deficits connected to the UK's mental health crisis. Research carried out by Westfield Health found that in 2020, mental health-related absences cost UK businesses £14 billion (Neville & Jones, 2021), while others 'put the cost of mental illness to the UK economy at more than £100 billion a year' (Spence, 2020). These costs converge with a decade of aggressive neoliberal policymaking and austerity measures, which Scott Weich, of the University of Sheffield's mental health research unit, notes has 'led to rising rates of psychiatric morbidity and, at the same time, reduced availability and access to care' (Duncan & Marsh, 2021).

While smartphones, and their app ecosystems, may offer cost-effective interventions for anxiety and depression, contemporary digital culture is also routinely linked to poor mental health (Lanier, 2018). The academic literature is rife with studies documenting the negative effects that social media and smartphone usage have on participants' mental wellbeing (e.g. Blackwell, Leaman, Tramposch, Osborne, & Liss, 2017). There, internet excess is often framed in terms of 'addiction' (D'Arienzo, Boursier, & Griffiths, 2019; Ponnusamy, Iranmanesh, Foroughi, & Hyun, 2020), and consistently correlates with higher rates of depression and anxiety and lower rates of self-esteem (Berthon, Pitt, & Campbell, 2019; Hawi & Samaha, 2017). Thus pathologised, digital culture is consistently positioned as a cause of mental illness, not a potential solution thereto.

This research regards such contradictions as productive. They offer ways of understanding the UK's mental health crisis in relation to the socioeconomic and technological contexts in which it has emerged. To that end, my research seeks to locate the coordinates at which depression and anxiety intersect with the smartphone era's values, infrastructures and affordances.

Empirically, I focus on Britain's contemporary terrain of smartphone interventions for anxiety and depression. In mapping this space, I develop a four-part framework for understanding products and services in this crowded marketplace. This framework evaluates smartphone 'treatment' apps relative to their (1) intended audience; (2) communicative affordances; (3) business model; and (4) therapeutic approach.

Through this framework, I develop the notion of *me apps* to codify the individualised, commercialised, and desocialised mode of address enacted by most of the apps in my dataset. I show that the ideology of *me apps*, and the mode of address they employ, frame mental illness as an individual problem and regard treatment as an individual endeavour. Therein, mental illness is also framed as a technological problem (Mills & Hilberg, 2020). Ultimately, my analysis captures the virulent neoliberalism and 'technological solutionism' (Morozov, 2013) that inform the contemporary relationship between mental health and digital culture.

This chapter proceeds in four parts. First, I trace key shifts in digital culture relative to hardware, software, and content, in order to locate the historical trajectory through which me apps have emerged. Next, I reflect on this study's research methodology and map out my app dataset according to the original framework described above. In part three, I draw on this framework and my historical mapping in order to develop the idea of *me apps*. Me apps is a conceptual device by which this research understands the operative relationship between depression, anxiety and the smartphone, and its ideological implications. To close, I consider the extent to which the smartphone era's individualised, commercialised, and desocialised register can be undone and reoriented towards a more collaborative, socially grounded understanding of both digital culture and mental wellbeing.

Shifts in Digital Culture

It is my view that the UK's mental health crisis is intimately connected to contemporary digital culture. My use of the term 'digital culture' is deliberate. It suggests not only the hardware and software of connectivity, but also the discursive claims and contents of communicative practice therein. The social, in other words, is baked into how digital culture reads technology (e.g. Wajcman, 2010). Digital culture thus highlights the specific ways in which contemporary sociality is enmeshed in the technological infrastructures and materialities through which we currently understand and perform ourselves. In so doing, it offers insight into the socio-technical conditions against which today's prevalence of depression and anxiety can be understood.

But in order to understand the digital present, we first need to understand the digital past. Today, digital culture reifies the political economy of individualism. This was not always the case. To that end, I suggest below that we got here through three sets of parallel shifts: in hardware, software, and content. I argue that these changes have infused digital culture with a neoliberal politics and socio-technical ethos of atomisation. Over time, these shifts have substantially reconfigured the relationship between digital culture and its users, and ultimately delivered the contemporary *me apps* moment in which mental health is individualised, commercialised, and desocialised. I explore the three shifts below.

Hardware Shifts

In the early days of computing, the machinery was gargantuan. Consider the familiar story of a computer filling up an entire room (Arthur, 2011). These physically imposing objects were also extremely expensive and required substantial (and at that time, rarefied) specialist knowledge to operate. All of this rendered computing effectively inaccessible to ordinary people. Early digital culture was instead linked with big, well-funded institutions: universities, research firms, governments (Leiner et al., 1997).

With advances in nanotechnology, however, computing underwent a process of miniaturisation and domestication. Desktop computers arrived. These were small enough to fit in the home; affordable enough for (wealthy) individuals to own; and had accessible-enough interfaces to be useful to non-computer scientists. The era of the PC, as the moniker implies, made computing personal. Rather than purely institutional assets, computers were now consumer goods as well.

When laptops surpassed desktop sales (Ofcom, 2015), computers became ever more personal and individualised. During the desktop's reign, a single machine was often shared by an entire household (Lally, 2002, pp. 18, 22). It was a communal resource, like a household's refrigerator. Once upon a time, radio and television were also communal resources (Livingstone, 1992; Williams, 1974). But, like the desktop computer, their sociability was substantially reduced by the hardware's eventual miniaturisation. As desktops, radios, and television sets shrank in size, their venues of consumption changed. Raymond Williams (1974, 1985) dubbed this move from the living room to the bedroom 'mobile privatisation'.

In today's smartphone age – where computing hardware is smaller and cheaper than ever, and internet speeds faster than ever – computers have become personal property in the strictest sense of the term. Every member of a household is now likely to have their own machine. Indeed, they are each likely to have multiple internet-enabled devices. The hegemony of the smartphone, thus, represents the apex of computing's transformation from shared resource to a product which caters to an audience of one.

Software Shifts

Alongside shifts in hardware, changes in computing software contributed to a similar transformation. The early, institutional days of computing consisted of broad-ranging sociality and a collaborative ethos aimed at technological innovation and network development (O'Regan, 2016). Here, people worked together – in their own labs and with remote colleagues – to build and improve the tech that would allow them to share resources and communicate across time and space. These digital pioneers regarded software – the programmatic means of 'doing' things with and through computer hardware (Manovich, 2013) – as a way of connecting people and ideas (Leiner et al., 1997). Indeed, '[c]ommunity spirit has a long history, beginning with the early ARPANET, whose early researchers worked as a close-knit community' (Leiner et al., 1997, p. 106). This is an inherently social reading of, and engagement with, software. Here, connectivity is in service to communication, collaboration, and knowledge production.

This prioritisation of sociality and communality also marked the early years of personal computing, with listservs, Internet Relay Chat (IRC), Bulletin Board Systems (BBS), and Usenet now capable of connecting users around the world (Sajithra & Rajindra, 2013). Networking software transformed the world into an 'electronic global village' (McLuhan, 1968; Targowski, 1990) and facilitated the birth of the online community (Rheingold, 1993). In 1989, Tim Berners-Lee gifted humanity with the World Wide Web (WWW) (O'Dwyer, 2014), making it possible for ever-greater numbers of people to connect with others in the 'electronic elsewhere' (Berry, Kim, & Spigel, 2010).

But with the emergence of web 2.0 in the early aughts (O'Reilly, 2005), the social register of networking software changed. The web 2.0 framework heralded a radical shift in software production, upending received wisdom about what software was for, how it was made and who made it. The new framework emphasised 'Trusting users as co-developers' and 'Harnessing Collective Intelligence' through peer-production, but it also encouraged developers and companies to see the value of user data capture and multi-device operability (O'Reilly, 2005). Web 2.0 was a set of design principles *and* a business model.

This approach to software development is seen clearly in today's social media ecosystem. These platforms are peer-produced, multi-device spaces of user-generated content in which users' personal data is extracted and commodified. In their emphasis on harvesting user data and monetising user participation, contemporary social media are routinely critiqued as agents of exploitation (Fuchs, 2017; van Dijck, 2013). For these same reasons, others celebrate social networking software for 'empowering' savvy entrepreneurs (Olanrewaju, Hossain, Whiteside, & Mercieca, 2020). Either way, computing software in this context has shifted from prioritising socialisation for its own sake and in the interest of knowledge sharing, to regarding sociality and connectivity predominantly as instruments for commercial gain.

The rise of social media has also been linked to emancipatory claims about these platforms' ability to challenge long-standing inequalities between ordinary people and media powerbrokers. Technology therein is conceived as an instrument of liberation. As I have written elsewhere (Feldman, forthcoming), social media platforms were seen to disrupt gatekeeper power by enabling 'anyone' with an internet connection to compete directly with institutions and professional content creators. Here, the software of connection centres and reifies the individual user and the marketplace.

Content Shifts

This connects to the third shift through which this research understands the contemporary register of digital culture: a shift in content. Whereas the early internet was a non-commercial endeavour, the WWW began incorporating commercial interests and artefacts alongside non-commercial ones. Banner ads became a fixture on many websites (Hofacker & Murphy, 2000). Companies started buying their way into (and positions on) search engine results (Bagnall, 2003). Still, most advertising expenditure continued to go to print and broadcast media (cf. Shaban, 2019). Where firms did develop an online presence, it was generally through static websites.

Things changed with the arrival of web 2.0 technologies, and their commercial underpinnings. A sophisticated digital marketing industry was born, with agencies specialising in search engine optimisation; eCommerce innovators selling online payment solutions and wrangling big data sets to segment audiences into markets; developers writing code to track user journeys; firms bidding in real-time on keywords; advertisers vying for click-throughs and virality, and consumers greasing the wheels with their everyday digital footprints.

Contemporary digital culture reflects this political economy. Content therein is increasingly commercialised and algorithmically personalised. Whether in a web browser, smartphone app or social networking site, algorithms aim to predict what content we will like and show us only that content. Algorithmic production is a mechanism of if → then (Bucher, 2018). These systems of content and knowledge production tell us what we want by watching what we see. The sophistication with which these algorithms parse our online behaviour and personalise our individual experiences is uncanny. This system enables a degree of content personalisation so intimate and accurate that it can feel intrusive. It can feel like a violation that an algorithm should know us so well. Yet, this emphasis on individualised content and the individual user – while technically accurate – can also be misleading. It can obscure the power of the global data monopolies, from Amazon to Google, that constitute today's digital content industries (Moore & Tambini, 2018).

As online content has become more personalised, the dialogic, independent, and text-based social systems of the early web – the BBS and the listserv – have receded from the mainstream. In their place, one finds platforms like Instagram, TikTok and Snapchat, which favour short formats and visuality, and are saturated in advertising, sponsored content, and aspiring influencers. Here, online content has transformed from non-commercial talking and idea exchange to a space of showing, looking, and selling. This shift coincides with a related phenomenon: content overload (nb. Toffler, 1970).

Consumer capitalism quickly adapted to this by producing more stuff, including myriad disconnection apps, self-help books, and digital detox holidays (Syvertsen & Enli, 2020) with rhetorical directives towards better 'digital hygiene', 'digital dieting', and 'digital wellness' (Beattie & Daubs, 2020; Pittaway, 2020; Sutton, 2017).

The above shifts in hardware, software, and content gesture to a contemporary digital culture that is overwhelmingly transactional, privatised, and unsocial. These are the values informing mental health care in the smartphone age, and the context in which *me apps* operate.

Methodology

Before proceeding to my analysis of *me apps*, it is essential to unpack the empirical portion of this project, together with its methodological approach and limitations. Because a primary aim of this research is to understand the contemporary landscape of mental health apps, much of this project resembles a scoping exercise (Arksey & O'Malley, 2005). I deployed keyword search (Bhalotia, Hulgeri, Nakhe, Chakrabarti, & Sudarshan, 2002) as a key instrument in helping me map this landscape.

Table 8.1.   Googling for Mental Health (Accessed 11 February 2021).

Digital Intervention	*Mental Health Concern*		
	Depression	**Anxiety**	**Mental health**
App for [concern]	472,000,000 results	306,000,000 results	828,000,000 results
Smartphone app for [concern]	20,200,000 results	17,800,000 results	43,700,000 results
AI app for [concern]	15,800,000 results	10,100,000 results	36,500,000 results
Chatbot for [concern]	690,000 results	826,000 results	1,890,000 results

My first use of keyword search focussed on getting to grips with the scale of mental health app representation on Google – the UK's leading search engine (Johnson, 2021). Were apps addressing depression and anxiety abundant, or was this a niche product category? I conducted 12 keyword searches on www.google.co.uk to answer this question. These searches centred on three mental health concerns and their links to four digital interventions, represented in Table 8.1.

This enquiry showed an abundance of digital technology aimed at mental health. For instance, the 'app for depression' search yielded nearly half a billion results. Unsurprisingly, the broad category of 'mental health' is much more frequently attended to by digital interventions, compared with a specific mental health condition or diagnosis like depression or anxiety. Nonetheless, those diagnoses are well-catered for by various apps, from generic 'apps' to smartphone apps, AI apps, and chatbots.

Of the three specific technologies I searched for, smartphone apps were the most popular digital interventions for addressing mental health. This was closely followed by AI apps. In contrast, chatbots for mental health care were comparatively underrepresented. This may indicate an area of future growth in mental health technologies. Interestingly, depression is the more frequently addressed condition relative to anxiety in all technical categories except chatbots. This suggests chatbots may be better suited to addressing anxiety, particularly anxiety around social interaction.

In conducting these Google keyword searches, I also sought out social networking sites and social media platforms for depression, anxiety, and mental health. I anticipated these technologies would also be useful digital interventions, alongside smartphone apps, AI and chatbots. After all, there is a rich history in early internet studies around online support networks (Wellman, 2001).

However, I found a significant qualitative difference in how social media in relation to mental health was represented in search results. That representation – although abundant – foregrounded a causal link between social media use and poor mental health (e.g. anxiety, depression). Whereas apps, AI and chatbots were presented by Google search as solutions to mental health conditions, social media platforms were positioned as detriments thereto.

Table 8.2. Google Play Store Search (Accessed 11 February 2021).

	Keyword		
	Depression	**Anxiety**	**Mental health**
No. of apps	251	250	250

From Google search, I moved onto the Google Play Store in order to understand how mental health was being catered for by the smartphone and specifically by Android app developers. Within the UK Google Play Store, I searched for 3 keywords: depression; anxiety; and mental health. This yielded a total of 751 apps (Table 8.2), of surprisingly even distribution between the three categories. This figure was reduced to 635 unique apps once duplicate listings across the three searches were identified and removed.

In a spreadsheet, I then captured each app's name, developer and download fee. Of the 751 total apps, I found that 57 appeared in 2 of the 3 keyword searches while 31 apps appeared in all 3 searches (Table 8.3).

Across these datasets, I read each app's Play Store description, user reviews and the app's product website (where available) in order to understand what was

Table 8.3. Android Dataset: Apps Across All Three Keywords.

App Name	
Ascension Wysa	MindDoc
7 Cups	Mood Potatoes
Ada	Mood Tracker
Anxiety Tracker	MoodMission
Aurum	MoodSpace
BetterHelp	MoodTools
BlissU	My Online Therapy
CBT Thought Diary	Online therapy
Cognitive Behavioural Therapy	Sanvello
Dealing with Depression	TalkLife
eMoods Bipolar Mood Tracker	Talkspace
InnerHour Self-Care Therapy	Unburden
Lift	WellMind
Mental Health Tests	What's Up?
Mental Health Tracker	Wysa
Mind journal	

on offer. To make sense of my observations, I developed a four-part framework by which to map them and tease out recurring features in my sample. In the next section, I introduce this framework and my findings in relation to it.

Limitations

Before proceeding, I wish to briefly highlight two limitations of this research. First, is the linguistic bias of this study, which addresses only English-language literature and empirical data. This linguistic bias matters because it operates as a cultural filter. Language is a cultural articulation *par excellence* (Wong, 2010), and culture – as a normative framework – affects topics of public discourse and how those topics get talked about. It also influences which topics are considered taboo. Mental health is one of these culturally marked fields. Discursively, going to therapy has long been regarded as 'so American' (Havis, 2017). This suggests that American biases and dispositions towards mental health may be built into my dataset and analysis.

Secondly, this research did not talk to any users or developers of the apps analysed. Indeed, the purpose of this study was to map the current landscape of mental health apps, and armchair research is well-suited to this task. However, understanding the experiences of app users and the intentions of app developers could add considerable depth to this scoping exercise.

Mapping Mental Health Apps: A Framework

This section proposes a framework by which analysts can conceptualise today's mental health app ecosystem and the products available therein. Using the data-sets defined above, I evaluated apps relative to four variables: an app's intended audience; its communicative affordances; its business model; and its therapeutic approach. These variables, taken together, provide a means of understanding how mental health and illness are being conceptualised and addressed by contemporary digital culture.

Audience

My analysis of the 635-app dataset shows that most apps targeting depression, anxiety, and mental health are aimed at single users. Although a handful of these offer practice test materials to mental health professionals (e.g. Psychiatric & Mental Health Nurse Exam Prep 2019), the vast majority of apps address individuals who are presumed to be experiencing symptoms of depression and anxiety.

Locating an app's intended audience reveals who an app is designed for (and who not). For developers, attending to the needs of the imagined user will inform an app's messaging and design, its aesthetic, language, and technical features. So, I was struck by that fact that most of the apps seemed to regard audiences as blank slates devoid of any identifying qualities other than their interest in mental health. For instance, no apps are gender-specific. And bar one exception (i.e. BlissU), the apps do not target audiences according to age or profession. In other words, mental health apps try to reach as broad an audience as possible. I found this 'one-size-fits-all' approach striking because it felt almost transgressive in the era of sophisticated audience segmentation and content personalisation that I described earlier.

However, my hopes of a robust departure in audience address were short-lived. Examination of the apps' communicative affordances revealed that personalisation and individualisation remained dominant modes of user engagement.

Communicative Affordances

This part of my framework considers the sorts of communication pathways built into my dataset. How did users communicate within the apps, and who (or what) were they communicating with? My findings suggest that mental health apps can be distinguished between two broad categories of communicative possibility: conversational and non-conversational.

The former facilitates engagement with a conversational agent, whether in real-time or asynchronously. That agent may be machinic, wherein the user 'talks' to a chatbot or AI (e.g. Wysa). Alternately, the conversational agent may be human, with several apps offering peer support chatrooms (e.g. Online Therapy, Sanvello) and others connecting users with qualified therapists (e.g. Better-Help) for one-on-one care. This latter app type reflects a traditional tele-health approach, wherein digital technology is deployed to replicate an offline clinical setting (Lupton, 2014).

In my dataset, apps that involved a conversational agent – whatever its specificities – were by far the minority app type. Instead, most apps fell into the second category of communicative possibility, wherein users communicated with no one (or arguably, only with oneself). Such apps provided a wide range of activities, from games, self-help exercises and self-guided study materials to instructional videos and quizzes to mood tracking and gratitude journaling (e.g. Mood Potatoes). But across this populated range of apps, none facilitates the possibility of talking to others.

Instead, users are siloed off from one another. This marks a significant departure from the group-based solidarities and care collectivities of the early WWW (Rheingold, 1993; Orgad, 2005a). But it also reminds us that other kinds of communicative futures are possible.

Business Model

Most of the apps in my dataset were free to access. Of the 635 unique apps identified, only 38 – less than 6% – charged a one-time download fee. Half of those apps were anxiety-specific, with fees ranging from £0.59 to £26.99; this may suggest app developers view anxiety as a mental health condition people are willing to pay to 'fix'.

Of free-to-download apps, some operate according to a freemium model (Seufert, 2014) wherein certain features are accessible to all users for free while other features are hidden behind a paywall (e.g. 7 Cups). Other free-to-download apps employ a subscription model, with users paying a monthly fee to access the app's services. The subscription model is most commonly used by apps that connect users to qualified mental health professionals for individual therapy (e.g. Talkspace). This subscription may entitle users to send an unlimited number of text messages to their dedicated therapist or to receive a specific number of text replies from that therapist. A monthly subscription usually also comes with a set number of therapy sessions – consultations that mimic in-person therapy but are promoted by apps as a much more affordable alternative.

Finally, the most common business model in my dataset is one that relies on advertising. Here, free-to-download apps remain free to users but integrate ads into the user experience. Free-to-download apps, thus, almost always come at a cost.

Therapeutic Approach

The final spoke in my framework concerns the therapeutic approach deployed by mental health apps. A small subset of apps in this research were purely diagnostic tools, aimed at helping users ascertain whether they were suffering from depression or anxiety and helping them identify the severity of their condition.

Of the remaining apps, some facilitated talking therapy. This group of apps overwhelmingly foregrounded cognitive behavioural therapy (CBT) techniques. CBT aims at identifying and modifying an individual's patterns of thought and behaviour (Beck, 2021). Rather than considering the layered complexities of a person's life and how these may contribute to their individual experiences with mental illness, CBT focuses on locating 'bad' behaviour (action or thought) and retraining an individual to behave or respond differently.

This emphasis on CBT also saturates the biggest category of mental health apps relative to therapeutic approach: apps offering self-help resources. As stated earlier, these largely non-conversational apps offer tools for mood tracking, journaling, learning about depression and anxiety, and testing one's knowledge. Many of these apps also feature an analytics dashboard which quantifies a user's engagement. It may show things like number of learning modules completed, chart mood fluctuation over time, or track quiz performance.

Finally, some self-help apps offer guided meditation scripts, mindfulness exercises, and other prompts aimed at relaxation and stress reduction (e.g. Calm). Within this category, I was struck by the prevalence of positive affirmations and gratitude journals. Deriving from the positive psychology movement (Gable & Haidt, 2005), these techniques of self-care long predate smartphones. Mitch Horowitz (2014), for instance, traces the roots of the 'positive thinking gospel' to nineteenth century America. The individualised centring of positivity also appears in psychology's autosuggestion movement of the early twentieth century, developed by French hypnotherapist Émile Coué. Coué (1922) claimed self-talk alone could improve one's wellbeing, and popularised the mantra 'Every day, in every way, I'm getting better and better'.

Regardless of therapeutic approach deployed, the apps analysed all legitimise themselves with reference to clinical mental health research, describing themselves as 'research-backed' or 'research-led'. Yet at the same time, these apps disavow their clinical legitimacy with various disclaimers. MoodMission, for instance, states that it 'is not a replacement for professional help'. Similarly, MoodTools describes itself as a 'mental health application (that) is not intended to be a replacement for treatment nor any sort of medical intervention'. This disavowal of responsibility is something I explore more fully below.

Me Apps

This section considers the app mapping framework presented above in relation to this project's aim of understanding how contemporary digital culture – particularly in the context of smartphone ubiquity – addresses mental health and mental illness. What does this ecosystem's response to depression and anxiety reveal about broader normative expectations of technology-for-health?

I propose the concept of *me apps* to respond to this question, and to capture the mode of address most commonly deployed by the mental health apps in this study. That mode of address is predominantly individualised, commercialised, and desocialised. *Me apps* thus extend from and articulate the virulent neoliberalism that marks contemporary life in the UK. Neoliberalism here is regarded as a social, economic, and political ideology that valourises individual choice above all (Chen, 2013). It is a worldview governed by the fetishisation of individualism – an orientation that holds profound consequences for social, economic, and political ideations of the 'good life' and how one might achieve it.

The neoliberal register of *me apps* also has consequences for how mental health is being conceptualised and attended to within contemporary digital culture. It is precisely this convergence of technology, mental health, and ideology that the concept of *me apps* gestures towards. *Me apps* refer to the technical, economic, and social features of my dataset. Taken together, these characteristics frame depression and anxiety as individual problems to be solved alone. Responsibility for care, and the work of caring, is individualised and delinked from broader contextual factors, structural critiques, and support infrastructures. *Me apps* seem to absolve society from the need to care by privatising, silencing, and compartmentalising mental illness into the smartphone.

It is a problem for me that so few of the apps in my dataset pair users with mental health professionals for therapeutic conversation. Instead, most apps cherry pick prescriptive features of CBT that can be self-administered, rendering mental health care and wellness tasks to be done by the self, for the self, with one's pocket computer. This positioning is replicated by the disclaimers mentioned earlier. App developers want no responsibility for user outcomes, so much so that they disavow their products' own clinical legitimacy. This divestment from responsibility is a central technique of neoliberalism (Rottenberg, 2014), and one which thoroughly individualises – rather than collectivises – the 'problem' of mental illness.

The individualisation of wellbeing is not unique to mental health. Indeed, the idea of 'me apps' was inspired by Donna Dickenson's (2013) compelling account of changes in biomedical research and development. Dickenson documents a sector-wide move away from investing in what she calls 'we medicine' – pharmaceutical and biotech innovations aimed at helping big swathes of the population. This universalist orientation has produced life-saving treatments like the polio and measles vaccines, penicillin, and now the Covid vaccine. But Dickenson traces the industry's move away from this type of collective solution towards investment in what she dubs 'me medicine'. This is personalised and privatised health care encompassing a broad range of interventions, from bespoke cancer therapies, umbilical cord blood banks and stem cell therapy, to retail genetics.[1]

Dickenson understands this shift towards 'me medicine', in part, as indicative of 'the dominance of personal choice as a cultural value'. As mentioned earlier, the fetishisation of choice is a key feature of neoliberalism and the digital culture produced therein. Consider the fact that the Google Play Store had 251 apps targeting depression! This abundance strikes me as more paralysing than empowering. As Zygmunt Bauman (2001) suggested, 'one shivers in front of the endless possibilities as one hesitates when facing choice', aware that if one makes a bad decision and things go wrong, there is no one to blame but oneself.

Dickenson (2013) also notes that the rise of me medicine reflects a rise in patient narcissism – an accusation remarkably similar to the one routinely launched at today's social media users (McCain & Campbell, 2018). Social media platforms – their content and their modalities – foreground the individual user. Therein, self-fascination, self-expression and solipsism are highly valued and valuable. As discussed previously, this political economy is a stark departure from earlier generations of 'social media', which foregrounded togetherness, community cultivation and sustained (often text-based) sociality.

The fact that digital culture today promotes individual choice and self-articulation is consistent with the logics, imperatives, and impositions of neoliberalism. Neoliberalism shifts responsibility onto the individual, where life outcomes are seen purely as a consequence of personal decision-making, rather than existing in relation to wider structures of power, organisation, and social reproduction (Bauman, 2001; Beck & Beck-Gernsheim, 2002). In this ideological context, people can no longer rely on a social safety net nor on the 'affiliations and ties that once provided a stable framework' (Beck-Gernsheim, 2013). Instead, 'people learn to see themselves as "the centre of action, [–] the planning office ... [of one's] own biography"' (Beck in Skelton, 2005, p. 321).

Within neoliberal digital culture, success and knowledge are privatised and individualised. And the responsibility for mental health, thus, shifts from a wider community (e.g. family, the state) to the individual. Robert Bellah (1995, see also Bellah, Madsen, Sullivan, Swidler, & Tipton, 1985) wrote with prescience that

---

[1]E.g. ancestry tracing, personal genome scans, prenatal gene editing.

If our society says, in effect, life is a race in which there are winners and losers and you'd better end up a winner, then it is natural for people to think of private opportunity alone.

It is in this context that today, psychological wellbeing has become a task in which the individual is charged with 'the responsibility for performing that task and for the consequences (also the side effects) of their performance' (Beck & Beck-Gernsheim, 2002). So mental health here is an individual responsibility and an individual problem that can only be solved *by* the affected individual.

This helps explain the prominence of positive affirmations and gratitude journals in my app dataset. The currency of these ideas makes particular sense in a neoliberal context, where, lacking recourse to social safety nets, optimism and self-confidence become personal tools for survival. As Barbara Ehrenreich (2010) laments, 'Optimism [isn't] just a psycho-spiritual lifestyle option... it [has] become increasingly mandatory'.

The individualisation of self-care and responsibility also extends to the problem of digital content overload mentioned earlier, with many of the world's tech giants wading into the tide. For example, Apple introduced the Screen Time app for iPhones in 2018 (Albergotti, 2019), to help users track and visualise their device usage. YouTube and Gmail now allow 'users to opt in to screen time limitations [as] a means of controlling addictive behavior and (by) reminding users to take a break' (Huang, 2020). But the discursive and clinical relationship between mental health and digital technology is complicated. On the one hand, positive health outcomes are linked to stepping back from hyperconnectivity and reducing one's digital footprint. Yet at the same time, the Quantified Self movement – of which *me apps* are part – argues that connectivity is key to optimising and improving one's health. Quantified Self adherents regard digital tracking and data capture technologies – whether apps, smartwatches, or other wearables – as means of achieving wellness (Ajana, 2018; Lupton, 2016). Likewise, the political economy of *me apps* seems to urge ever-greater connectivity.

The inward focus of *me apps* represents a radical departure from the ethos of the early internet. Even before Tim Berners-Lee announced the WWW in 1989, the internet was being used as a collaborative tool for supporting people concerned about mental health. One of the earliest examples is the *Whole Earth 'Lectronic Link* (the WELL), which launched as a text-based online community in 1985 and was a social media platform before we started using the term 'social media' or 'platform'.

On the WELL, there were discussion forums for just about any topic imaginable, including forums for 'Mind, Spirit and Health', with groups on Psychology, Health and Medicine, Buddhist Practice and Principles, Alcohol and Drug Recovery, and various others. As Howard Rheingold's (1993) seminal work shows, these forums operated as spaces of information sharing, sociality, and short- and long-term emotional support. Shani Orgad (2005b) writes about similar types of collective support in operation on SharedExperience.org, a social networking site for breast cancer sufferers and survivors. She homes in on the emotional support, sociality, and mutuality that this online community afforded its participants.

Today's personalised, desocialised and commercialised digital culture ecology represents a shift away from such communities of solidarity and information sharing. In place of these networks of collectivity and care, we see platforms of individualisation. Or to appropriate Dickenson's (2013) formulation, we see a shift from 'we apps' to 'me apps'.

Conclusion

Aspirations around tele-health have been with us for a long time (Gogia & Hartvigsen, 2020). But the current ubiquity of the smartphone, coupled with Covid-related social restrictions, suggests this may be a golden age for telemedicine – particularly so for mental health care. Today, computing afford-ability, high-speed internet availability and video conferencing accessibility mean patients and clinicians can easily connect and replicate many of the conditions of in-person therapy.

Despite these possibilities, digital technologies are often linked with poor men-tal health rather than with mental health treatment. As this chapter has shown, this is due in large part to the neoliberal values and modes of address that cur-rently operate in digital culture. These values are today crystalised in the smart-phone, which offers a commercialised and highly curated ecosystem of apps for connecting to ideas, people, and things. It is also a key interface through which we connect with and articulate ourselves. Despite the social potentialities of the smartphone, my analysis of *me apps* gestures to a profoundly desocialised and inward-looking technoculture.

As such, smartphones represent a profoundly individualised moment in the history of digital culture. If the medium is the message, as McLuhan (1964) sug-gested, and today's medium is the smartphone screen, then the message seems to be one of solipsism. My research has contextualised this solipsistic register, first by tracing historic shifts in computing hardware, software, and content. I then mapped the contemporary terrain of mental health apps in the UK via a four-part framework. Through this I have located the individualised, commercialised, and desocialised features of *me apps*, reflected on how they have emerged and explored how they coincide with neoliberal understandings of health and self.

This chapter's mapping work, its attention to digital culture history, and its development of *me apps* all offer a powerful reminder that other kinds of techno-socialities are possible. As David Graeber (2015, p. 89) wisely observed, 'the ulti-mate, hidden truth of the world is that it is something that we make, and could just as easily make differently'. The intersection of mental health care and digital culture can be reimagined and redesigned.

In the UK (as elsewhere), building that alternative vision matters. Public Health England (2020) found that between 2017 and 2018, 17% of England's adult population was prescribed antidepressants. This figure has since increased, even as the number of 'new referrals to adult mental health services' declined (Armitage, 2021). Depression and anxiety are rampant. They are also highly gendered. In England, almost twice as many women as men 'are diagnosed with depression in their lifetime' (MHFA England, 2020). Women are also much more likely to experience major depression (Leach, et al., 2008) and be diagnosed with anxiety (Remes, Brayne, van der Linde, & Lafortune, 2016).

These are conditions that digital culture can be used to address. But as this chapter has shown, we need to consider carefully the outcomes implied by the modes of address our technologies deploy. Likewise, we need to consider how mental health care apps can be designed without reproducing existing neoliberal structures of power and disempowerment.

References

Ajana, B. (Ed.) (2018). *Metric culture: Ontologies of self-tracking practices*. Bingley: Emerald Publishing Limited.

Albergotti, R. (2019). Teens find circumventing Apple's parental controls is child's play. *The Washington Post*. October 15. Retrieved from https://www.washingtonpost.com/technology/2019/10/15/teens-find-circumventing-apples-parental-controls-is-childs-play

Arksey, H., & O'Malley, L. (2005). Scoping studies: Towards a methodological framework. *International Journal of Social Research Methodology, 8*(1), 19–32.

Armitage, R. (2021). Antidepressants, primary care, and adult mental health services in England during COVID-19. *The Lancet Psychiatry, 8*(2). Retrieved from https://www.thelancet.com/journals/lanpsy/article/PIIS2215-0366(20)30530-7/fulltext

Arthur, C. (2011). The first computer was as big as a room. Now they're the size of a full stop... and getting even smaller. *The Independent*, October 23. Retrieved from https://www.independent.co.uk/news/first-computer-was-big-room-now-they-re-size-full-stop-and-getting-even-smaller-1349636.html

Bagnall, J. (2003). New technology briefing: Search engine marketing. *Interactive Marketing, 4*, 388–394.

Bauman, Z. (2001). *The individualized society*. Malden, MA: Polity Press.

Beattie, A., & Daubs, M. S. (2020). Framing 'digital well-being' as a social good. *First Monday, 25*(12). doi:10.5210/fm.v25i12.10430

Beck-Gernsheim, E. (2013). Interview with Elisabeth Beck-Gernsheim on 'Individualization'. *Theory, Culture & Society*. Retrieved from https://www.theoryculturesociety.org/interview-with-elisabeth-beck-gernsheim-on-individualization

Beck, J. S. (2021). *Cognitive behavior therapy: Basics and beyond* (3rd ed.). New York, NY: The Guildford Press.

Beck, U., & Beck-Gernsheim, E. (2002). *Individualization: Institutionalized individualism and its social and political consequences*. London: SAGE Publications.

Bellah, R. N. (1995). Individualism and Commitment: "America's Cultural Conversation". Lecture at Portland State University, March 7. Retrieved from http://www.robertbellah.com/lectures_6.htm

Bellah, R. N., Madsen, R., Sullivan, W. M., Swidler, A., & Tipton, S. M. (1985). *Habits of the heart: Individualism and commitment in American Life*. London: University of California Press.

Berry, C., Kim, S., & Spigel, L. (2010). *Electronic elsewheres: Media, technology, and the experience of social space*. Minneapolis: University of Minnesota Press.

Berthon, P., Pitt, L., & Campbell, C. (2019). Addictive De-Vices: A public policy analysis of sources and solutions to digital addiction. *Journal of Public Policy & Marketing, 38*(4), 451–468.

Bhalotia, G., Hulgeri, A., Nakhe, C., Chakrabarti, S., & Sudarshan, S. (2002). Keyword searching and browsing in databases using BANKS. In *Proceedings 18th International Conference on Data Engineering* (pp. 431–440), San Jose, CA, USA.

Blackwell, D., Leaman, C., Tramposch, R., Osborne, C., & Liss, M. (2017). Extraversion, neuroticism, attachment style and fear of missing out as predictors of social media use and addiction. *Personality and Individual Differences, 116*, 69–72.

Bucher, T. (2018). *If… Then: Algorithmic power and politics*. New York, NY: Oxford University Press.

Chen, E. (2013). Neoliberalism and popular women's culture: Rethinking choice, freedom and agency. *European Journal of Cultural Studies, 16*(4), 440–452.

Chesney, E., Goodwin, G. M., & Fazel, S. (2014). Risks of all-cause and suicide mortality in mental disorders: A meta-review. *World Psychiatry, 13*(2), 153–160.

Correll, C. U., Solmi, M., Veronese, N., Bortolato, B., Rosson, S., Santonastaso, P., … Stubbs, B. (2017). Prevalence, incidence and mortality from cardiovascular disease in patients with pooled and specific severe mental illness: A large-scale meta-analysis of 3,211,768 patients and 113,383,368 controls. *World Psychiatry, 16*(2), 163–180.

Coué, E. (2019 [1922]). *Self mastery through conscious autosuggestion*. New York, NY: Gildan Media LLC.

D'Arienzo, M. C., Boursier, V., & Griffiths, M. D. (2019). Addiction to social media and attachment styles: A systematic literature review. *International Journal of Mental Health and Addiction, 17*, 1094–1118.

Dickenson, D. (2013). *Me medicine vs. we medicine: Reclaiming biotechnology for the common good*. New York, NY: Columbia University Press.

Duncan, P., & Marsh, S. (2021). Antidepressant use in England soars as pandemic cuts counselling access. *The Guardian*, January 1. Retrieved from https://www.theguardian.com/society/2021/jan/01/covid-antidepressant-use-at-all-time-high-as-access-to-counselling-in-england-plunges

Ehrenreich, B. (2010). Overrated Optimism: The Peril of Positive Thinking. *Time*, October 10. Retrieved from http://content.time.com/time/health/article/0,8599,1929155,00.html

Feldman, Z. (forthcoming). On quitting social media: Agency is a red herring. In A. Chia, A. Jorge, & T. Karppi (Eds.), *Reckoning with social media: Disconnection in the age of the techlash*. London: Rowman & Littlefield.

Fuchs, C. (2017). *Social media: A critical introduction* (2nd ed.). London: SAGE Publications.

Gable, S. L., & Haidt, J. (2005). What (and Why) is positive psychology? *Review of General Psychology, 9*(2), 103–110.

Global Burden of Disease Study Collaborators. (2013). Global, regional, and national incidence, prevalence, and years lived with disability for 301 acute and chronic diseases and injuries in 188 countries, 1990-2013: A systematic analysis for the Global Burden of Disease study. *The Lancet, 386*(9995), 743–800.

Gogia, S., & Hartvigsen, G. (2020). Rationale, history, and basics of telehealth. In S. Gogia (Ed.), *Fundamentals of telemedicine and telehealth* (pp. 11–34). London: Academic Press.

Graeber, D. (2015). *The Utopia of rules: On technology, stupidity, and the secret joys of bureaucracy*. London: Melville House.

Havis, R. J. (2017). The US Versus UK: Comparing mental health care and stigma. *Talkspace*, July 10. Retrieved from https://www.talkspace.com/blog/us-versus-uk-comparing-mental-health-care-stigma

Hawi, N. S., & Samaha, M. (2017). The relations among social media addiction, self-esteem, and life satisfaction in university students. *Social Science Computer Review, 35*(5), 576–586.

Hofacker, C. F., & Murphy, J. (2000). Clickable World Wide Web banner ads and content sites. *Journal of Interactive Marketing, 14*(1), 49–59.

Horowitz, M. (2014). *One simple idea: How positive thinking reshaped modern life*. New York, NY: Crown Publishers.

Huang, M. (2020). On the rise of digital wellness. Retrieved from https://medium.com/social-media-stories/on-the-rise-of-digital-wellbeing-ca648e68e873

Johnson, J. (2021). Search engines ranked by market share in the United Kingdom (UK) as of January 2021. *Statistica*, February 11. Retrieved from https://www.statista.com/statistics/280269/market-share-held-by-search-engines-in-the-united-kingdom

Lally, E. (2002). *At home with computers*. Oxford: Berg Publishing.

Lanier, J. (2018). *Ten arguments for deleting your social media accounts right now*. London: Vintage.

Leach, L. S. et al. (2008). Gender differences in depression and anxiety across the adult lifespan: The role of psychosocial mediators. *Social Psychiatry and Psychiatric Epidemiology*, *43*(12), 983–998.

Leiner, B. M., Cerf, V. G., Clark, D., Kahn, R. E., Kleinrock, L., Lynch, D. C., ... Wolff, S. S. (1997). The past and future history of the Internet. *Communications of the ACM*, *40*(2), 102–108.

Livingstone, S. (1992). The meaning of domestic technologies: A personal construct analysis of familial gender relations. In E. Hirsch & R. Silverstone (Eds.), *Consuming technologies: Media and information in domestic spaces* (pp. 113–130). New York, NY: Routledge.

Lupton, D. (2014). Critical perspectives on digital health technologies. *Sociology Compass*, *8*(12), 1344–1359.

Lupton, D. (2016). *The quantified self*. Malden, MA: Polity.

Manovich, L. (2013). *Software takes command*. London: Bloomsbury Academic.

McCain, J. L., & Campbell, W. K. (2018). Narcissism and social media use: A meta-analytic review. *Psychology of Popular Media Culture*, *7*(3), 308–327.

McLuhan, M. (1964). *Understanding media: The extensions of man*. New York: McGraw-Hill.

McLuhan, M. (1968). *War and peace in the global village*. New York, NY: Bantam Books.

McManus, S., Bebbington, P., Jenkins, R., & Brugha, T. (Eds.) (2016). *Mental health and wellbeing in England: Adult Psychiatric Morbidity Survey 2014*. Leeds: NHS Digital. Retrieved from https://webarchive.nationalarchives.gov.uk/20180328130852tf_/http://content.digital.nhs.uk/catalogue/PUB21748/apms-2014-full-rpt.pdf

MHFA England. (2020). Mental health statistics. Retrieved from https://mhfaengland.org/mhfa-centre/research-and-evaluation/mental-health-statistics

Mills, C., & Hilberg, E. (2020). The construction of mental health as a technological problem in India. *Critical Public Health*, *30*(1), 41–52.

Moore, M., & Tambini, D. (Eds.) (2018). *Digital dominance: The Power of Google, Amazon, Facebook, and Apple*. New York, NY: Oxford University Press.

Morozov, E. (2013). *To save everything, click here: Technology, solutionism, and the urge to fix problems that don't exist*. London: Allen Lane.

Neville, S., & Jones, V. (2021). Mental health absences 'cost UK businesses £14bn in 2020'. *WalesOnline*, February 10. Retrieved from https://www.walesonline.co.uk/news/uk-news/mental-health-absences-cost-uk-19803458

NHS Digital. (2020). Psychological therapies: Annual report on the use of IAPT services 2019-20. Retrieved from https://digital.nhs.uk/data-and-information/publications/statistical/psychological-therapies-annual-reports-on-the-use-of-iapt-services/annual-report-2019-20

O'Dwyer, D. (2014). Berners-Lee gifted us the web 25 years ago and changed our communications forever. *The Irish Times*, March 12. Retrieved from https://www.irishtimes.com/business/technology/berners-lee-gifted-us-the-web-25-years-ago-and-changed-our-communications-forever-1.1721085

O'Regan, G. (2016). The first digital computers. In *Introduction to the history of computing: A computing history primer* (pp. 55–72). Cham: Springer.

O'Reilly, T. (2005). What Is Web 2.0: Design patterns and business models for the next generation of software. Retrieved from https://www.oreilly.com/pub/a/web2/archive/what-is-web-20.html

Ofcom. (2015). The Communications Market Report 2015. Retrieved from https://www.ofcom.org.uk/research-and-data/multi-sector-research/cmr/cmr15

Ofcom. (2016). *Communications Market Report: Scotland.* Retrieved from https://www.ofcom.org.uk/__data/assets/pdf_file/0024/43476/CMR_Scotland_2016.pdf

Olanrewaju, A.-S., Hossain, M. A., Whiteside, N., & Mercieca, P. (2020). Social media and entrepreneurship research: A literature review. *International Journal of Information Management, 50,* 90–110.

ONS. (2020a). Internet access – Households and individuals, Great Britain: 2020. Retrieved from   https://www.ons.gov.uk/peoplepopulationandcommunity/householdcharac-teristics/homeinternetandsocialmediausage/bulletins/internetaccesshouseholdsand-individuals/2020

ONS. (2020b). Coronavirus and depression in adults, Great Britain: June 2020. Retrieved from   https://www.ons.gov.uk/peoplepopulationandcommunity/wellbeing/articles/coronavirusanddepressioninadultsgreatbritain/june2020#introduction

Orgad, S. (2005a). The transformative potential of online communication: The case of breast cancer patients' Internet spaces. *Feminist Media Studies, 5*(2), 141–161.

Orgad, S. (2005b). *Storytelling online: Talking breast cancer on the internet.* New York, NY: Peter Lang.

Pittaway, D. A. (2020). Digital hygiene: Pandemic lockdowns and the need to suspend fast thinking. *Filosofia Theoretica: Journal of African Philosophy, Culture and Religions, 9*(3), 33–48.

Ponnusamy, S., Iranmanesh, M., Foroughi, B., & Hyun, S. S. (2020). Drivers and outcomes of instagram addiction: Psychological well-being as moderator. *Computers in Human Behavior, 107.* doi:10.1016/j.chb.2020.106294

Public Health England. (2020). Prescribed medicines review: Summary. Retrieved from https://www.gov.uk/government/publications/prescribed-medicines-review-report/prescribed-medicines-review-summary

Remes, O., Brayne, C., van der Linde, R., & Lafortune, L. (2016). A systematic review of reviews on the prevalence of anxiety disorders in adult populations. *Brain and Behavior, 6*(7). Retrieved from https://onlinelibrary.wiley.com/doi/full/10.1002/brb3.497

Rheingold, H. (1993). *The virtual community: Homesteading on the electronic frontier.* Reading, MA: Addison-Wesley.

Robinson, J. (2020). Rate of depression in Great Britain doubled during COVID-19 pandemic, ONS figures reveal. *The Pharmaceutical Journal,* August 19. Retrieved from https://pharmaceutical-journal.com/article/news/rate-of-depression-in-great-brit-ain-doubled-during-covid-19-pandemic-ons-figures-reveal

Rottenberg, C. (2014). The rise of neoliberal feminism. *Cultural Studies, 28*(3), 418–437.

Sajithra, K., & Rajindra, P. (2013). Social media – History and components. *IOSR Journal of Business and Management, 7*(1), 69–74.

Seufert, E. B. (2014). *Freemium economics: Leveraging analytics and user segmentation to drive revenue.* Waltham, MA: Elsevier.

Shaban, H. (2019). Digital advertising to surpass print and TV for the first time, report says. *The Washington Post,* February 20. Retrieved from https://www.washington-post.com/technology/2019/02/20/digital-advertising-surpass-print-tv-first-time-report-says

Skelton, C. (2005). The 'individualized' (woman) in the academy: Ulrich Beck, gender and power. *Gender and Education, 17*(3), 319–332.

Spence, A. (2020). Britain's struggling mental health services are on the brink of a new crisis. *OpenDemocracy,* December 18. Retrieved from https://www.opendemocracy.net/en/ournhs/britains-struggling-mental-health-services-are-on-the-brink-of-a-new-crisis

Sutton, T. (2017). Disconnect to reconnect: The food/technology metaphor in digital detoxing. *First Monday*, *22*(26). Retrieved from http://firstmonday.org/ojs/index.php/fm/article/view/7561/6310.

Syvertsen, T., & Enli, G. (2020). Digital detox: Media resistance and the promise of authenticity. *Convergence: The International Journal of Research into New Media Technologies*, *26*(5–6), 1269–1283.

Targowski, A. (1990). Strategies and architecture of the electronic global village. *Information Society*, *7*(3), 187–202.

Toffler, A. (1970). *Future shock*. New York, NY: Random House.

van Dijck, J. (2013). *The culture of connectivity: A critical history of social media*. Oxford: Oxford University Press.

Wajcman, J. (2010). Feminist theories of technology. *Cambridge Journal of Economics*, *34*(1), 143–152.

Wellman, B. (2001). Computer networks as social networks. *Science*, *293*(5537), 2031–2034.

Williams, R. (1974). *Television: Technology and cultural form*. London: Fontana.

Williams, R. (1985). *Towards 2000*. Harmondsworth: Penguin.

Wong, J. (2010). The "triple articulation" of language. *Journal of Pragmatics*, *42*(11), 2932–2944.

Part IV

Body Quantification and Smart Machines

Chapter 9

The 'Smart' AI Trainer & Her Quantified Body at Work

Phoebe V. Moore

Abstract

Most scholarly and governmental discussions about artificial intelligence (AI) today focus on a country's technological competitiveness and try to identify how this supposedly new technological capability will improve productivity. Some discussions look at AI ethics. But AI is more than a technological advancement. It is a social question and requires philosophical inquiry. The producers of AI who are software engineers and designers, and software users who are human resource professionals and managers, unconsciously as well as consciously project direct forms of intelligence onto machines themselves, without considering in any depth the practical implications of this when weighed against human actual or perceived intelligences. Neither do they think about the relations of production that are required for the development and production of AI and its capabilities, where data-producing human workers are expected not only to accept the intelligences of machines, now called 'smart machines', but also to endure particularly difficult working conditions for bodies and minds in the process of creating and expanding the datasets that are required for the development of AI itself. This chapter asks, who is the smart worker today and how does she contribute to AI through her quantified, but embodied labour?

Keywords: Artificial intelligence; quantified work; smart machine; smart worker; big data; content moderator

The Quantification of Bodies in Health: Multidisciplinary Perspectives, 181–194
Copyright © 2022 by Phoebe V. Moore
Published under an exclusive license by Emerald Publishing Limited
doi:10.1108/978-1-80071-883-820211014

Most scholarly and governmental discussions about artificial intelligence (AI) today focus on a country's technological competitiveness and try to identify how this supposedly new technological capability will improve productivity. Some discussions look at AI ethics. But AI is more than a technological advancement. It is a social question and requires philosophical inquiry. From the time of the Victorians who built tiny machines resembling maids, to the development of humanoid carebots such as those seen in Japan today, we have been reifying machines with our characteristics. Malabou (2015) discusses the cyberneticians' assumptions that intelligence is primarily associated with reason as per the Enlightenment ethos. Indeed, cyberneticists' fascination with similarities between living tissue and nerves and electronic circuitry 'gave rise to darker man-machine fantasies: zombies, living dolls, robots, brain washing, and hypnotism' (Pinto, 2015, p. 31). Pasquinelli (2015) argues that cybernetics, AI and current 'algorithmic capitalism' researchers believed and still believe in instrumental or technological rationality and the ontological and epistemological determinism and positivism that permeate these assumptions. The mysticism and curiosity of how smart machines can be, and how smartness and intelligence are manifest, definitely predate our current era of algorithmic management (see Adams-Prassl, 2020).

But unlike the first stages of AI research, where scholars such as Hubert Dreyfus (1979) directly challenged the idea that it would be relatively easy to get a machine to behave as though it were a human, today, very little AI research looks for a relationship between the machine and the workings of the human mind at all. Nonetheless, software engineers and designers – and software users, who in the cases set out below are human resource professionals and managers – unconsciously as well as consciously project direct forms of intelligence onto machines themselves, without considering in any depth the practical implications of this when weighed against human actual or perceived intelligences. Neither do they think about the relations of production that are required for the development and production of AI and its capabilities, where workers are expected not only to accept the intelligences of machines, now called 'smart machines', but also to endure particularly difficult working conditions for bodies and minds in the process of creating and expanding the datasets that are required for the development of AI itself.

The quantified workplace is one where workers' productivity is monitored and even possibly 'surveilled' via electronic performance monitoring (EPM) techniques (Moore 2018a, b). Most workplaces and what I have called workspaces are now digitalised and rely on the ontological premise of Cartesian dualism, with mind dominant over body. Contributing to debates in new materialism, this chapter demonstrates that a new employment relationship is emerging, with the machine as a third actor. The body of the worker and her corporeality can be separated from the cognitive aspects of work via metrics and key performance indicators, which are often delineated and measured by an invisibilised, digitalised, management system. Ajana has written extensively about the increase in metricisation of everything (Ajana, 2018, 2020) and this increasingly occurs in workplaces, from the factory and warehouse to the office and streets. Meanwhile, as digitalisation of workplaces and spaces has increased, workers still experience intensified precarity, austerity, intense competition for jobs, and anxieties about the replacement of labour-power with robots and other machines as well as ourselves being seemingly replaceable, by other humans. Workers are being asked to internalise the imperative to perform as both a mental and a manual entirety in specific productive tasks that themselves contribute to the development of AI via databases.

This chapter queries the ontological premise for recognising human 'intelligence' in machines by way of interrogating how intelligence, through textual and image recognition, is depicted and derived. The questions we must ask are how categorisation of meaning is decided and what kind of embodied labour goes into that process of categorisation via the production of data. If there is a possibility for machinic symbolic understanding, the designers, engineers and developers of such machines and the philosophers and scientists looking at these cases, still must identify labelling, that is, how are symbols themselves introduced into human understanding. This chapter aims to look at a new category of workers who are working along the AI value chain and the impact that their work is having on their bodies and minds. In digitalised workplaces and workspaces in for example, the gig work environment, labour process relations are now widely reported, where algorithmic management coupled with poor labour contracts and the lack of social protections has led to ongoing struggle. Workers resist against exploitative aspects of the working conditions, often in highly creative ways. So, forms of control discussed in digital work studies address the sophisticated or 'smart' technological capabilities of algorithmically enhanced tools. However, neither Marx nor subsequent Marxist, Marxian and post-Marxist researchers have fully acknowledged or interrogated the assumptions around an important feature: datasets. Large sets of data are necessary to scientifically build an intelligent machine, or what we today call a smart machine, given a 'smart' and 'intelligent' human is a highly problematic assumption in and of itself. What is missing is sufficient discussion of the role of ourselves as data producers and explicitly, how some people work in highly unprotected and vulnerable workplaces/spaces carrying out work that ultimately contributes to the precise datasets that are necessary to train machine learning and to produce, ultimately, AI.

After outlining smart machines' demonstrations of seeming and hoped intelligences, and then indicating how that is translated into working conditions for data-producing bodies, this chapter makes the argument that workers, in collaboration with other workers, should currently be appropriating the definition of 'smart', to critique and challenge the dominant ideas surrounding ideal types for supposed machinic smartness or intelligence. Human resources assistive machine seen in people analytics have, after all, shown evidence of discriminatory, racist, sexist, and psychosocially violent traits of human intelligence in digitalised work contexts. If these are the core tenets of the dominant forms of human intelligence today, then we should take a closer look at how these data sets are produced and the surrounding issues.

Smart Machines

We hear about smart cars, smartphones, smart watches, and even smart cities in the news and in scientific research, but there seems to be no critique around what 'smart' means. Heuristically, we can say that 'smart' as a definitional category for these kinds of objects refers to machines' ability to perform an activity on behalf of humans, or to perfect reality for us by performing menial tasks, providing convenience and services, and enhancing possibilities for ecological sustainability. Smart cars are smaller than average and can run on electricity instead of petrol, thereby helping the environment and so hopefully extending humans' stay on this planet. Smart cars are also expected to eliminate the need for the driver's body. Low productivity in the UK has been attributed to time wasted in transportation to work. If people are being driven to work by robots, we could read our Kindles and write on our I-pads in the back seat, relying on the intelligence of machines and at the same time ideally developing our own, perhaps even eliminating 'bullshit jobs' (Graeber, 2018) through achieving more quality work, upskilling and so on, and improving the country's productivity altogether.

Of course, these utopian ideas could be stymied due to the global Covid-19 pandemic, where many knowledge workers are increasingly being required to stay home to work. Thus, the 'smart office' may be increasingly defined within the laboratory of personal environments, where a range of devices used to calculate working time electronically and to measure other aspects of work are normalised via experimentation. Quantified bodies in this sense are the body at home, where productivity is abstracted by numeration and measure carried out by people analytics. Smartphones further offer a chance for work mobility and e.g., their capture of general data positioning (GPS) so workers' bodily movements can be quantified, and data generated. Smartphones can document workers' geographical data and offer the use of the internet and a camera for recorded data. Phone conversations in which we can see people's face, as well as a whole array of applications enable to find our way to the nearest restaurant or shop, listen to almost any music we want, track patterns in our steps and heart rate, order transport, set goals, do yoga, read books, and get the latest news, are other features of smart phones that can be used for workplace benefit. 'Smart cities', furthermore, are those which provide convenience for citizens and tourists via better connectedness and travel options.

While smart products and environments sound quite attractive and exciting, they rely on the acquisition of big data sets extracted from human activity or objects that are based originally in human activity. Self-driving cars must learn to recognise specific images which are originally categorised by human labour. Smart phones' provisions such as digital maps rely on data provided by humans input of locations. The smart office relies on data such as that collected from workers' keystrokes, timestamps for entering and exiting work platforms, and so on. With regards to smart services and social media, the product is provided in exchange for, in some cases, a small monetary fee, or, often, is provided with the expectation for reams of data gathered about us, used to profile our 'selves' for advertising and possibly for governmental use.

Based on human data, smart technologies, via machine learning, algorithms, robotics, emotion coding and a number of other techniques, demonstrate forms of active 'smarts' or intelligences, which I have previously called collaborative, assistive, prescriptive, and proscriptive intelligence (Moore, 2020), where machines' functionality towards these active intelligences is facilitated and augmented by AI. These are human/machine mirror intelligences, but these are based more on the *active potential* than on expected *social cognitive conditions* which then are evidenced in what Marx talked about as the social relations of production. The current chapter therefore builds on my previous arguments about human/machine reflections of intelligence, looking more closely at the social relations of production and surrounding expectations placed on the smart worker.

AI Trainers and the Relations of Production

Karl Marx observed in the *Fragment on Machines* section of *Grundrisse: Foundations of the Critique of Political Economy* (Marx, 1993) that we as humans often attribute to machines our own characteristics, and, by association, also intelligence. However, the site of introduction into the labour process is one of class struggle and the attribution of intelligence to machines relies on specific categories of 'intelligence' in socially dominant understandings of that sphere, to preside. The employment relationship in the early stages of industrialisation was dividing people along class lines as Marx wrote, whereby a handful of people were assumed to have superior mental capabilities and the intelligence to design machines and to organise and manage workplaces, as well as to manage workers and control labour processes and operations. The other main category for intelligence in fact, explicitly subordinated workers, who were expected to carry out physical labour and to mechanistically build and maintain the very same machines which ultimately were considered to be more intelligent than the average person.

All this being said, intelligence is by no means a homogeneous category. Nevertheless, so-called symbolic and connectionist AI researchers have never got to grips with nor agreed on what the most important features of intelligence are. Haugeland (1985), who coined the term 'GOFAI', described intelligent beings as demonstrating the following characteristics:

> our ability to deal with things intelligently... due to our capacity to think about them reasonably (including subconscious thinking); and the capacity to think about things reasonably[which] amounts to a faculty for internal 'automatic' symbol manipulation.

Marcus Hutter, who designed a well-known theory of universal AI, later argued:

> The human mind... is connected to consciousness and identity which define who we are... Intelligence is the most distinct characteristic of the human mind... It enables us to understand, explore, and considerably shape our world, including ourselves. (Hutter, 2012, p. 1)

AI research, Hutter indicates, reflects this sentiment, since the 'grand goal of AI is to develop systems that exhibit general intelligence on a human-level or beyond' (Hutter, 2012). Memory and the distinctly human ability to process thoughts and ideas and turn those ideas into analysis; the ability to make choices rather than simple decisions; and empathy and sentience are necessary for intelligence to be manifest, which is particularly important as machines are ascribed more forms of intelligence. In these ways, the machine may soon be understood to be autonomous.

Autonomous 'Smarts'

The most important prediction and hope in 1956, which is still widely appreciated today, is that machines can *learn* and even *teach themselves*, and this is what defines them as being intelligent, or what we now refer to as smart and what is expected by machine learning. While there have been various phases in expectations of their capability, to finalise the goal towards universal AI, the goal in the current phase of research and development is for machines to be fully autonomous.

'Universal', autonomous AI is where a single universal agent can learn to behave optimally in any environment and where universal competences are demonstrated by a robot, such as walking, seeing, and talking, where machines can teach themselves based on errors used to adapt and optimise algorithms to 'perform' better the next time. Today, as computer memory capacity increases and programs become more sophisticated, universal AI is becoming an increasingly likely prospect. This would lead to machines that can learn, teach themselves, and now, even teach people and of course, workers.

Despite the current expectation for machines to be autonomous, however, direct comparisons with human thought, being and competences in AI research have all but disappeared. This is a problem, because AI is bursting back into public discourse and experiencing a huge resurgence in corporate interest, and huge pots of government funding are being invested in this area (even as local austerity initiatives and the funding of unpopular wars continues). The European Commission's definition indicates that AI 'refers to systems that display intelligent behaviour by analysing their environment and taking actions – with some degree of *autonomy* [italics added for emphasis] – to achieve specific goals' (European Commission, 2018). This definition should facilitate a clear discussion about what is at stake as AI systems and machines are integrated into workplaces, where systems demonstrate competences that allow decision-making and prediction much faster and more accurately while exhibiting human-like behaviour and assisting workers without having, it is hoped, full autonomy. Indeed, workers are now expected to not only be controlled and managed by machines, but also potentially mimic and learn from machines, which are portrayed as universally reliable calculators, rather than the other way round.

The idea of *autonomy* is central to all discussions about AI today. But the agency ascribed to the human by definition is not identical to the concept applied to machines. A series of social movements and activist groups have taken autonomy exceedingly seriously since the 1960s such as the Italian movement now known as *autonomia* where groups took issue with the dominance of the Catholic church and of the power of the bourgeoisie to impose work and working conditions that eliminated human capacity for expression and solidarity. So human autonomy is here linked explicitly to activism and social justice. The autonomous robot is rarely described as agential in that regard. New materialism and post-humanist research have gone some way in exploring conatus and material objects and our relations to them, but to align the way that human autonomy is and has historically been comprehended with how AI autonomy is hoped, would be absurd.

Instead, autonomous machines, rather than posing a challenge to existing status quo, in the workplace context, they are expected to simply add another actor that apparently has agency and autonomy, to the standard employment relationship. This actor is of course, a supposedly autonomous machine itself. Autonomy is understood to be demonstrated via a machinic capabilities for analysis and prediction, in 'people analytics'; via automation and semi-automation which is part of a machine's supposed 'assistive' and 'collaborative' intelligence; and all of this, via machines' extensive surveillance capabilities.

Who Trains the AI?

Having looked at the types of intelligence attributed to machines both consciously and sub/unconsciously by the engineers and software developers designing and building such tools and applications and the ways that their products can be adopted, we turn to a discussion of the backbone of AI and its development, which relies upon the production of big datasets that require human labour, at least in the initial stages, to exist. In that context, swathes of semi- and unskilled workers in both the Global North and South are carrying out what is called digital 'dirty work' (Roberts, 2016) in social media and data services. This category of what we can even call AI 'trainers' (AIT) are for example (a) content moderators, who curate content for social media platforms such as Facebook and other news and video services, and (b) data service workers, who work with data via annotation and natural language process training for such products as Amazon's chatbot Alexa. Both categories have been named 'information service workers' (Gray, 2019) and they usually work in opaque conditions (Anwar & Graham, 2019). The main, and very lucrative, asset that AIT provides is information for huge databases of images and text which are used to train machines for AI, which add significant value to social media and smart devices and contribute to the development of AI. AI trainers are talked about as 'ghost workers' (Gray & Suri, 2019), and 'internet custodians' (Gillespie, 2018) where workers are expected to behave like machines (Ruckenstein & Turunen, 2019).

While there are trade secrets around what precisely happens to the data sets that these workers create, discussions I have had with several technical experts reveal that companies use the datasets which AIT work contributes to, to train other products. For example, Facebook uses deep learning networks to recognise human emotion from images (Facebook, 2020). Google offers the product 'Explicit Content Detection' where five different categories of contents can be correctly identified (Google, 2019) and Microsoft offers an Azure Content Moderator for the detection, moderation and filtering of various images, text, and videos (Microsoft Azure, 2020). Paradoxically, some of these products could be argued to eventually automate AIT work itself, however, AIT roles at present, are prevalent in today's digital workforce and are not likely to be fully automated any time soon, if at all. Currently, the tasks that AI trainers carry out require human involvement and cognitive work that is not possible, yet anyway, to fully automate (Gillespie, 2018). In fact, all algorithmic enforcement and decision-making systems are difficult, if not impossible, to automate (Perel & Elkin-Korean, 2017) because of the sensitive, subjective nature of the work as well as liability issues surrounding decision-making.

Companies do not publicly release data on how many workers are currently carrying out content moderation nor natural language process training specifically, but there were 6.1 million data workers in Europe in 2016 (IDC & Open Evidence, 2017), and at least 41,000 content moderators globally (Levin, 2017; Newton, 2019a, 2019b). The World Bank indicated that the online outsourcing industry would grow from 4.8 billion in 2016 to up to 25 billion 2020 (World Bank, 2015). Given these trends, predictions and the enormous ongoing investment into AI, this workforce is highly representative of the future of work (Gray, 2019). However, in both hemispheres, like gig workers, AIT are an unskilled and semi-skilled, low paid and insecure tier of digital workers who are most at risk in times of crisis and change. Research about, and exposure of gig work is now impacting policy across the world, but these workers have no correspondent coverage. But like gig workers, AI trainers are 'on-demand,' non-standard, carry out task-based jobs and are offered limited work contracts with very little in the way of social protections such as union membership rights. Digital workers in lower skilled tiers face very high levels of exposure to psychosocial violence (D'Cruz & Noronha, 2018; Moore, 2020), experience exceedingly unsafe workplaces (Newton, 2020), and are subject to extreme levels of monitoring and surveillance (Noronha & D'Cruz, 2009). Indeed, a group of content moderators sued Facebook due to work related post-traumatic stress disorder (Wong, 2019). Content moderators were asked to work from home by Facebook soon after Covid-19 hit, which was ethical in principle, but which introduced lots of questions about data security and about how prepared this lower tiered, mostly socially unprotected group of workers, could reasonably be. Furthermore, psychological help was not available after workers were asked to work from home. Facebook proceeded to carry out testing to automate this labour altogether, but the effectiveness was quickly exposed as faulty (Facebook Content Moderators, 2020).

On top of these violations, AI trainers perform an element of unpaid and unseen work that adds significant value to the development and products augmented by AI. The paid work of AI trainers is recognised, and their productivity measured, through intensive ticketing systems, time tracking and digitised performance monitoring. In contrast, the unpaid work of AIT is not ticketed nor tracked in the way their productive work is, and is rather, carried out through 'affective labour'. Affective labour is the mostly unseen surplus work performed by AI trainers to protect themselves from trauma, for example horrifying images that content moderators report seeing many times daily, as well as the stress of being heavily digitally monitored/tracked, and internal mechanisms unconsciously adopted to manage (Levin, 2017; Newton, 2019b; Punsmann, 2018).

The Smart Worker's Data Rights

So far, I have discussed the types of intelligences ascribed to machines and then the relations of production that are required for the very datasets upon which those perceived intelligences are build. Indeed, AI cannot exist without human data. Thus, in this section, I look at the rights that a 'smart worker' has or should have to protect her working conditions in situations where she is the data trainer, or the gig worker, or any other digitalised worker, when it comes to the protection of the data that is gathered and used about her/him whilst they simultaneously produce data themselves.

The General Data Protection Regulation (GDPR) is the focus for this set of arguments, because, as a policy instrument, it introduces extensive updates to older version of data and privacy policy, and a new playing set of possibilities for workers' rights in institutional data collection, processing, and usage. This Regulation, introduced to replace the 1995 Data Protection Directive, allows for better discussions between workers and data for the seeming necessity for data collection; the proportionality between a company's stated necessity to collect data and workers' data protection and privacy rights and other needs; requires transparency when data collection and other tracking and monitoring processes are considered; the importance of data minimisation, where companies should only collect as much data as needed to achieve an intended goal and to avoid function creep; and many other areas that concern workers. While many assume the GDPR is most applicable for consumers, there are also extensive protections imbued by this Regulation.

The GDPR is a game-changer in terms of providing ammunition for trade union representatives, in collective bargaining. For example, the area of 'consent' is important. The concept of consent was defined within the 1995 DPD (EU 95/46/EC) as 'any freely given specific and informed indication of his[/her] wishes by which the data subject signifies his agreement to personal data relating to him[/her] being processed' (EU 1995). The GDPR definition goes further, where the way that consent is sought, and given, is now also under scrutiny. The GDPR's Art.4(11) now makes it clear that consent is:

> any freely given, specific, informed and unambiguous indication
> of the data subject's wishes by which he or she, by a statement or
> by a clear affirmative action, signifies agreement to the processing
> of personal data relating to him or her.

Art. 7 and recitals 32, 33, 42 and 43 of the GDPR provide guidance for the ways the Data Controller (usually the organisation or institution which employs workers and collects data about them) must behave to meet the main elements of the consent requirement. Recital 32 of the GDPR provides particularly good clarification:

> Consent should be given by a clear affirmative act establishing a freely given, specific, informed and unambiguous indication of the data subject's agreement to the processing of personal data relating to him or her, such as by a written statement, including by electronic means, or an oral statement.

'Freely given', of course, can only exist in a situation where a data subject has a say and a real choice, and as the 2020 update published by the EDPB outlined below indicates, 'if the data subject has no real choice, feels compelled to consent or will endure negative consequences if they do not consent, then consent will not be valid'. Furthermore, if it is 'bundled up' and 'non-negotiable' or whereby a subject cannot refuse or withdraw consent without detriment, then consent has not been freely offered (European Data Protection Board (EDPB), 2020, p. 7). While these explicit interventions are promising for the consumer, where for years now, data accumulation has substituted more traditional forms of payment for services, consent is difficult to authentically obtain in the employment relationship due to its inherently imbalanced nature. However, given the discussion around whether workers can meaningfully give consent for data collection and use, meaningful *dissent* to the possible violations to privacy and data protection that workers face is also increasingly possible. GDPR Recital 32 lists some important aspects of new requirements, indicating radical new regulations, such as the stipulation that "silence, pre-ticked boxes or inactivity should not... constitute consent".

The EDPB in its 2020 Guidelines 05/2020 emphasises that:

> [...] requirements for consent under the GDPR are not considered to be an 'additional obligation', but rather as *preconditions for lawful processing*. (EDPB, 2020, p. 6, emphasis added)

While consent is only one of six criteria that may be selected by a company to identify lawfulness of actions, consent to data collection and processing is nevertheless worth keeping alive in discussions particularly if co-determination is legislated and during collective bargaining phases of discussion between employers and worker representative groups. Consent could take a different form, intellectually overhauled and reconsidered in definitional terms when discussing unions to be meaningful *if obtained via unions* rather than simply individually. This is one of the recommendations for smart workers, for example that they should link to unions and worker groups for a collective voice.

For quite obvious reasons, the concept of consent does not necessarily sit easily with worker/manager relationships. However, today's smart workers have new tools at their disposal to become vigilant in the face of location and biometric data gathering and to protect themselves via collective bargaining and co-determination activities, thanks to the new provisions set out in the GDPR. Art. 22, called 'Automated individual decision-making, including profiling', indicates that:

> 22(1): The data subject shall have the right not to be subject to a decision based solely on automated processing, including

profiling, which produces legal effects concerning him or her or similarly significantly affects him or her.

The foundations for the Regulation also make it quite clear that:

(71): The data subject has the right not to be subject to a decision, which may include a measure, evaluating personal aspects relating to him or her which is based solely on automated processing and which produces legal effects concerning him or her or similarly significant affects him or her, such as... e-recruiting practices without any human intervention. Such processing includes profiling that consists of any form of automated processing of personal data evaluating the personal aspects of a natural person, in particular to analyse or predict aspects concerning the data subject's performance at work... reliability or behaviour, location, or movements, where it produces legal effects concerning him or her or similarly significantly affects him or her.

The GDPR is written with the individual as a focal subject. However, data collection operates at more levels and impact people not only individually but also as groups. Therefore, data governance should be seen as a collective good, where all social partners must be involved. The bigger the dataset, the more powerful it is, because it can be used to train algorithms for decision-making. Therefore, responses to large datasets and their collection should not be individualised but should be *collective*. Consent is usually perceived to be a unidirectional arrangement and considered intrinsically impossible in the employment relationship. However, in countries which enjoy co-determination rights, digital workspace transformations require negotiation and bargaining between workers and management to proceed and to be collectively governed rather than only individually consented.

In this light, precise identification of the necessity for technological tracking must be infused with worker/employer negotiations about what can be deemed proportional to workers' privacy and taking their wider interests seriously, which is particularly important for the smart worker AI trainer, whose jobs are explicitly traumatic and are the most surveilled than any other category of digital worker today. Privacy and dignity are more than 'interests', they are a fundamental human right. But there is a whole range of interests surrounding aspects of privacy which are at stake in the monitored workplace and space, which have relevance for discussions of necessity and proportionality. Privacy and related worker interests should be discussed and agreed in consultation and collective bargaining with unions. All and any monitoring and tracking processes must be made transparent to workers, where Data Protection Officers and trained trade union representatives work together to agree on proportionality and necessity.

Conclusion

Against this backdrop, it is not sensible to assume that technologies entering workplaces is part of 'business as usual'. The mirror for AI is repositioning, but this still reflects human behaviour and has significance for relations of production and their correspondent working conditions for the embodied labour of the smart worker, including the AI trainer discussed above. The relations of production associated with specific forms of intelligence in digitalised, AI-augmented workspaces, mostly reflect the standard employment relationship. Correspondent legislation, as it exists within capitalism, while offering some capacity for augmented collective bargaining, does not function to overturn these strictures. Ideally, smart workers should remain vigilant and aware of the structure within which AI activities are carried out, realising that the history of AI falls within this structure, and that the understanding of what makes an intelligent/smart machine, or an intelligent/smart human is no *fait accompli*. Smart workers today will be those who use the types of intelligence ascribed to machines, such as collaborative or assistive capabilities, to collaborate with and assist each other in ways that can facilitate a democratic workplace. Potentially, technologies can be repurposed and appropriated to overcome the hegemony of competition and growth models that impact the digitalised employment relationship.

While some policy characteristics within AI refer to *meaningful consent*, there are perhaps better possibilities for *meaningful dissent*. For example, co-determination could operate to at least provide some democratic social relations around the possible violations of privacy rights. Most of the EU's post-Brexit members enjoy some kind of co-determination in state-run firms and the private sector. Those countries which do not enjoy the right to co-determination are Belgium, Bulgarian, Cyprus, Estonia, Italy, Latvia, Lithuania, and Romania. To provide a platform for meaningful dissent at this stage, all EU member countries should implement some form of co-determination. In countries where co-determination rights exist, all data collection and processing activity should ideally be co-determined. Companies and labour authorities must take note of the legal apparatuses in countries with co-determination rights and ensure they are adhered to.

Another possible avenue for meaningful dissent is as follows. If workers had access to all the data that is being gathered about them as they should, given GDPR requirements, in people analytics processes discussed above, smart workers and AI trainers could be empowered by accessing new forms of data that would help them identify areas for improvement, stimulate personal development, achieve higher levels of engagement as well as to identify data that is potentially discriminatory, and challenge this through collective bargaining. The data could be used by worker representatives and workers themselves to secure better pay, for example, if they could prove they consistently worked overtime, or to demonstrate the need for time off based on data relating to sickness or stress. Therefore, with access to data about their work patterns, workers and their representatives could also negotiate with employers in areas of the employment relationship where they had not done so before. On the basis that numbers do not lie, then for example, overtime could be remunerated appropriately, sick leave taken seriously, and discrimination and stress could be avoided, where a connection could be made between sickness levels and working conditions that are exacerbated in the AI-augmented workspace.

This issue has become more pressing than ever, in the context of the global Covid-19 pandemic, where labour processes are being re-organised at high speed with the help of digital technologies. In this situation, it is important for labour scholars to ask: Which forms of 'intelligence' will dominate the design and execution of AI-augmented tools and applications into the workplace? Will workers be expected to not just mirror that intelligence, but also, to provide datasets that train AI in very difficult working conditions? In this context, who is a 'smart worker' expected to be now, given the rise of smart machines? Who will the smart(est) worker need to be in the coming years, given the rise in AI in the workplace?

References

Adams-Prassl, J. (2020). What if Your Boss Was an Algorithm? The Rise of Artificial Intelligence at Work. *Comparative Labor Law & Policy Journal, 41*(1).

Ajana, B. (Ed.) (2018). *Metric culture: Ontologies of self-tracking practices.* Bingley: Emerald Publishing.

Ajana, B. (2020). Personal metrics: Users' experiences and perceptions of self-tracking practices and data. *Social Science Information.* Retrieved from https://journals.sagepub.com/doi/full/10.1177/0539018420959522

Anwar, M. A., & Graham, M. (2019). Digital labour at economic margins: African workers and the global information economy. *Review of African Political Economy.* Retrieved from https://ssrn.com/abstract=3499706

D'Cruz, P., & Noronha, E. (2018). Target experiences of workplace bullying on online labour markets: Uncovering the nuances of resilience. *Employee Relations, 40*(1), 139–154.

Dreyfus, H. (1979). *What computers can't do.* New York, NY: MIT Press.

European Commission. (2018). *Communication on artificial intelligence for Europe.* Brussels: European Commission. Retrieved from https://ec.europa.eu/digital-single-market/en/news/communication-artificial-intelligence-europe

European Data Protection Board (EDPB). (2020). Guidelines 05/2020 on Consent Under Regulation 2016/679 Version 1.1. Accessed on May 2020.

Facebook. (2020). Computer vision. Retrieved from https://ai.facebook.com/research/computer-vision

Facebook Content Moderators. (2020). Open letter to Facebook. Retrieved from https://www.foxglove.org.uk/news/open-letter-from-content-moderators-re-pandemic

Graeber, D. (2018). Bullshit Jobs: A Theory (Allen Lane).

Gillespie, T. (2018). *Custodians of the internet: Platforms, content moderation, and the hidden decisions that shape social media.* New Haven: Yale University Press.

Google. (2019). Google Vision API (Part 13) – Detect Explicit Content (Safe Search Feature). Retrieved from https://learndataanalysis.org/google-vision-api-part-13-detect-explicit-content-safe-search-feature/

Gray, M. L. (2019). Ghost work and the future of employment. Microsoft Research June 11 2019 EmTech Next. Retrieved from https://events.technologyreview.com/video/watch/mary-gray-microsoft-ghost-work/

Gray, M. L., & Suri, S. (2019). *Ghost work: How to stop silicon valley from building a new global underclass.* New York, NY: Mariner.

Haugeland, J. (1985). Artificial Intelligence, the Very Idea (MIT Press).

Hutter, M. (2012). One decade of universal artificial intelligence. In P. Want & B. Goertzel (Eds.), *Theoretical foundations of artificial general intelligence* (Vol. 4, pp. 67–88). Amsterdam: Atlantis.

IDC and Open Evidence. (2017). *The European Data Market Study.* Retrieved from https://datalandscape.eu/study-reports/european-data-market-study-final-report

Levin, S. (2017). Google to hire thousands of moderators after outcry over YouTube Abuse Videos. *Guardian*, December 4. Retrieved from www.theguardian.com/technology/2017/dec/04/google-youtube-hire-moderators-child-abuse-videos

Malabou, C. (2015). Post-trauma: Towards a new definition? In M. Pasquinelli (Ed.), *Introduction. Alleys of your mind: Augmented intelligence and its traumas* (pp. 187–198). Lüneburg: Meson Press.

Marx, K. (1993). *Grundrisse*. London: Penguin.

Microsoft Azure. (2020). Content moderator. Retrieved from https://azure.microsoft.com/en-us/services/cognitive-services/content-moderator

Moore, P. (2018a). *The quantified self in precarity: Work, technology and what counts.* London: Routledge.

Moore, P. (2018b). Tracking affective labour for agility in the quantified workplace. *Body & Society, 24*(3), 39–67.

Moore, P. V. (2020). The mirror for (artificial) intelligence: In whose reflection? *Comparative Labour Law and Policy Journal, 41*(1), 47–67. Special Issue: 'Automation, Artificial Intelligence and Labour Law', edited by V. De Stefano.

Newton, C. (2019a). Bodies in Seats. *The Verge*. Retrieved from https://www.theverge.com/2019/6/19/18681845/facebook-moderator-interviews-video-trauma-ptsd-cognizant-tampa

Newton, C. (2019b). The Trauma Floor: The secret lives of Facebook moderators in America. *The Verge*. Retrieved from https://www.getrevue.co/profile/caseynewton/issues/coronavirus-and-the-emergency-in-content-moderation-233920

Newton, C. (2020). Coronavirus and the emergency in content moderation. The Interface Issue #474. 17 March 2020. Retrieved from https://www.getrevue.co/profile/caseynewton/issues/coronavirus-and-the-emergency-in-content-moderation-233920

Noronha, E., & D'Cruz, P. (2009). *Employee identity in Indian call centres: The notion of professionalism*. New Delhi: Sage/Response.

Pasquinelli, M. (Ed.) (2015). *Alleys of your mind: Augmented Intelligence and its Traumas.* Lüneburg: Meson Press.

Perel, M., & Elkin-Korean, N. (2017). Black Box Tinkering: Beyond disclosure in algorithmic enforcement. *Florida Law Review, 69*, 181–222.

Pinto, A. T. (2015). The Pigeon in the machine: The concept of control in behaviourism and cybernetics. In M. Pasquinelli (Ed.), *Alleys of your mind: Augmented Intelligence and its traumas* (pp. 23–36). Lüneburg: Meson Press.

Punsmann, B. G. (2018). Three Months in Hell. What I learned from three months of content moderation for Facebook in Berlin. Retrieved from https://sz-magazin.sueddeutsche.de/internet/three-months-in-hell-84381

Roberts, S. (2016). Commercial Content Moderation: Digital Laborers' Dirty Work . In S. U. Noble & B. Tynes (Eds.), *The Intersectional Internet: Race, Sex, Class and Culture Online*. Peter Lang Publishing.

Ruckenstein, M., & Turunen, L. (2019). Re-humanizing the platform: Content moderators and the logic of care. *New Media and Society, 22*(6), 1026–1042.

Wong, Q. (2019). Content moderators protect Facebook's 2.3 billion members. Who protects them? *Net News*. Retrieved from https://www.cnet.com/news/facebook-content-moderation-is-an-ugly-business-heres-who-does-it/

World Bank. (2015). The global opportunity in online outsourcing. Retrieved from http://documents.worldbank.org/curated/en/138371468000900555/The-global-opportunity-in-online-outsourcing

Chapter 10

Towards a Quanto-Qualitative Biological Engineering: The Case of the Neuroprosthetic Hand

Laura Corti

Abstract

This chapter investigates the need to focus on the gap between the pure quantification of the body, expressed by robotic implants, and recent research aiming to recover qualitative aspects of touch, such as sensation. The solution proposed is to analyse new implant technologies with a stereoscopic vision that is able to consider sensation both as intensity of neural signals and as something that we feel. The central question is: what is the value of introducing qualitative analysis into typically quantified robotics research, governed by data?

Keywords: Quantified body; neuroprosthetics; raw feels; embodiment; perception; sense

Introduction

This chapter examines the problem of implementing qualitative aspects in the evaluation of technologies. In particular, it focusses on the problem of sensation in the prosthetic hand. This issue is of interest because it reveals a more general problem concerning the relations between qualities and quantities in the scientific domain.

From a historical perspective, a large number of studies based on the concept that the *book of nature* is written in the *language of mathematics* (Galilei, 1960), indicate that modern science is founded on Galilean methods. Galileo thought that mathematics is the fundamental means for investigating the world. Consequently, Galileo distinguished between primary and secondary qualities. Primary,

The Quantification of Bodies in Health: Multidisciplinary Perspectives, 195–211

Copyright © 2022 by Laura Corti

Published under an exclusive license by Emerald Publishing Limited

doi:10.1108/978-1-80071-883-820211015

or real, qualities include shapes, positions and all the dimensions inherent in the nature of the object. Secondary qualities, such as tastes, odours, colours, are related to a relationship between the object and the subject's perception. John Locke, in *An Essay Concerning Human Understanding* (Locke, 1997) analysed in depth the general topic of qualities in relation to simple ideas. He called *primary qualities of the body* all the ideas pertaining to the structural or objective dimension, such as 'solidity, extension, figure, motion or rest, and number'; secondary qualities, in contrast, were for him

> nothing in the objects themselves but power to produce various sensations in us by their primary qualities, i.e. by the bulk, figure, texture, and motion of their insensible parts, like colours, sounds, tastes (...). (Locke, 1997, p. 135)

We can say that objects have in themselves both primary and secondary qualities. The difference lies in the fact that secondary qualities are relational and dispositional traits. For example, colour can be described both as a perceptual subjective quality and as an electromagnetic radiation, defined by wavelength and intensity.

In the twentieth century, this way of thinking was fundamental for the development of Artificial Intelligence, which is based on a *mathematisation* of computational thoughts similar to that of the Turing's machine. Today, even with technology shaping our world in an ever more profound way (Liberati, 2015; Verbeek, 2011), secondary qualities are not entirely excluded from the scientific perspective, nor have they been completely formalised. This is evident in the case of the ongoing trend in engineering that is moving towards more and more cross-contamination between primary and secondary qualities.

We can think about the field of research called Affective Computing, describable as 'computing that relates to, arises from, or deliberately influences emotions' (Picard, 1997, p. 3). The general domain of affect is studied from an informational point of view to generate models that are able to detect and recognise the emotional state of the interlocutor, and also to generate emotions and their expression in machines themselves. In robotics, a good example of this pathway is the Kismet, the robot with elements resembling human facial features: ears, eyebrows, eyelids and lips (but not a nose). The movement of these elements creates facial expressions which simulate emotions (Breazeal, 2002).

More and more robotics engineers are thinking about modelling aspects that concern the subjective sphere, and in particular, sensitive and affective response. At the same time, a large number of philosophical works are discussing the need to revise the categories concerning the qualitative dimension in various fields of research, such as cognitive sciences, artificial intelligence, robotics, and biology. For example, in 2016 the journal *Humana.Mente* dedicated a special issue to the question in order to develop an ontology because

> the new categories of qualitative ontology can simultaneously serve as a framework for those disciplines that are in the need of a qualitative, dynamic and relational analysis of their object. (Lanfredini, Liberati, Pace Giannotta, & Pagni, 2016, p. V)

In this chapter, I will address this problem from a philosophical point of view, exploring specifically the prosthetic upper limb, as an example of a quantified engineering perspective on bodies, which has to take into account also the first-person experience. As Maria Chiara Carrozza affirms, writing from an engineering perspective,

> the incentive for the creation of the artificial hand stems from the desire of the amputees to completely recover their skills, and above all to feel and explore the external environment. (Carrozza, 2019, p. 58)

Therefore, the focus of this chapter is the gap between the quantification of the body, expressed by robotic implants, and the need to consider the subjective aspects of sensation and perception.

The creation of autonomous robots capable of having emotions, as opposed to medical devices, poses different challenges that can be assigned to two main categories: (1) the neurophysiological perspective on human-device interface and (2) the phenomenological aspect, concerning for example embodiment, the relationship with the patient's living body and perceptual qualities. The chapter is comprised of five sections. Section 1 gives a brief overview of Wilfid Sellar's philosophical position regarding the problem of the relation between a scientific vision and the manifest image of man-in-the-world. Section 2 presents the bioengineering perspective on upper limb prosthesis, focussing on how touch is restored in active prostheses. Section 3 contextualises the engineering perspective in a new vision of perception as active manipulation instead of passive reception of impressions from outside the body. Section 4 ties together the theoretical inputs from the previous sections in order to propose a stereoscopic vision of the prosthetic body. Section 5 summarises the main findings of this project and highlights why phenomenology can provide a useful methodology for a complete analysis of the human-prosthesis relationship.

From the Two Images of Man to a Stereoscopic Vision

This section presents an overview of the problem of two conceptions of man-in-the-world through the reflections of Wilfrid Sellars who addresses the problem of how to build a stereoscopic vision in which the scientific and the manifest image can coexist. From the point of view of the present discussion, his work is significant as it helps identify the problem of qualities in the scientific domain and opens the way to new perspectives. In *Philosophy and the scientific image of man* (1991), Sellars distinguishes between the manifest and scientific image of man-in-the world, defined as two projections of man *in the human understanding* (Sellars, 1991). The manifest image reflects man's encounter with himself that can be described as self-awareness. It produces a kind of paradox (Gabbani, 2007) because, as Sellars claims, we cannot define a human being as a man until he encounters himself. The manifest image is a 'sophisticated' and refined image of man which becomes awareness of himself; it is a recurrent topic in the philosophical traditions which consider this image as completely true and real. Sellars suggests that, even if many philosophers have tried to subordinate the theoretical categories to this framework, it is more fruitful to avoid a 'piecemeal task' and to build a stereoscopic vision in which the two visions of man-in-the-world are articulated. His declared aim is to sketch a description of the scientific image, similar to that of the manifest image. This image is also an idealisation. It is not complete because of constant new scientific developments. The term 'scientific' does not call to mind the difference between a pre-scientific/un-scientific vision and a scientific one. It implies a more fine-grained difference between one conception, the manifest image, limited to the correlation technique applied to the 'perceptible and introspectable events' and another, the scientific image, which 'postulates imperceptible objects and events for the purpose of explaining correlation among perceptible' (Sellars, 1991, p. 19).

We can conclude that the significant difference between these two perspectives is how a relation is established between us and the world. In the case of the manifest image, the relation is based on the concept of correlation, while the scientific image is founded on the postulation.

The scientific image is a complex structure composed of a series of images founded in scientific theories, each of which is 'supported by' the manifest conception. From this perspective, it seems possible to conclude that the manifest image is 'prior in a substantive sense'. Even if the emergence of a scientific image is based on different specific images that come from various theories, the dependency between manifest and scientific image becomes clear through a methodological analysis in which the manifest image is presented as an 'inadequate but pragmatically useful' conception of reality. The number of scientific images corresponds to the number of sciences, among which Sellars includes, for example, physics and biochemistry. The scientific image itself reveals a difficulty in the unification of several different images into one coherent image. The central point is that a scale of equivalence is needed to create a balanced equation between different scientific conceptions.

The clash between these two images concerns all the philosophical dualisms in which there are two different realms, one based on a concept of the mind, which also includes sensations, and the other, the physical one, which is governed by physical laws. This dualistic theory of man is a consequence of the denial of the reality of perceptible objects. The body is seen as a system of particles and cannot be the subject of feelings and thoughts that are not explainable as a complex interaction between physical elements. Sellars proposes, as an alternative solution, the primacy of the scientific image. He decides to work on the conceptual elaboration of thought as a series of cerebral processes. He considers conceptual thought as related to but not equated with qualitative dimensions, such as sensations or feelings. Sellars draws an analogy between conceptual thinking and overt speech that can be extended to 'the analogy between speech and what sophisticated computers can do' (Sellars, 1991, p. 33) and, more in general, between computer circuits and neurophysiological organisation in patterns.

In response to the central question, What are thoughts? Sellars replies that they are 'items' conceived in terms of the roles they play (Sellars, 1991, p. 34).

This concept allows him to identify conceptual thoughts and neurophysiological processes, recalling also thoughts in the field of scientific vision. In the case of sensation, the most significant difficulty in constructing the same argumentation is located in the specific context because the analogy based on thought concerns its role. In contrast, the case of sensation involves quality itself in an ontological perspective. The question, for Sellars, is 'can we define, in the framework of neurophysiology, states which are sufficiently analogous in their intrinsic character to sensation to make identification plausible?' (Sellars, 1991, p. 35). Sellars seems to conclude that it is not possible to define, from a scientific/neurophysiological point of view, all the states connected with sensation. Consequently, the whole qualitative dimension is absent in the contemporary scientific image.

The resulting issue is 'how to reconcile the ultimate homogeneity of the manifest image with the ultimate non-homogeneity of the system of scientific objects' (Sellars, 1991, p. 36). The trajectory seems to draw a pathway to dualism, even if it is an unsatisfactory solution. The resulting antinomy is (a) the neurophysiological analysis is not complete and new objects, such as sensations, have to be added, (b) the scientific image is complete and the 'sense qualities' are mere 'appearances' that do not exist. Sellars proposes a plausible solution:

> although for many purposes the central nervous system can be construed without loss as a complex systems of physical particles, when it comes to an adequate understanding of the relation of sensory consciousness to neurophysiological process, we must penetrate to the non-particulate foundation of the particulate image, and recognize that in this non-particulate image the qualities of sense are a dimension of natural process which occurs only in connection with those complex physical processes. (Sellars, 1991, p. 37)

Therefore, the neurophysiological analysis of the category of person sees the human person as a complex system of physical particles up to the point where the sensory consciousness has to be analysed and requires a non-particulate foundation in which qualitative statements are dimensions of natural processes. The final section of Sellars' study is dedicated to recovering the general category of person, where person is defined as he 'who finds himself confronted by standards (ethical, logical etc.)' (Sellars, 1991, p. 38). A possible alternative is to define the full personal dimension of desires and duty not as a 'scientific specimen' but as an 'irreducible core of the framework of persons'. Sellars' conclusion is that

> a person can almost be defined as a being that has intentions. Thus, the conceptual framework of person is not something that needs to be *reconciled with* the scientific image but rather something to be *joined to* it. (Sellars, 1991, p. 40)

So, a complete analysis of person comprehends both the scientific image and the dimension of the language of community and individual intentions in order to transcend the dualism between the manifest and scientific image of man-in-the-world. Actions enrich our scientific vision in such a way that they directly relate the world as conceived by scientific theory to our purpose, and make it our world and no longer an alien appendage to the world in which we do our living. (Sellars, 1991, p. 40)

In conclusion, this section helps to identify the central issue of this chapter which is to question whether the perceptual qualities that could be described as raw feelings, sensations or just feelings are reducible only to neurophysiological signals. Sellars identifies many problems in affirming and sustaining this identification and finishes with a complex paradigm in which the connection between sensation and neural signals is not direct. Sellars' most important contribution here is offering the chance to problematise the idea that scientific analysis might also include a qualitative dimension and, for example, raw feelings when applied to the human being. I do not provide a scientific inquiry into the nature and foundation of raw feelings. Nevertheless, I am sure that for a complete knowledge of the man-in-the-world, a qualitative analysis could include something that is not considered in the physical and biochemical inquiry. From my perspective, Sellars identifies a clear pathway to reconsider the role of the person either in the philosophy of science or in epistemology. The factual situation clearly describes the primacy of the scientific image and I do not consider alternatives to this solution or to Sellars' position on the relation between the two images because of the objectiveness, efficacy and status of science. The point is to try to get science to focus on, include and discuss qualitative methods and the qualitative dimension in its approach to the world. I am not convinced that we need to reconstruct the scientific image of man if we want to take into account also raw feelings, as Gabbani argues (see Gabbani, *Between Two Images? An Introduction*, 2012). It might be enough to reconsider the scientific parameters of analysis and methodology, which is also an aim of this chapter. In line with Sellars' idea of constructing a synoptic view, I will argue below for the possibility of constituting a quanto-qualitative view in the analysis of upper limb prostheses.

The Robotic Hand: State of the Art

The previous section identified the philosophical problem of a synoptic vision of man-in-the-world to affirm the need to include the qualitative dimension in an integrated perspective on the human person. This section starts by considering the importance of the hand as an 'operative opening' and focuses on how bioengineering is working on the possibility of restoring the entire sense of touch.

Even if we consider only an ancient philosophical conception of the hand, as expressed for example in Anaxagoras' statement that the hand is the reason why human beings are the most intelligent animals or Russo's affirmation to explain Aristotle's position that 'intelligence is the reason why we have hands' (Russo, 2017, p. 100), the importance of the hand is crystal clear for our actions and cognition. The most crucial role of the hand is the active manipulation and grasping of objects. For this reason, it has an 'operative opening, which means that it can be used in many different ways' (Russo, 2017, p. 100). We can also recall the formulation of ready-to-hand, expressed by Heidegger in Being and Time, Part 1,

Section 1, Chapter 3, as an 'ontological categorical definition of beings as they are in themselves' (Heidegger, 1996, p. 67). According to José Manuel Chillòn,

> Ready-to-hand is the ontological status of things in the world from the perspective of the ontological difference that distinguishes between the way of being of the being that is *Dasein* and the other worldly beings that are there to use, to grasp, to touch. (Chillón, 2017, p. 117)

Therefore, the loss of these functionalities has many implications during the lifespan and daily routine of a person. The problem of manufacturing general prostheses is very ancient: the pioneers were the Egyptians who made prosthetic limbs from fibres to give them a sense of 'integrity', but also from ancient Greece and Rome to the nineteenth century we can find examples of prostheses made from iron, bronze and wood (Norton, 2007). For example, in the early sixteenth century a German mercenary soldier, Gotz von Berlichingen who lost his right arm in a battle had an iron prosthesis that could be moved by a series of releases and springs.

The history of prostheses is divisible in a series of dichotomies: upper limb versus lower limb which implies a focus on active manipulation versus stability, and cosmetic wholeness versus personal autonomy which implies a dualism between passive and active. One of the main goals of biomedical engineering in the field of active upper limb prosthetics is to restore the complete sense of touch in the active and passive components. The prostheses of today have achieved new functionalities, like the feeling of what is touched and precise grasping, compared with the hook prostheses of the past. The scientific literature on prostheses documents the emergence of two different approaches: vibrotactile substitution and neural interface. The first approach is less invasive and consists of applying a series of vibrotactile motors on the skin near the stump. The second, more invasive approach uses on a series of internal electrodes implanted in the muscles and nerves.

Hannes, a prosthetic hand developed by Italian National Health Service (INAIL), is a perfect example of the first kind of prosthesis, based on sensory substitution. It is described as the perfect solution to

> bridge the gap between complex poly-articulated and multifunctional prostheses, which are capable of very high performance, but which are very expensive and contain very delicate and complex mechanisms, and on the other hand, tri-digital prostheses, which are characterized by robustness and ease-of-use, but offering limited versatility and poor aesthetics. (Rehab Technologies – INAIL – IIT Lab, n.d.)

In this type of prosthetic hand, stimulation of the skin through mechanical vibration, provides mostly vibrotactile feedback. It is the most frequently used non-invasive technique to restore a kind of feedback in grasping (Cordella et al., 2016). Hannes stimulates the skin by using local electrical current. One of the main problems of this signal is its incapacity to isolate sensation in a specific task. Message decoding is inaccurate.

The second approach, involving the invasive technique, is based on a long tradition. At the end of the 1980s a preliminary project that aimed to create 'a neural controlled hand, based on electrodes implanted in the arm's peripheral nerves' (LifeHand2, n.d.), was launched by Paolo Dario at the Scuola Superiore Sant'Anna in Pisa, thanks to a series of international collaborations. The current approach to the dichotomies is to build 'a cybernetic anthropomorphic hand intended to provide amputees with functional hand replacement' (Carrozza et al., 2006, p. 629), like CyberHand or LifeHand 2. The core idea is to design a prosthesis which is bio-inspired 'in terms of modular architecture, physical appearance, kinematics, sensorisation, actuation, and its multilevel control system' (Carrozza et al., 2006, p. 629). The aim is to design a prosthetic hand controlled by the human subject that can interpret the intention of the user and actuate an appropriate action in terms of grasp type and force level. The principal aim is to control the active manipulation of objects by controlling the different types of grasps (or DoF, Degree of Freedom), such as the power grasp of cylindrical and spherical objects, or precision grasps, such as pinch or tripod. This is achieved by a neural interface that allows the use of the 'sensorimotor mechanisms for controlling the action' (Carrozza et al., 2006, p. 629), made by the hand. The robotic hand is based on the biomechanical modelling of the natural hand, optimising the kinematics for humanlike action.

In the last decade, many studies have been published concerning the frontier of neural elicitation of tactile sensation. Among these, one of the most important is *Restoring natural sensory feedback in real-time bidirectional hand prostheses* (Raspopovic et al., 2014).

> In this case study, our aim was to restore touch sensation in a person with hand amputation using transversal intrafascicular multichannel electrodes (TIMEs) connected to artificial hand sensors and to intuitively use this sensation to achieve bidirectional control of a hand prosthesis. Our hypothesis was that the participant would be able to exploit the dynamic tactile information induced by neural stimulation that is triggered by the sensors of the hand prosthesis, during real-time simultaneous control of a dexterous prosthetic hand, to adaptively modulate grasping force, thus closing the user-prosthesis loop. (Raspopovic et al., 2014, p. 2)

In this paper, Raspopovic opens a concrete and clear pathway to stimulating peripheral nerves through electrical signals to restore the sensation in a bidirectional prosthesis. From a theoretical point of view, this conception implies the possibility of encoding the entire tactile sensation in electrical signals. From both an engineering and a philosophical perspective, another relevant paper is *Restoring tactile sensations via neural interfaces for real-time force-and-slippage closed-loop control of bionic hands*, published in February 2019 in *Science Robotics*. The primary aim was to provide an example of the use of sensory information 'to finely control a prosthetic hand in complex grasp and manipulation tasks' (Zollo et al., 2019, p. 1). The authors use the muscle electrical activity to decode the user's intention in the efferent canal, while they restore the afferent canal with electrical stimulation of peripheral nerves. Thus, the communication between the body and the prosthesis works in two different ways: the muscle is the principal interpreter of the electrical signal, coming from the brain. At the same time, the nerves, with the addition of cuff and intraneural electrodes, are the units employed for the sensorial feedback. The article is based on a single case trial, conducted at Campus Bio-Medico University Hospital of Rome. The participant was blindfolded and acoustically shielded and was asked to grasp various objects with and without neural feedback. The training was designed to test four different tasks:

(i) lateral grasp of large and small objects; (ii) pick and place of large object with a power grasp; (iii) pick and place of small objects with a precision grasp; (iv) manipulation tasks of pouring water from a bottle to a cup and shape sorter with small cylinders and discs. (Zollo et al., 2019, p. 3)

Several different Degrees of Freedom were identified: (1) manipulation of objects of different shapes (cylinder, parallelepiped, disk, cube, and triangle), that can be small or large; (2) different type of grasp (lateral, power or 'pick and place'); and (3) precision and power manipulation involving the fingers. The experiment proved clearly that the ability to manipulate the object was increased significantly by the sensation because 'when the contact area between the hand and the object decreased, grasp stability was more difficult to ensure, and the role of sensation became paramount' (Zollo et al., 2019, p. 6).

This section highlights the importance of sensory feedback for the control and dexterity of upper limb prostheses and the best ways to achieve this feedback. From a philosophical point of view, we can conclude that the bioengineering pathway approaches life in a unique perspective that distances itself from forms of eliminativism of qualities (Ramsey, 2020) and, instead, seeks to increasingly integrate aspects such as sensations.

From a Functional View to an Integrate Approach

The previous section showed that, generically, the recovery of functionality is based on dualism, active perception versus passive quality. Even if the studies proposed by Raspopovic (Raspopovic et al., 2014) and Zollo (Zollo et al., 2019) proved respectively the relevance of sensory feedback in dexterity and the centrality of sensation in the active exploration and manipulation of the world, the engineering perspective remains settled in a quantitative dimension in which sensation is still a residual afferent trait. This perspective is present also in the Human Activity Assistive Technology (HAAT) model (Cook & Polgar, 2015) and the International Classification of Functioning, Disability and Impairment (ICF) model because in ICF the activity is described as 'the execution of a task or action by the individual'. In this general definition, it is possible to distinguish two main dimensions: performance, that describes 'what the person actually does', and capacity, or potential performance.

In the third chapter of Cook and Polgar (2015) book *Assistive Technologies: Principles and Practice*, there is a note-worthy definition of sensation as one of several other sensory functions which refers, as we can see in the following example, to the other senses.

> Seeing classification involves functions related to vision. (...) the functions of hearing include both auditory (hearing) functions and those related to the vestibular function in the inner ear. (...) Tactile functions involve the ability to detect various physical stimuli, including temperature, vibration, pressure, and noxious stimuli. (Cook & Polgar, 2015, p. 45)

This quotation is fundamental to comprehend that the qualitative aspect of the experience is considered in Assistive Technology (AT) as for example an additional sensory function.

In the Oxford English Dictionary, the term 'function' has three meanings:

> 1. a special activity or purpose or thing; 2. a social event or an official ceremony; 3. a quantity whose value depends on the varying values of others, and a part of a program that performs a basic operation. (Wehmeier, McIntosh, & Turnbull, 2005, p. 630)

Considering that the senses are defined in the same dictionary as 'the five powers that your body uses to get information about the world around you' (Wehmeier et al., 2005, p. 1382), we can conclude that this definition is, possibly, based on a quantification or mathematization of the body and a passive understanding of perception. The main goals in recovering/recreating bodily functionalities are related to recovering the Activities of Daily Life (ADLs). The six basic ADLs are: eating (self-feeding), bathing, getting dressed, toileting, mobility and personal hygiene. In this functional perspective, the main objective is to recover the ability to fulfil these tasks without attention to the lived experience of these actions.

Thus, a functional-based perspective is not sensitive to a fine-grained analysis of the relation between quality and quantity. It remains settled in a dualistic approach. Bioengineering tries to overcome this shortcoming even if it is based only on a reductionism to electrical signals. I would like to show that a philosophical approach can help to develop a stereoscopic vision in which quality is considered as something more than a signal.

The two models of active prosthesis discussed in the previous section, based on vibrotactile substitution and neural interface, do not produce the same quality of feedback. The less invasive technique, vibrotactile substitution, is not able to perceive 'isolated sensations in a specific task' (Cordella et al., 2016, p. 10) despite the fact that sensory substitution has been a disruptive research topic from the second half of the last century (Bach-Y-RIta, 1972; Bach-Y-Rita, Tyler, & Kaczarek, 2003; Lundborg, Rosén, & Lindberg, 1999). In contrast, the more invasive technique can restore the tactile sensation in a more precise way not only to identify the object touched but also in the active manipulation of it. I think this indicates that the body, the perceived quality and 'raw feels' are important in the human–prosthesis relationship (Corti, 2019).

An alternative framework for considering the problem of raw feels and overcoming a passive account of perception, from a philosophical point of view, is enactivism in which the relation between subject and object is a 'dependent co-origination in the process of experience' (Giannotta, 2016, p. 1). For a general understanding of enactivism (Varela, Thompson, & Rosch, 2016; Thelen, 1994), we can look to the work on the sensorimotor approach, a philosophical and psychological perspective developed in the twenty-first century by the philosopher, Alva Noë and the psychologist, Kevin O'Regan. They propose a vision in which perception is considered as a complex phenomenon that implies different modalities, 'governed by different laws', for different sensory domains, such as vision, smell, tasting and so on (O'Regan & Noë, 2001). For them, perception becomes an active attitude of the subject that oversteps the conception of perception as passive receiving of qualitative information from the world.

In relation to the problem of qualities of perception, O'Regan (2011) tries to provide a scientific explanation of perceptual qualities based on the interaction between the agent, the environment and four characteristics of the new interpretation of perception: bodiliness of the experience, richness, partial insubordinateness and grabbiness of the world. For O'Regan, this explanation solves the four problems connected with qualities in perception: (1) that we feel something that cannot be reduced to brain functions; (2) the different qualities perceived; (3) the structure of different qualities and (4) the ineffability of raw feels. In particular, the phenomenality plot, a graph representing bodiliness on the x axis, and grabbiness on the y axis, produces a quantifiable estimation of the qualitative dimension and could be useful for also including a qualitative dimension in the evaluation of prosthesis.

This approach, encoded in the ICF in experience-based criteria, could be relevant because it addresses the following points:

1. The importance of the body as an active player in perception.
2. The analysis of the qualitative dimension based on subject-environment interaction.
3. The structure of the qualitative dimension.

Addressing this perspective in the evaluation of ADL means that the how-dimension of the recovered functions is also important; in particular, as I have shown, sensation is crucial also in the execution of tasks that, from a philosophical point of view, are more than functions to recover.

In conclusion, this section demonstrates that a functional-based analysis of perception is not adequate because it does not focus on sensation, described as something that cannot be encoded completely in electrical signals because there is something more, the feeling of what is touched that we experience and communicate. This synoptic vision is possible only if, at the same time, the engineering perspective and the philosophical analysis reflect on the concept of the body, central in the new vision of perception proposed in this paper. The topic of the body is explored in the following section.

Which Meaning for the Body?

The previous section shifted the focus from a functional-based perspective to a synoptic vision of corporeity in which perception is seen in an active way. The questions that guide this section are: how can we describe prostheses? and what is the concept of the body behind the possibility of restoring the sense of touch?

The Robot Inside Us

In *The Robot and Us*, Maria Chiara Carrozza dedicates a chapter to *The Robot Inside Us* that offers an excellent description of the spatial position of the mechanical device inserted into the body of the user. Two related themes are bio-inspiration and the neural interface. 'One of the dreams of neuro-robotics is the connection between a patient's brain and a robotic system, with the aim of transmitting commands and receiving sensory feedback' (Carrozza, 2019, p. 54). This is a very interesting observation, connected to a pure quantification of the body that is explainable as an entity governed by electric current. Even in the case of the prosthetic limb, this physical perspective reigns. For example, Carrozza affirms that

> the neural interfaces implanted in the peripheral nervous system do not interact with the primary motor intention in the brain but are less invasive. They offer the advantage that with a single electrode implant you can connect both with the efferent fibers that transmit the motor command from the central nervous system to the limb, and with the afferent fibers that follow the reverse path and stimulate the central nervous system by transferring the tactile sensory feedback from the hand to the brain. (Carrozza, 2019, p. 58)

In this case, is the body seen as a physical entity controlled by electrical signals? Can a quantified description of body function be adequate to comprehend better the living mechanism? Carrozza points out an important element when she states that the prosthesis is not a robot but a *wearable medical device*. Her classification of the prosthesis in relation to the user, describing it as a medical device *on us*, specifying that 'it converses with the intimate part of us thanks to the neuro-prosthesis' is crucial to the central aim of this paper (Carrozza, 2019, p. 59).

The prosthesis is located close to the body, having a continuative co-operation with the nervous system. This is an excellent description combining the physical and physiological perspectives, even if the kind of relationship between the user and the neuro-prosthesis is not specified.

We can conclude that an active robotic prosthesis should not be considered as a robot per se but rather as a mechanical part, embedded in the subject who uses it to perceive the environment.

The Body as Machine

The concept of the body beyond this engineering approach proposed by Carrozza is a quantitative one. It corresponds to the concept of the body described by Scheller et al. as an electrical and complex machine that includes various types of receptors: electromagnetic, mechanoreceptors, chemoreceptors, thermo and pain receptors (Scheller, Petrini, & Proulx, 2018). For these authors, the primary function of the receptors they identify is to transform different kinds of energies into electrical signals in a process called transduction. These impulses, so encoded, are sent to the central nervous system via a neural pathway where the information is combined and processed in a 'way that makes us perceive and recognize the world around us' (Scheller et al., 2018, p. 2). A crucial aspect of this process is clearly expressed in chapter 15 of *Stevens' Handbook of Experimental Psychology and Cognitive Neuroscience*, titled *Perception and Interactive Technology*, written by Meike Scheller, Karin Petrini, and Michael Proulx. It is

> not a unidirectional process but stays in constant dynamic interaction with the action we make. We actively use our body to facilitate perception by sampling our environment in the best way possible. (Scheller et al., 2018, p. 2)

Here the body, interpreted as a 'neurophysiological' machine, (Boden, 2008) is seen in a dualistic vision as a mediator/medium of exchange between our mind and the world, as a useful box that relates with the external world or it could be seen as a unitary element. Their analysis is based on *a non unidirectional process* in a vision that contains both a bottom-up (from peripheral stimulis to the central nerve) and a top-down (from the brain to activation of muscles) direction. It is a circular process in which the active and passive reciprocally influence each other in a dynamic way and the action is not only based on the perceptual information but is continuously changed by passive receptivity.

Returning to the study by Zollo and Di Pino (Zollo et al., 2019), I discussed in Section 2, we can now reframe its relevance in relation to this study by raising the following question: Is it possible to consider the prosthesis as a device that reproduces this loop? We can affirm that even though prostheses without sensory feedback can provide some information about the object being manipulated, the corporeal loop can only be fully realised through sensation. To address this question we need to consider two different circular processes; the first one is a close linear cycle process in which the feedback is the end of the afferent circuit. The second one is a loop in which the passive information received by manipulation is a dynamic concept, related to the discrimination of softness, form, and warmth of the object as well as a progression in action and precise manipulation. This second type of circular process is iterative and dynamic.

In conclusion, based on the scientific evidence provided by Zollo and Di Pino (Zollo et al., 2019), the new vision of action proposed in the previous section and the need to re-configure a philosophical approach focussed on a stereoscopic vision, I would like to underline the challenge to rethink about the body and experience in an integrated way in which both the quantitative and qualitative dimensions are present at the same time.

The Other Side of the Coin: Embodiment

The philosopher Don Ihde investigates how technology plays a role in human-world relations (Ihde, 1990) and introduces the term *embodiment relationship* to describe technological devices like eye glasses or prostheses that are linked closely with the subject and become part of the way he or she perceives the world Specifically, as Verbeek argues, prosthetic devices actually specify the relation of embodiment in the relation of cyborg intentionality. It can be seen as a form of "radicalization" (Verbeek, 2008) of the embodied relation identified by Ihde. The cyborg relation describes not only a proximal relationship between the technological device and the human being but rather a new entity, developed from a "merge" between the subject and the technology (Caronia 2008). This paper does not focus on the problem of whether the prosthesis may represent a body-extension, body-incorporation or a part of the body, as in the works of De Preester (De Preester, 2011; De Preester & Tsakiris, 2009). Instead, it focusses on the concept of embodiment from a phenomenological point of view. Following Hubert Dreyfus, to avoid the concept of body as a 'meat machine', we must bring phenomenological analysis into the discussion (Dreyfus, 1992). To begin with, Edmund Husserl, the founding father of phenomenology, distinguished two different types of bodies: *Körper*, the physical and inanimate body, and *Leib*, the living and lived body (Husserl, 1983). For Husserl, the body finishes being the zero point of orientations because all the things we perceive are related to the position of the perceiver and his movement. Maurice Merleau-Ponty goes beyond this conception affirming that we are experiencing the world through our own body because we are *embedded in* the environment (Merleau-Ponty, 1962). He underlines the active role of the body in the perception of the environment. Thus, for him the body is describable as a medium of experience because it 'plays a critical role in shaping our cognitive life' (Zipoli Caiani, 2014, p. 152).

In phenomenology, the core idea is that the body is a 'constitutive condition of experience and understanding' (Durt, 2020, p. 1). Instead of a machine which tests hypotheses, the human body is able to

> modify its expectations in terms of a more flexible criterion: as embodied, we need not check for specific characteristics or a specific range of characteristics, but simply for whether, on the basis of expectations, we are coping with the object. (Dreyfus, 1992, p. 250)

Thus, it is through the body that we experience the world (Clark, 1999), because only corporeity allows for perception. This conception is based not on the idea of man as a functional-based machine but as a living, biological entity (Corti & Bertolaso, 2020). It represents a way to go beyond the mind–body dualism and consider the body as the constitutive principle of experience and human–world relationship. As Merleau-Ponty affirms, embodiment provides a third approach to the ongoing physiological and psychological approaches (Merleau-Ponty, 1962).

With these considerations of the body in mind and rather than proposing a paradigmatic shift for engineering, I propose a methodological pathway for the analysis of all technological devices closely connected with the body. Phenomenology could offer a very clear and innovative way to approach the topic of the interplay between prosthesis and the lived body.

Perspectives

This study set out to explore the possibility to a stereoscopic vision in the analysis and evaluation of the prosthetic hand. This synoptic vision brings together the physiological analysis of stimuli and the phenomenological perceptual quality to consider globally the experience of prosthesis. The first section addressed the problem from a philosophical point of view and discussed the problem of reducing sensation to a brain function but also its importance for a complete analysis. The second section showed that sensation is an irreducible element also from an engineering perspective on upper limb prosthetics. Feeling what is touched has a crucial impact on the identification of the object being manipulated but also in its active exploration. The third section of the chapter focussed on the problem of function-based analysis of prostheses and underlined the importance of sensation as something that cannot be reduced to brain function. This section also showed that it is possible to affirm a new approach to perception, through a sensorimotor account which can be integrated into the perspective of analysis. The fourth section examined how it is possible to consider the concept of body in a synoptic vision. This contribution is a preliminary work aimed at identifying an integrated and intermixed pathway for the analysis of the embodied relation between human and prosthetics implants in order to propose a quanto-qualitative approach to technological assessment. In particular, I propose phenomenological analysis as a useful empirical methodology for a comprehensive approach in the evaluation of prostheses from both a theoretical and practical point of view.

References

Bach-Y-RIta, P. (1972). *Brain mechanisms in sensory substitution*. New York, NY: Academic Press.

Bach-Y-Rita, P., Tyler, M., & Kaczarek, K. (2003). Seeing with the brain. *International Journal of Human-Computer Interaction, 15*(2), 285–295.

Breazeal, C. (2002). *Designing sociable robots*. Cambridge, MA: The MIT Press.

Boden, M. A. (2008). *Mind as machine: A history of cognitive science*. Oxford, Oxford University Press.

Caronia, A. (2008). *Il cyborg. Saggio sull'uomo artificiale*. Milano: ShaKe.

Carrozza, M. C. (2019). The robot and us. *An 'Antidisciplinary' Perspective on the Scientific and Social Impacts of Robotics*. Cham: Springer International Publishing (Biosystems & Biorobotics, 20).

Carrozza, M. C., Cappiello, G., Micera, S., Edin, B. B., Beccai, L., & Cipriani, C. (2006). Design of a cybernetic hand for perception and action. *Biological Cybernetics, 95*, 629–644.

Chillón, J. M. (2017). Ready-to-hand in Heidegger. Philosophy as an everyday understanding of the world and the question concerning technology. In M. Bertolaso & N. Di Stefano (Eds.), *The hand perception, cognition, action* (pp. 115–126). Cham: Springer.

Clark, A. (1999). An embodied cognitive science? *Trends in Cognitive Sciences, 3*(9), 345–351.

Cook, A. M., & Polgar, J. M. (2015). *Assistive technologies: Principles and practice*. St. Louis, MO: Elsevier.

Cordella, F., Ciancio, A. L., Sacchetti, R., Davalli, A., Cutti, A. G., Guglielmelli, E., & Zollo, L. (2016). Literature review on needs of upper limb prosthesis users. *Frontiers in Neuroscience, 10*, 209.

Corti, L. (2019). How the neuroprosthetic hand shapes the embodied perception, I-RIM Conference, 74–75.

Corti, L., & Bertolaso, M. (2020). Embodiment from philosophy to life science and back. *Ludus Vitalis, 27*(52), 137–142.

De Preester, H. (2011). Technology and the body: The (im)possibilities of re-embodiment. *Foundations of Science, 16*(2), 119–137.

De Preester, H., & Tsakiris, M. (2009). Body-extension versus body-incorporation: Is there a need for a body-model? *Phenomenology and the Cognitive Sciences, 8*(3), 307–319.

Dreyfus, H. L. (1992). *What computer still can't do*. Cambridge, MA: The MIT Press.

Durt, C. (2020). Bodily, embodied, and virtual reality. *Phänomenologische Forschungen, 1*, 1–13.

Gabbani, C. (2007). *Per un'epistemologia dell'esperienza personale*. Milano: Edizioni Angelo Guerini e Associati.

Gabbani, C. (2012). Between two images? An introduction. *Humana. Mente Journal of Philosophical Studies, 21*, V–XXIX.

Galilei, G. (1960). The Assayer. In G. Galilei, H. Grassi, M. Guiducci, J. Kepler (Eds.), *The controversy on the Comets of 1618* (pp. 151–336). Translated by S. Drake and C. D. O'Malley. Philadelphia: University of Pennsylvania Press, 151–336.

Giannotta, A. P. (2016). Epistemology and ontology of the quality: An introduction to the enactive approach to qualitative ontology. *Humana.mente Journal of Philosophical Studies, 31*, 1–19.

Heidegger, M. (1996). *Being and time*. New York, NY: State University of New York Press.

Husserl, E. (1983). *Ideas pertaining to a pure phenomenology and to a phenomenological philosophy – First Book: General introduction to a pure phenomenology*. Leiden: Martinus Nijhoff Publishers.

Ihde, D. (1990). *Technology and the life word*. Bloomington, IN: Indiana University Press.

Lanfredini, R., Liberati, N., Pace Giannotta, A., & Pagni, E. (2016). The enactive approach to qualitative ontology: In search of new categories. *Humana.mente, 9*(31), III–XIII.

Liberati, N. (2015). Technology, phenomenology and the everyday world: A phenomenological analysis on how technologies mould our world. *Human Studies*, 1–28.

LifeHand2. Retrieved from http://www.unicampus.it/eng/current/lifehand-2. Accessed on July 30, 2021.

Locke, J. (1997). *Essay concerning human understanding*. London: Penguin Classics.

Lundborg, G., Rosén, B., & Lindberg, S. (1999). Hearing as substitution for sensation: A new principle for artificial sensibility. *Journal of Hand Surgery, 24*(2), 219–224.

Merleau-Ponty, M. (1962). *Phenomenology of perception*. London: Routledge & Kegan Paul.

Norton, K. M. (2007). A brief history of prosthetics. *Motion, 17*(7), 11–13.

O'Regan, K. J., & Noë, A. (2001). A sensorimotor account of vision and visual consciousness. *Behavioural and Brain Sciences, 24*, 939–1031.

O'Regan, K. (2011). *Why red doesn't sound like a bell*. Oxford: Oxford University Press.

Picard, R. (1997). *Affecting computing*. Massachusetts: MIT Press.

Ramsey, W. (2020). Eliminative Materialism. Retrieved from <https://plato.stanford.edu/archives/sum2020/entries/materialism-eliminative/>

Raspopovic, S., Capogrosso, M., Petrini, F. M., Bonizzato, M., Rigosa, J., Di Pino, G., … Micera, S. (2014). Restoring natural sensory feedback in real-time bidirectional hand prostheses. *Science Translational Medicine, 6*(222), 222ra19–222ra19.

RehabTechnologies–INAIL–IITLab.(n.d.).RetrievedfromINAIL–IITLab:https://www.iit.it/research/lines/rehab-technologies-inail-iit-lab

Russo, M. T. (2017). The human hand as a microcosm. A philosophical overview on the hand and its role in the processes of perception, action, and cognition. In M. Bertolaso & N. Di Stefano (Eds.), *The hand perception, cognition, action* (pp. 99–113). Cham. Springer.

Scheller, M., Petrini, K., & Proulx, M. J. (2018). Perception and interactive technology. In J. T. WixtedS & S. L. Thompson-Schill (Eds.), *Stevens' handbook of experimental psychology and cognitive neuroscience* (Vol. 2, pp. 1–50). Hoboken: Wiley.

Sellars, W. (1991). Philosophy and the scientific image of man. In W. Sellars (Ed.). *Science, perception and reality* (pp. 1–41). Atascadero, CA: Ridgeview Publishing Company.

Thelen, E. a. (1994). *A dynamic system approach to the development of cognition and action.* Massachusetts: MIT Press.

Varela, F. J., Thompson, E., & Rosch, E. (2016). *The embodied mind: Cognitive science and human experience.* Massachusetts: MIT press..

Verbeek, P. P. (2008). Cyborg intentionality: Rethinking the phenomenology of human–technology relations. *Phenomenology and the Cognitive Sciences, 7*(3), 387–395.

Verbeek, P.-P. (2011). *Moralizing technology. Understanding and designing the morality of things.* London: The University of Chicago Press.

Wehmeier, S., McIntosh, C., & Turnbull, J.. (2005). *Oxford Advanced Learner's Dictionary.* Oxford: Oxford University Press.

Zipoli Caiani, S. (2014). *Mindsets.* Sesto San Giovanni: Mimesis International.

Zollo, L., Di Pino, G., Ciancio, A. L., Ranieri, F., Cordella, F., Gentile, C., ... Denaro, L. (2019). Restoring Tactile sensations via neural interfaces for real time force-and-slippage closed-loop control of bionic hands. *Science Robotics, 4*(27), eaau9924.

Index